401
M59H
1899

HOW TO LEARN PHILOLOGY

A SIMPLE AND INTRODUCTORY BOOK FOR TEACHERS AND LEARNERS

BY

EUSTACE H. MILES, M.A.

HONOURS COACH IN CLASSICS AND PHILOLOGY, AND LECTURER IN CLASSICS AND PHILOLOGY FOR THE SPECIAL BOARD OF CIVIL SERVICE STUDIES (1897-99), AT CAMBRIDGE UNIVERSITY

LONDON

SWAN SONNENSCHEIN & CO., LIM.

NEW YORK: THE MACMILLAN CO.

1899

THOUSANDS OF SCARCE BOOKS
ON THESE AND OTHER SUBJECTS:

Freemasonry * Akashic * Alchemy * Alternative Health * Ancient Civilizations * Anthroposophy * Astrology * Astronomy * Aura * Bible Study * Cabalah * Cartomancy * Chakras * Clairvoyance * Comparative Religions * Divination * Druids * Eastern Thought * Egyptology * Esoterism * Essenes * Etheric * ESP * Gnosticism * Great White Brotherhood * Hermetics * Kabalah * Karma * Knights Templar * Kundalini * Magic * Meditation * Mediumship * Mesmerism * Metaphysics * Mithraism * Mystery Schools * Mysticism * Mythology * Numerology * Occultism * Palmistry * Pantheism * Parapsychology * Philosophy * Prosperity * Psychokinesis * Psychology * Pyramids * Qabalah * Reincarnation * Rosicrucian * Sacred Geometry * Secret Rituals * Secret Societies * Spiritism * Symbolism * Tarot * Telepathy * Theosophy * Transcendentalism * Upanishads * Vedanta * Wisdom * Yoga * *Plus Much More!*

DOWNLOAD A FREE CATALOG
AND
SEARCH OUR TITLES AT:

www.kessinger.net

TO

THE REV. E. S. ROBERTS

THIS WORK IS DEDICATED

BY KIND PERMISSION

PREFACE.

There has long been great need of a simple and introductory work on such subjects as, for example, Etymology, Textual Criticism, Analysis, the Indo-European Language, the Greek Dialects, and the leading Scholars of the past: the need has been felt by Tutors and Lecturers at the Universities, by Masters at Schools, and by students and learners generally; and this little work of mine is an attempt to satisfy it.

1. I have tried *to cover a very wide ground*, and so I hope that my method will have the advantage of ensuring variety.

2. The Chapters on each subject are *short and especially adapted for Beginners*—most learners of Philology *are* beginners; the work pre-supposes very little knowledge beyond that of the ordinary declensions and conjugations and vocabulary, in Greek and Latin and English. Wherever it has been possible, I have avoided Sanskrit and other unfamiliar languages.

3. These pages are intended *only as an Introduction*, but it is sincerely hoped that they will so interest the reader that afterwards he will study and appreciate the more advanced works by Giles, King and Cookson, Lindsay, Victor Henry, and others.

I wish, above all, to emphasise the fact that this book is not a "Cram-book": it does not cover the whole ground, but merely forms an Introduction.

4. *References* are given to many of the more special works, in the appropriate Chapters.

5. Among the new features I may mention an attempt to show people how to *teach* Philology (e.g. by working out examples). In fact, I have tried to explain the method *both for Teachers and for Learners:* and not the least important part of this will be

6. *the Exercises*, and the *Criticism of common Mistakes* (e.g. see pp. 40, 64, 153).

7. At the beginning of the work I have tried to *avoid details*, wherever I have been able to do so, and I have also tried to avoid Laws and Rules.

8. The understanding has been helped by *Maps and Diagrams*, and by

9. the principle of *starting with Instances*—the *simplest and most familiar* Instances (especially English words) coming first—and not of starting with Rules and then giving Instances.

From the Instances General Rules are drawn, which Rules are further illustrated by new Instances.

10. I have also ventured to add certain helps for remembering the Rules, among which will be found (e.g. see pp. 153, 251) *one or two Rhymes*. The obvious objections to Rhymes as a means of remembering I shall answer elsewhere. Tennyson seemed to have considered Rhymes to be chiefly valuable as an aid to the memory.

11. Besides this, I suggest *Hints as to how to Practise;* thus I suggest (pp. 1, 22) that the learner should start by doing the simpler Instances slowly and again and again, until he knows them thoroughly, and until he sees the Principles which underlie these simple Instances. Then I suggest Exercises in which he could apply these Principles, and to these *Exercises* I add the *Answers* (see, for example, pp. 64, 65).

12. I have also suggested (e.g. p. 43) some useful and interesting *Subjects for Research.*

13. Wherever I have been able to, I have given illustrations and analogies from daily life and from Science (see pp. 72, 217).

14. In the Chapters dealing with the Analysis of Words, I have tried to treat the subjects *in a logical order* (p. 20 foll.), and

15. I have also tried (e.g. pp. 42, 151) to give *the Evidences* for every answer which I have suggested, *explaining the process* of Analysis (p. 152) and

16. showing *the Interest* of the subject, e.g. by mentioning the other subjects on which it will throw light (see pp. 43, 56).

17. Right at the end of the Analysis will come the Technical Terms, the Formulas and Rules, and the Details.

18. It has been my aim to give the most up-to-date theories, or, rather, the theories to which Dr. Giles and Messrs. King and Cookson give their support in their excellent Manuals: my work is mostly orthodox, and has very little originality except in its *Method.* I have

tried to ensure accuracy, although in a work of this kind it is certain that some misprints must 'creep' into the text. I must here express my genuine thanks to the staff of the Aberdeen University Press for the care they have taken with the Printing.

If this book should be favourably received it might be followed by a series of Examination-papers with Answers, and by a work similar to this but dealing with Syntax.

A few words must be said about the many *Books which have already been published* on these various subjects. It would be easy to make a large list of those which are excellent for Specialists, and which are up-to-date in their theories, and have a capital index. But as yet there has appeared no comprehensive work on *all* the subjects: no work, for instance, which comprises such departments as Greek Dialects, Latin Inscriptions, and Textual Criticism.

The severest censures which have been passed on many of the Text-books have been due to a misconception. It is true that these Text-books are expensive; it is true—at least so my pupils and others have told me—that they are not adapted for Beginners (who, when they read them, are plunged into a sea of details); that they may often seem dull and uninteresting, and wanting in variety; that they give no advice as to how to teach Philology; that they give too many details which beginners can and ought to pass over; that they do not lay stress on the important points, throwing the rest into the background; that they are full of

Technical Terms, such as *Anaptyxis;* that they consist of Abstract Rules followed by Instances, thereby ignoring the foundation of all teaching, viz. that we should proceed to the Abstract Rule *from* the easy and concrete Instance (which, for English learners, should be, if possible, an English Instance).

Again, these books have no Diagrams or Maps, although a Map of the Indo-European Language, and of Greece and of Italy, and a Diagram of the Organs of Speech, would have thrown much light on the subject and would have given it additional interest.

Then, again, these books suggest no convenient ways of remembering the long Lists in which they abound ; they give no advice (either to Teachers or to Learners) as to how to practise the subject ; they suggest no Exercises for practice ; they comparatively seldom suggest subjects as worthy of research ; they rarely give those illustrations, from everyday life and from Science, which might redeem the subject from dulness. They seem to have no logical order or arrangement ; they do not show the Teacher or the Learner how to set about answering an Examination Question ; still less do they give the Evidence on which an Answer should be based.

Many of them are so ill-adapted for reference that the average man might almost be allowed to take his Text-book into the Examination, and to use it there, without any fear of his getting full marks. The enormous value of the various subjects is not explained, although this would itself give an interest to each subject ; and the books are by no means free from inaccuracies, such as the want of distinction between Long Vowels and Short Vowels—a serious mistake.

But much of the above criticism would not have been passed by students, had those students come to these books *already well equipped*: they needed to be introduced to the subjects first before they tried these learned treatises; had they gone through a simple and preparatory course like this, I think they would have thoroughly appreciated most of these Text-books. But they were "obliged to jump before they had learnt to walk".

In conclusion, it may not be uninteresting to the reader to learn how it was that I came to write this book.

Whilst I was an Undergraduate at Cambridge, I went through some of the regular training in Philology, and I read most of the English works on the subject. I even ventured to write certain works myself, which received more criticism than praise.

After that, I went to teach at Rugby, and there, as well as at one or two other Public Schools, I lectured on the subject of Philology; it was not till I thus tried to *teach* the subject to Beginners that it occurred to me to give up the old methods of teaching it and to try to find *a Method which should be more logical and better adapted for Beginners.*

The last few years, while coaching some hundreds of Honours pupils, at Cambridge and at Girton, I have been constantly changing, and (I hope) improving, my ways of teaching, in the light of what I have read and of what I have found out by actual experience as to the universal Principles of Teaching in all subjects.

But, throughout my teaching my great difficulty has been *the want of a Text-book*, which should at once be easy enough for beginners and up-to-date and comprehensive.

Again and again I have been asked to recommend such a book, and again and again I have been obliged to say that I did not know of one.

Last of all, I received a good many letters from various Teachers and students, urging me to embody my experiences, as to the best way of teaching the subject, in a small Text-book adapted for Beginners; and this I have tried to do.

It is needless to say that *any* suggestions as to improvements will be very welcome, whether they be made in private letters or in periodicals: for I cannot but feel that, in dealing with this most complicated subject, I have scarcely mastered even a few of the best methods by which it might be taught.

EUSTACE H. MILES.

5 St. Paul's Road,
Cambridge, 1899.

CONTENTS.

PART I.

INTRODUCTORY.

PART II.

PREPARATION FOR ANALYSIS OF WORDS.

PART III.

ANALYSIS OF WORDS.

PART IV.

GENERAL QUESTIONS ON SOUND-CHANGES, ETC., AND TECHNICAL TERMS EXPLAINED.

PART V.

PRONUNCIATION, ACCENTS, AND SPELLING.

PART VI.

HOW SOUNDS ARE MADE (PHYSIOLOGY).

PART VII.

THE ALPHABETS.

PART VIII.

ETYMOLOGY AND SÉMANTIQUE, OR THE MEANINGS OF WORDS.

PART IX.

SOME IDIOMATIC USES OF GREEK PARTICLES, WITH LATIN EQUIVALENTS.

PART X.

TEXTUAL CRITICISM, AND HOW TO EMEND.

PART XI.

A FEW SCHOLARS AND PHILOLOGISTS, AND THEIR SERVICES.

APPENDIX.

LIST OF USEFUL BOOKS (MOSTLY IN ENGLISH).

A FEW SUGGESTIONS TO THE READERS OF THIS BOOK.

1. First go very quickly through the book so as to get a general idea of it.

2. Before reading the Answer to any Question, try to make your own Answer to it.

3. While reading the Answers, be content to work very slowly at first, practising and thoroughly mastering the elementary and foundation facts: this will save time in the end, just as, in fencing, it saves time to spend many hours in thoroughly mastering the elementary positions and movements of the feet, body, wrists, etc.

4. After having begun to read the book for the second time, i.e. slowly and carefully, go through the old work before beginning the new. Be like the Early Romans. Make sure of the ground which you have already passed over, make it your own, before you proceed to new acquisitions.

5. When you are comparing your Answers with the Answers suggested here, do not merely

(*a*) notice the actual mistakes and

(*b*) the more correct Answers; but also

(*c*) find out *why* you have made the mistakes, *why* your Answer is wrong, and

(*d*) *how* the mistakes might have been avoided. See p. 153, foll.

6. Keep a notebook for this purpose.

7. After an Examination Paper has been tried, go through it again with books, and try to arrive at the correct Answers: don't be satisfied merely with having finished the Paper itself.

8. Whenever you find anything in this book which is not clear, or which is or may be a mistake, make a memorandum of it, and do me the great favour of pointing it out to me.

PART I.

INTRODUCTORY.

1. Advantages of studying Philology.
2. Origins of Language.
3. The Indo-European or Māter-Language, and its descendants.
4. What 'Analyse tremunt (or τρέμουσι)' really means.

1. Advantages of Studying Philology.

1. *Mention the chief advantages of Studying Philology.*

At the outset it is needless to say that Philology has few advantages unless it is taught properly; this applies to most subjects.

1. In Philology, which tells us how words are formed and how their meanings change, there should be a particular interest; for the words themselves, which form the subject-matter, are familiar to every one. It is this that gives Philology its great advantage over other studies, viz. that it takes as its starting-point something which is *familiar to all its learners* and also *interesting to them.*

2. Again, Philology supplies *the link between the present and the past.* It should show as well as (or perhaps better than) any other subject *the principles of Evolution*, such as we have had in recent years expounded to us by Darwin and others in the province of Science (see p. 218, foll.). But Philology might be superior to Science as a subject of teaching, especially for the young, because it is absolutely harmless; whereas a superficial knowledge of Science has often led to Agnosticism or to Atheism.

Philology should tell us as much as Science can about 'Laws' and 'Exceptions' (p. 66). It should tell us almost as much as Psychology can about our methods of thinking and remembering.

3. Moreover, it is one of the most valuable branches of *Evidence,* not only for Psychology, but also for Mythology, History (especially the early Indo-European history, the mixture of races, and the connection of various peoples with one another); and also for ancient Geology and Geography. E.g., see pp. 43, 56.

Philology teaches us to weigh evidence, to arrive at different degrees of probability; and it also teaches us to see the causes of phenomena.

4. If rightly studied, it should be found most useful *in the learning of various Languages:* not only in the learning of foreign languages, their words, their order of words, and their Syntax, but also in the learning of *the Technical Languages* of various Sciences and Arts and Trades. With regard to Greek and Latin, Philology will show their connexion with one another (p. 16): this should make their study easier as well as pleasanter.

5. By means of Philology we may learn to expose fallacies—for many fallacies arise from a loose use of words—and we are thus taught part of the great lesson of *accuracy in reasoning.*

6. In one department of Philology (p. 201) some useful facts about voice-production would be the result of a more special study.

7. To innumerable people, in the past and in the present, Philology has formed a convenient hobby for odd moments: one of its great advantages is that it needs for ordinary purposes no special apparatus, the problems being stored in the mind ready for use.

2. Origins of Language.

2. *What different theories have been suggested as to the Origins of Language? State your own view.*

A. A certain kind of language can start as '*Gesture*' alone. Children convey a great deal of their meaning by gesture alone, for instance by pointing; and in recent years we have seen a whole play acted simply by gesture.

Under the general heading of '*Gesture*' we must include the different movements of the body and of its various parts, especially of the arms and fingers, and of the head and eyes and mouth and forehead.

Under this heading we must also put *pictures and other signs which represent gesture.*

B. Secondly, there is a language of *Music,* a language of *notes* alone. For instance, a cat scarcely has any consonants in its speech, and speaks mostly by varying its tones.

C. There is also a language of *Sounds alone,* 'vowels and consonants'—mere sounds apart from change of musical note. An instance of this will be the intoned services in the Church, where meaning is conveyed without any change of note.

D. Fourthly, *Words alone, without any sound* at all, can convey meaning; and writing is the clearest example of this.

E. As a rule, however, we *combine* two or more of these methods of conveying meaning. For instance, in a sentence like 'The cat's gone in there, hasn't it? What?' we may find all four methods combined.

A question arises, however, as to *how meanings came to be attached to sounds or forms;* and to this question several answers have been given.

1. There are some who think that all language arose through *Imitation*. This was advocated by Professor Max Müller, and may be called *the 'Puff-puff' theory* or the 'Cuckoo' theory, because obvious instances of words which have originated in this way are 'puff-puff' and 'cuckoo'; but this will not account for very much.

2. (*a*) The second theory is that sounds were originally only the *expressions of Emotions*. In other words, men who had certain emotions, such as fear or anger, could not help expressing themselves by means of certain sounds.

Under this heading may be mentioned the involuntary yell of pain, or the growl of anger.

2. (*b*) To this we add that certain actions, especially violent actions, would naturally be accompanied by certain sounds. But this would not be in itself sufficient to explain all language as it is; and the following theory must be added to the other two. It does not exclude them, it only supplements them.

3. We know how a child *invents* for certain persons or things *certain names or sounds which have little or nothing to do with the thing itself*. But by degrees, and owing to gesture and repetition especially, every one around comes to understand what the child means when it utters some particular sound.

Now it is probable that *in very early times* there existed *a great wealth of sounds*, which were used (from various causes and on various occasions) with no particular and definite meaning of their own.

Supposing a primitive man wished to speak of a sheep—he might point to a sheep and utter some one of these sounds. His hearers would associate together this sound and the idea of a sheep, and this sound would be (tacitly) agreed on as a sign for sheep. From these two or more people this sound for sheep might have extended to many other people.

4. Lastly, when people had already acquired a certain number of words or sounds for simple ideas (such as *heat*

or *fire*), then they might come to apply these words to new ideas.

Thus the word used for heat or fire might come to be applied Metaphorically to the *heat or fire of anger :* the word for *see* might be metaphorically used for seeing with the mind or understanding. See p. 223.

Other principles in the history of language will be illustrated on p. 217, foll., in the Chapter on 'Etymology' (Sémantique).

3. The Indo-European or Māter-Language.

3. (*a*) *What is meant by the Indo-European Language? Draw a Plan to illustrate your answer.*

What was the Indo-European Language? A good idea of it will be given by the following sentences (see p. 159):—

mā́ter yuℊóm bhere: séptṃ agróis esti.

How are these sentences restored? for there is no doubt that they are 'restorations': the Indo-European Language itself has perished.

We restore them by taking certain Greek forms and Latin forms and English forms, and pairing them together, and finding *what the parent-form might have been.* The parent-form must be such as will naturally develope into *all* the forms which are found *in the descendants: it must account for all of them*, if they *are* direct descendants.

In answer to the question *when* this Language was spoken, it may be said that it was spoken at any rate more than three thousand years ago. As to *where* it was spoken, authorities are not agreed. Some hold that its earliest home was in Asia, while others are equally certain that its earliest home was in Europe.

Wherever the home was, it was certainly *a large plain*, and whoever the people were they were certainly not barbarous but were yet in a somewhat primitive state of civilisation.

How do we know this? Chiefly from the restored language, in which we find words for such ideas as horse, ox, plough (?), home, door, wealth, wine, milk, liver, father, mother, daughter, the numerals, and so on: see the Pairs of Words, on p. 83, foll.

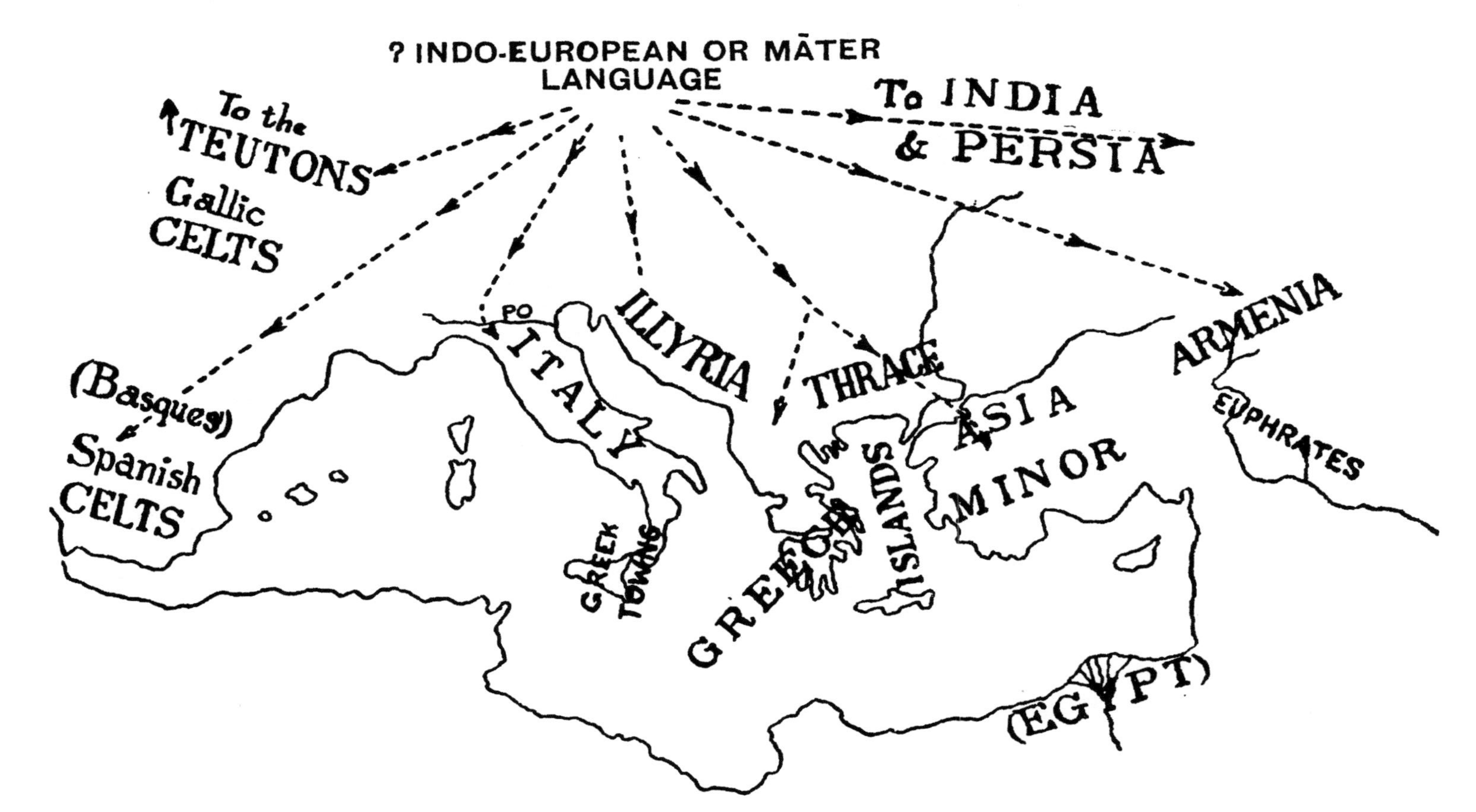

A. ROUGH MAP OF THE INDO-EUROPEAN LANGUAGE, AND ITS EXTENSION, *IF* ITS EARLY HOME WAS IN EUROPE. Non-Indo-European Languages are in Brackets.

How then did this single language give rise to a number of languages, including Greek, Latin, and English?

Well, it seems that the people in this large plain grew *more and more numerous*, and sent out different *waves* in various directions, especially in the direction of the Mediterranean. One or more waves went to Greece, one or more waves went to Italy: other waves went elsewhere.

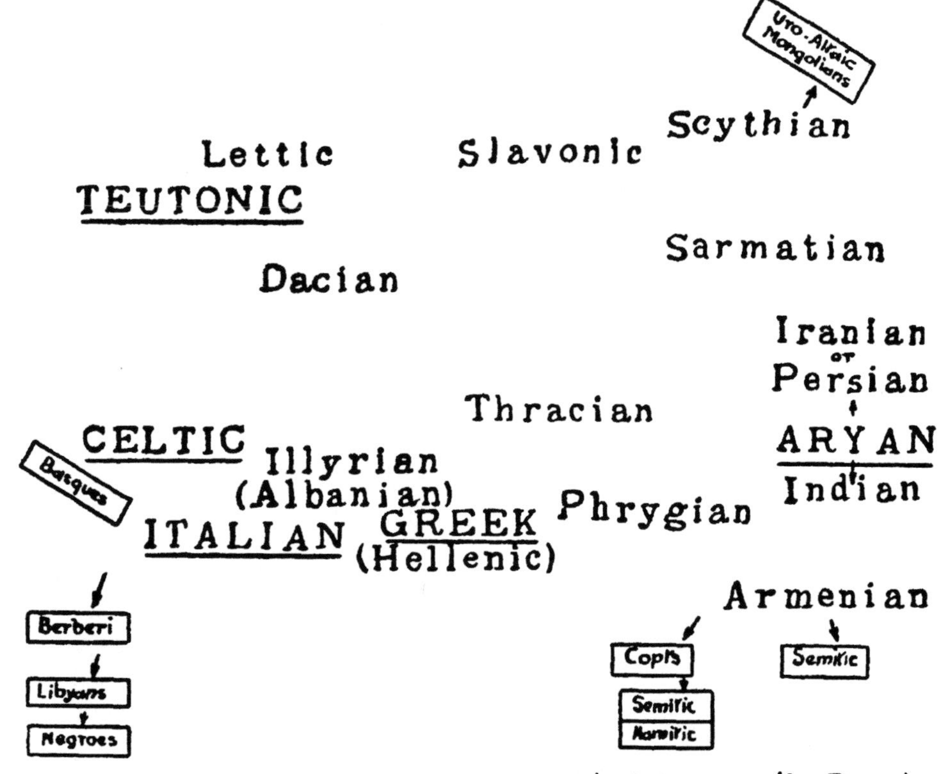

B. PLAN OF INDO-EUROPEAN LANGUAGES (not necessarily Races). Non-Indo-European Languages are in Brackets.

The Plan will give some idea of the directions which the various waves may have taken, and the list (below) will show how one parent-language may have given rise to several daughter-languages.

LIST OF INDO-EUROPEAN LANGUAGES.

The following is an inaccurate and incomplete List.

1. *Aryan*:—

(*a*) *Indian,* of which Sanskrit is the chief Language. It was the Literary Language of the Brahmans, the Indian priests: the older

Sanskrit is found in the Vedic Hymns, the later or Classical Sanskrit in the Epics, etc.

(*b*) *Iranian*, of which the Old Persian is found on the Cuneiform Inscriptions, while Old Bactian is found in the Zendavesta, the sacred books of Zoroaster.

2. *Armenian.*
3. *Greek* (see pp. 17, 31).
4. *Illyrian or Albanian.*
5. *Italic* (see pp. 17, 55).
6. *Celtic:* (*a*) Irish, Gaelic, and Manx, in the North;
   (*b*) Cymric, Cornish, and Armorican, in the South.
7. *Teutonic:* (*a*) Old Gothic and Scandinavian (including Icelandic, Norwegian, Danish, and Swedish), in the East;
   (*b*) in the West, English, Frisian, and Low and High German.
8. (*a*) *Baltic*, including Old Prussian, Lithuanian, and Lettish;
   (*b*) *Slavonic*, including Russian, Bulgarian, Servian, and Croatian in the South, and Polish and Czechish in the West.

It is necessary here to guard against a mistake that is very commonly made, viz. that language is the same as race. People can speak the language of a race without belonging to that race by blood; for instance, in France we find people who spoke a dialect of the Latin language, but who were not Latins by blood, but (largely) Celts. So it must be clearly remembered that we are here speaking not of an Indo-European race and its descendants, but of an Indo-European *language* and its descendants.

The Indo-European Language was only one Language and was at first spoken within a small area: in other areas many other Languages were spoken which had quite a different origin, for instance, the African Languages. The number of different Languages or Dialects over the world is reckoned by some at upwards of 1000, by others at over 3000.

3. (*b*) *What other names have been given to the Indo-European Language? Criticise them, and suggest new names if you can.*

The Indo-European Language has also been called

(i.) the '*Aryan*' Language: but 'Aryan' is a term which sometimes refers especially to the Asiatic group (Sanskrit and Persian);

(ii.) the '*Indo-Germanic*' Language: but the Asiatic group was not merely Indian, and the European group (see p. 14) was not merely German or Teutonic; the Slavonic and Latin-speaking peoples, for instance, are excluded by the term 'Indo-Germanic';

(iii.) '*Indo-European*' is better: but this does not include Persian;

(iv.) '*Eur-Aryan*' is still better, for this includes European Languages (mostly descended from this Language), and 'Aryan' in its special sense;

(v.) the '*Māter*'-Language might be suggested, as it would not only give an idea of a 'Mother-Language', but would also give a form which actually belonged to that Language. It should be pronounced Mah-ter, not May-ter.

3. (*c*) *Give a few Specimen-words of the Indo-European or Māter-Language, with Greek, Latin, and English descendants.*

The Indo-European or Māter-Language Sentences for

(*a*) mother, bear the yoke in the ten fields;

(*b*) there is a new family;

(*c*) which of those women is going alone?

would be something like the following, except that I have not here put in Accents (to mark the Notes, see p. 73):—

(*a*) *māter, dekm̥ agrois yuϑom bhere;*

(*b*) *neu̯om esti ϑenos;*

(*c*) *$q_u$is tāsōm oinā eiti?*

(*a*)	*māter*	μῆτερ	māter	mother
	dekm̥	δέκα	decem	ten
	agrois	ἀγροῖς	agrīs	acres
	yuϑom	ζυγόν	iugum	yoke
	bhere	φέρε	fer	bear
(*b*)	*neu̯om*	νέον	nouom	new
	esti	ἐστί	est	is
	ϑenos	γένος	genus	kin

(c)	*q_uis*	τίς	quis	whi(ch)
	tāsōm	τῶν	(is)tārum	th(ose)
	oinā	οἴνη	ūna	an, a
	eiti	εἶσι	īt (later ĭt)	...

See p. 83, foll.

3. (*d*) *State* (*and illustrate by a Plan*) *the relation of Greek and Latin to one another.*

A mother sometimes sees her children go out of the home country into other lands, where they find new neighbours and new conditions, and where one child may change in one special way and another child in another special way; the children of one child may thus become very different in appearance from the children of another child, and yet some family features may remain; the first and second cousins may still be like each other in some respects.

The Indo-European or *Māter*-Language sent out children into other lands, where these children found new neighbours and new conditions, and gradually became less and less like each other, as they moved further and further away from each other and communicated less frequently. At first the Māter-Language split up into Dialects, and then these Dialects became separate Languages (p. 28); one of these daughter-Dialects had been Italic, which had at its left hand Celtic, and at its right hand Greek: Greek again had, at its right hand, possibly Armenian but anyhow Aryan (Sanskrit and Persian). The order of these Dialects, from left to right, would be easily seen from a map of Europe (vide p. 11), and would be given by the word CIGAR (Celtic, Italic, Greek, *Ar*menian, *Ar*yan).

Thus Italic and Greek were once sister-Languages, living next to each other; they then moved further apart, and became in their turn mother-Languages, Italic having children who are (inaccurately) called Latin, Oscan or Sabellian, and Umbrian, and Greek having children who are (also inaccurately) called 'Aeolic', Ionic, and Doric: these are called Dialects.

C. PLAN OF ITALIC AND GREEK, AND THEIR DIALECTS.

Thus the Latin Dialect of the Italic Language, and the Ionic Dialect of the Greek Language, were first-cousin-Dialects, or they may be regarded as first-cousin-Languages; Attic was mainly a branch of Ionic, and would therefore be to Latin a first-cousin-once-removed.

Of these cousin-Languages, viz. Attic and Latin, we usually only see one side, the polished side; we usually see not the everyday conversational side but the Literary side of Attic and Latin, e.g. Attic and Latin as they were written by Sophocles and by Cicero.

Notes.—1. Thus 'Greek' and 'Latin', in the ordinary sense of the words, were cousins of one another and of Sanskrit: we must beware of saying that Latin forms came from Greek forms, or Greek forms from Sanskrit forms: this is a common mistake. As a matter of fact, Latin forms are often older than Greek forms (*e.g.* quoque than πότε, and see p. 100), and Greek or Latin forms are often older than Sanskrit forms.

2. As we shall see (p. 36), Latin is in some respects not so close to Attic Greek, as e.g.

(*a*) the Italic Dialects (p. 55) are to

(*b*) the 'Aeolic' Dialect.

4. What 'Analyse tremunt' really means.

4. (*a*) 'Analyse tremunt, or τρέμουσι'—*What does this question really mean?*

'*Analyse τρέμουσι*' is an example of a type of Philology Question which has long puzzled the beginner, who naturally supposes that he is meant to 'analyse τρέμουσι', and puts down e.g. τρεμ-ο-υσι, which is not the right Answer; the right Answer is nearer to

Root.	? Suffix (of Present)	Ending (of 3rd Plur. Act.).
trem	*o*	*nti.*

In fact, the question does not mean 'Analyse τρέμουσι', but 'Write down *the Early form* of τρέμουσι, and analyse *that*'. It cannot be too clearly understood, that 'Analyse *x*' does not mean 'Analyse *x*', but means 'Write down the Early form of *x*, and then analyse that'.

Now what is this Early form? It is the parent-form of the Greek word as we have it, and not only of this; for (often) it is also the parent-form of some Latin word as well; for instance, *tremonti* is the Indo-European or Māter-form which was the *parent-form* both of Greek τρέμουσι and of Latin tremunt; now tremousi would not be right as a parent-form, because it could not have produced Latin tremunt, and tremunt would not be right as a parent-form, because it could not have produced Greek τρέμουσι. No; we must find some parent-form which would have produced *both* Greek τρέμουσι *and* Latin tremunt.

4. (*b*) *What must be known before the Question 'Analyse . . .' can be safely answered? Suggest a logical process of learning how to 'Analyse' words.*

Our first Problem, in analysing words, is to arrive at the Early form, and, if possible, to arrive at the parent-form. How can we arrive at this form?

Obviously, the further back we go in Greek, and the further back we go in Latin, the nearer we shall be to the parent-forms; we must therefore be on the look-out for forms in Early Greek and in Early Latin.

What *Specimens of Early Greek and of Early Latin* have we? Well here we find (1) in the Doric Dialect τρέμοντι, (2) on a Latin Inscription tremonti. More generally speaking, then, we shall look out for Early forms in

(1) *Greek Dialects*, including the Homeric Dialect; many of the Dialect-forms we shall get from Greek Inscriptions (see p. 31);

(2) Old *Latin Inscriptions* and Old Latin wherever it survives.

It will be clear, from what has already been said about the Indo-European or Māter-Language (p. 13), that Sanskrit forms would also be valuable evidence, but, as the ordinary reader does not know Sanskrit, I shall not allude to them unless I am obliged, as in the case of the Early form of ἵππος, p. 88.

These two sources will give us *tremonti* as the Early form (here it was the parent-form): but how about a word like *bis?* For here we have δίς and bis; which was more likely to have been the Early form?

In a case like this, Sanskrit would be valuable evidence; but we shall often find

(3) *English forms*, especially Old English forms, to be of great use; here, for instance, to one who knows Grimm's Law (p. 63), 'twice' suggests that the Early form began with *dw*—, or, as it is usually written (p. 171), *du̯*—.

The beginner will therefore have to practise and to get experience in arriving at Early forms and, if possible, at parent or Indo-European forms, and he will best do this, not by looking at Early Greek forms alone, nor yet by looking at Early Latin forms alone, but by *comparing Early Greek and Early Latin forms together, taking Pairs of words to start with*, and from these Pairs restoring the parent- or Indo-European forms as nearly as possible; thus it will be easier for him to restore the Indo-European form (woikom or) *u̯oikom* by looking at the Pair of words οἶκον (Early Ϝοῖκον) and vīcum (Early ueicom) side by side, than by looking at either of these words *per se*.

But he will find this exercise becomes far easier if he has first grasped

(4) *some General Principles in the history of Sounds*, such, for instance, as the principle of *Association or Analogy* (p. 67), and other principles according to which parent-forms changed to Greek and Latin forms.

When he has seen these Principles at work, by means of a few simple instances, he will then be better prepared for this process of

(5) finding the parent or Indo-European forms of Pairs of words.

So much, then, for the process of *arriving at Early forms*.

We now come to the process of analysing these Early forms; and here our task is somewhat easier. But obviously we must first of all know

(6) *the various Parts of which Early words were composed*, or rather the parts into which it is convenient to analyse them; we must know what these parts are, i.e. where they are all to be found in one word (viz. Prefix, Root, Suffix, and Ending), and also what functions these parts have; we must know that, in aberis, for instance, the Early form *apo-eses* would be analysed into

Prefix, *apo* Root, *es* Suffix, *e* Ending, *s*;

and that, whereas we say 'you will be away', in four words, an analysis would be nearer to

away — be — will — you

in a single word, of which apo alone could be 'detached'.

(7) An *analysis of a few Greek and Latin words* would illustrate the parts and their functions, but it is needless to say that we should be very much helped if we knew something more about these parts in detail, especially about

(8) the commonest Endings (e.g. the Case-Endings), and the commonest Suffixes (e.g. the Suffix *-no-* of Adjectives).

Having worked thus by way of preparation, we could now proceed to

(9) *Exercises in the analysis of many Greek words*, with Answers by which the learner might correct his mistakes, and then

(10) of Latin words on the same plan.

(11) A *Summary*, giving the *Evidences* by which we analyse words in a certain way, and

(12) *Hints as to how to answer Questions and to avoid mistakes*, would finish the actual Analysis. And now the principles drawn from the various instances might be gathered up in

(13) a *Series of General Questions, collecting* various beads, as it were, that lie scattered here and there, and threading them upon their proper threads, or—to use a different comparison—a Series of Questions leading the learner to look at his facts from several points of view; for instance, some of the commonest and the hardest *Sound-changes* could be summarised and *tabulated.*

This, it seems, would give a really logical process; for instance,

(*a*) the Dialects would come before Analysis, because, without a knowledge of the Dialects, Analysis is not safe;

(*b*) Examples would come before Rules, because, without examples, Rules are too apt to be obscure and dull, whereas to take an example and to draw from it the Rule will give the learner clearer ideas, more interest, and—a most essential point—self-activity.

The process may be summed up as follows :—

After the Introduction on the Origins of Language, and on the Indo-European Language in particular, I then show what 'Analyse τρέμουσι' really means, and what one must know in order to analyse it correctly, and how one may best acquire skill in analysing words. The process will involve the following subjects :—

(1) Greek Dialects ;
(2) Latin Inscriptions ;
(3) Grimm's Law ;
(4) General Principles in the history of Sounds ;
(5) Pairs of Words, in Greek and Latin, with Parent-forms ;
(6) the various parts of words ;
(7) a few Greek and Latin words analysed ;
(8) common Endings and Suffixes ;
(9) many Greek words analysed ;
(10) many Latin words analysed ;
(11) Summary of Evidences ;
(12) Hints as to how to answer Questions and to avoid mistakes ;
(13) a Series of General Questions, showing various threads of Philology.

PART II.

PREPARATION FOR ANALYSIS OF WORDS.

Dialects.
Greek Dialects.
Latin Inscriptions.
English Consonants and Grimm's Law.
General Principles and useful facts in Philology
Pairs of Words in Greek and Latin, with Early or parent-forms.

5. Dialects.

5. (i.) *What is meant by 'Dialects'?* (ii.) *How do different Dialects arise, and* (iii.) *how do they disappear?*

As to (I.),

we hear a great deal about '*the* English Language', and we are apt to forget that the language has many varieties: thus there are, for instance,

(*a*) Literary English,

(*b*) Conversational English,

(*c*) the English of Dialects (e.g. the English of Cornwall, of Yorkshire, of Suffolk), to say nothing of

(*d*) the English of different Periods, and

(*e*) Poetic English.

Similarly, we hear much about '*the* Greek Language', and we are apt to forget that the Language had many varieties corresponding to the above; we are apt to forget, for instance, that the Greek for

'they (fem.) remain after sending messengers'

was not always

μένουσι πέμψᾱσαι ἀγγελούς,

but was, in one of the Greek Dialects (viz. 'Aeolic'),

μένοισι πέμψαισαι ἀγγέλοις [cp. (*c*) above];

and we are also apt to forget that there were certain Poetic Greek forms also [cp. (*e*) above].

Now what does a 'Dialect' mean? In its wider sense, it means 'something which differs from the standard Literary Language': thus Cornish would be a Dialect of English, and Doric a Dialect of Greek: supposing you could not understand what a Cornishman meant, then Cornish would rather be a separate Language than a Dialect of the English Language.

We may say, then, that a Dialect of a Language is (i.) a form of that Language which can be understood by one who knows the Standard form or ordinary form of the Language, but which (ii.) differs more or less from the Standard form or ordinary form of the Language.

The mutual relations of a Language to a Dialect will be clearer if we consider the history of Conversational (or 'Vulgar') Latin. This Language was spoken over a great part of the Roman Empire, e.g. in Italy, France, and Spain; and in these countries (owing to reasons which will be given directly) small differences arose, which by degrees grew greater and greater, till Italians, 'French', and 'Spaniards', instead of merely speaking different Dialects of a single Language and being able to understand each other, came to speak different Languages and to be unable to understand each other. The different Dialects had now become different Languages, and these different Languages were liable themselves to split up into different Dialects, and so on.

Note.—In treating of the Dialects, we must always remember that

(i.) there were many *sub-divisions*, many minor Dialects, with their own peculiarities, inside the large Dialect; and that

(ii.) there were some *mongrel-Dialects*, as when a conquering people imposed its Dialect on a conquered people, or where the land of two peoples met (see the Diagram).

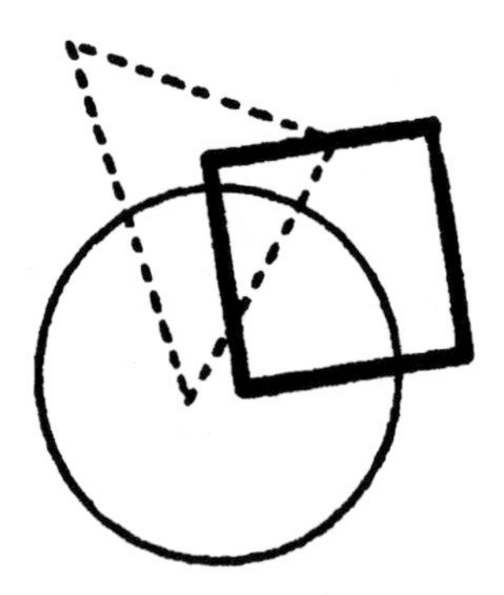

D. HOW DIALECTS OF A SINGLE LANGUAGE MAY OVERLAP.

(iii.) Each Dialect differed at different *stages* in its history.

(iv.) Dialect does not mean 'race'; to say that certain people spoke a certain Dialect does not imply that they belonged to a certain race, since conquered people, for instance, may speak the Dialect of their conquerors without changing their race; it is always as well to bear in mind the Norwegians who came to France and settled in Normandy; they spoke a Dialect of French, without being French by race. Those of them who, later on, went over to England, as Norman conquerors, came to speak a Dialect of English.

(v.) Dialect does not always mean Locality: i.e., because a man wrote in the Doric or 'Aeolic' Dialect, it does not follow that he was a native of a Doric or an 'Aeolic' place, or even that he lived there: for it was customary to write *Choral Odes* in Doric (partly or wholly), and this has left traces in the Chorus of Attic Tragedy, and it was customary to write Personal Lyrics in 'Aeolic', and Epic Poetry in 'Epic', irrespective of the author's birthplace. Pindar and Theocritus varied the Dialect according to the subject.

As to (ii.), *the reasons why Dialects arise*, among the chief are:—

(*a*) *Geography* and its effects: mountains, forests, the sea, and rivers may separate from one another and may cut off from intercommunication people who once spoke a single Language; moreover, a different Climate, etc., may produce differences in

(*b*) the organs of speech; Geography may also help to produce differences in

(*c*) the character, customs, constitutions, and occupations of the people; agriculture and a seafaring life would lead to differences in the Language itself;

(*d*) immigrants and travellers would especially tend to introduce into one place the conditions and the Language of other places, especially of neighbouring places;

(*e*) the previous population of the country, or, later on,

(*f*) an invading and conquering population might have a powerful effect.

As to (iii.) *the reason why Dialects disappear*:—

(*a*) Man breaks down the barriers set up by Geography;

mountains are cut through or passes over them are discovered, forests are cut down, ships go over the sea, and rivers are bridged;

(*b*) thus there is more communication, more interchange of ideas by travel and trade;

(*c*) sometimes one predominant State extends its Language, its poetry and its prose, to other States; this is especially the case with a great civilising or commercial State. A modified Attic Dialect was spread far and wide when Macedon and Greece conquered the East;

(*d*) or, again, States may band together to resist some common enemy; close union may be brought by danger or war when everything else has failed to unite.

In England we ourselves have seen the Dialects disappear very rapidly, owing to the influence of large towns, of railways, of the Bible, of newspapers and other forms of literature, of trade, of intercourse, of local government, and so on. The great Dialect Dictionary needs quick work if the fragments are to be rescued from oblivion.

6. Greek Dialects.

6. *Give the chief peculiarities of the—*

(i.) *Doric Dialect,*
(ii.) *Ionic Dialect,*
(iii.) *Old and New Attic Dialect, with instances; say where these Dialects were spoken.*

As to the position of the three main Dialects, it will be useful to remember the word A I D; for in most of the Northern States and islands and their colonies we have '*Aeolic*', in some of the Central States and islands and their colonies we have *Ionic* (*and Attic*), and in most of the Southern States and islands and their colonies we have *Doric.*

For details as to the Dialects, the reader may refer to Giles' *Manual* (Appendix B.), Roberts' *Greek Epigraphy*, Merry's *Greek Reader* ('The Greek Dialects'), Cauer's *Delectus*, Meister's *Die Griechischen Dialekte*, H. W. Smyth's *Ionic Dialect*, Boisacq's *Les Dialectes Doriens*, etc.

6. (i.) *The Doric Dialect.*

The Doric Dialect was spoken chiefly in the States of South Greece (in Europe and Asia), in the South Islands, and in the colonies from these: see Map, p. 17.

'Doric' was to be found—

(*a*) *in Peloponnese*—in Laconia (where we have its 'extreme' form), Messenia, Argolis, Aegina, and Corinth; Elis and Achaea did not have the pure Dorian Dialect;

(*b*) *in the Ægean Sea*—in Melos, Thera, and Rhodes;

(*c*) *in Colonies*—at Selinus and Byzantium (from Megara), Corcyra and Syracuse (from Corinth), Cyrene (from Thera), Gela and Acragas (from Rhodes). See a Map of Greece, and the Plan on p. 17.

'*Having conquered the strangers seven times in the first year, when he was playing the pipe, he sets up the pillar of the Muses, which we see, in the hope that they may accept it,*' would have been expressed in Old Laconian by νῑκᾱhᾱς (νῑκήσᾱς) τως ξηνως ἑπτακιν (τοὺς ξένους ἑπτάκις) τω πρᾱτω ϝετεος (τοῦ πρώτου ἔτους) ὁκα ἐσυριδδε (ὅτε ἐσύριζεν), ἱστᾱτι (ἵστησι) τᾱν στᾱλᾱν τᾶν Μωʽᾱν ἇν ὁρᾱμες (τὴν στήλην τῶν Μουσῶν ἣν ὁρῶμεν), αἰ κα λαβωντι (εἴ κε = ἐάν πως λάβωσι).

The peculiarities should be worked out in full; here it will be sufficient to notice a few, with Attic forms in Brackets: ᾱ (η), ω (ου), η (ει, sometimes), ᾱ (ω, sometimes), uncontracted vowels, ϝ (disappeared), δδ (ζ, Doric also had -σδ-), -τι (-σι), -μες (-μεν), -ντι (-σι).

There were other varieties of Doric, for which see, for instance, Giles (Appendix B.); thus Argive and Cretan had an Accusative Plural in -νς (e.g. τόνς).

Corinth had ἐνθὼν πεπόνθεις (ἐλθὼν πέπονθας).
Crete, besides τόνς (τούς), had ἀποϝειπάσθω δίκαδδεν (ἀπειπέσθω δικάζειν).

6. (ii.) *The Ionic Dialect.*

The Ionic Dialect was to be found in:—
(*a*) Euboea,
(*b*) Chios and Samos, and the coast-towns near them,
(*c*) the Cyclades.

Note.—Ionic is best known, to most readers, from Herodotus, but it is probable that the text of Herodotus was altered a good deal before it arrived at its present form. Smyth's work on the subject (see above) is excellent, but expensive.

Ionic would have expressed '*Thence, accordingly, you gained the whole thing as it was easiest to do it,*' by ἐνθεῦτεν ὦν (ἐντεῦθεν οὖν) οὖλον τὸ πρῆγμα (ὅλον τὸ πρᾶγμα) ὅκως ῥήϊστον ποιέειν ἐκτήσαο (ὅπως ῥᾷστον ποιεῖν ἐκτήσω).

Notice here, among other things, ω (ου, cp. Doric), no Aspirate in οὖλον (cp. Aeolic), ου (ο), ρη (ρᾱ), and Uncontracted Vowels.

6. (iii.) *Old and New Attic* were spoken chiefly in Athens and in those States to which the Athenian Dialect spread: see below.

The Old Attic of Thucydides would have said αἰετὸς αἰεὶ πράσσει ξὺν θάρσει, whereas the New Attic of Demosthenes said ἀετὸς ἀεὶ πράττει σὺν θάρρει.

6. (iv.) *What is meant by the* Κοινή, *and by the Language of the New Testament?*

When Alexander had conquered the East, he and his successors brought to it the Greek Language—not the Classical and Literary Greek of Athens, but a slightly different Dialect,

(*a*) nearer in many respects to the Conversational Language (of a later age than that of Demosthenes),

(*b*) with elements from other Dialects, and

(*c*) modified by the Language spoken in the countries to which it was imported.

This was called the Κοινὴ (διάλεκτος), and Polybius and Plutarch are usually called writers of the Κοινή; but they give us its Literary and more polished side.

The Colloquial side of the Κοινή gave rise to New Testament Greek, which was influenced—cp. (*c*) above—by the native Language of the Jews of Alexandria and elsewhere.

Thus in the New Testament we find much that was Literary Attic, but a certain amount that was due to Conversational Greek, to the Greek of other Dialects, and to the Language of the Jews.

Among New Testament features may be noticed

(i.) Case-Endings, such as νοΐ (νῷ), δυσίν (δυοῖν),

(ii.) Indeclinable Nouns, especially Hebrew proper names, e.g. Ἀαρών, Ἱερουσαλήμ or Ἱεροσόλυμα,

(iii.) Comparatives such as περισσοτέρως,

(iv.) 'Double-Augmented' forms like ἤμελλε, ἠδύνατο, ἀπεκατεστάθη,

(v.) Unaugmented Pluperfects, like δεδώκει,

(vi.) 2nd Aorist-forms like ἤλθατε,
(vii.) 3rd Plurals like εἴχοσαν (εἶχον),
(viii.) 2nd Singulars like δύνασαι,
(ix.) 'Middle' forms like ἤμην 'I was,'
(x.) a tendency to *discard* the Optative (and the Dual).

For details, see Winer's *Grammar of New Testament Greek*, which has long been the standard work on the subject. The book is, unfortunately, expensive.

7. ' Aeolic ' Dialect.

7. *Define the ' Aeolic ' Dialect, and mention its chief features, comparing it with Latin, as far as possible.*

' Aeolic ' was derived from αἴολος ' variegated ', and the name is used in more than one sense.

(*a*) It sometimes refers to Old Greek, such as was spoken in the Peloponnese in Early times: a better name would perhaps be ' *Achaean* ', applying to the Dialect of the Arcadians and Cyprians.

The ' Achaeans ' are the people of whom we hear so much in Homer: in fact sometimes Ἀχαιοί can almost mean ' Greeks ' in Homer. These ' Achaeans ' flourished especially in Peloponnese, but most of them seem to have been conquered or displaced by the Dorians who invaded the Peloponnese about 1000 B.C. It is possible that the *Arcadians*, who were protected by their mountains, may have remained as a relic of the older inhabitants, and some of the *Cyprians* were colonists from Arcadia.

The Arcadian and Cyprian for βάλλεται ἐξ οἰκίᾱς εἰς βάραθρον ἱερεύς would be δέλλεται ἐξ [ἐς could be used before Vowels] οἰκίαυ ἰν ζέρεθρον ἱερῆς.

(*b*) Usually, however, ' Aeolic ' applies especially to the Dialect of *Lesbos* and the coast of Asia Minor near Lesbos; and also to Thessaly (which may have been partly ruled by Dorian nobles), and to Boeotia (which may have been partly conquered by Dorians in early times). At any rate these two latter Dialects have some Doric features.

Perhaps many of the ' Achaeans ', who were driven out by the Great Migrations, fled to Lesbos and its neighbourhood.

(*c*) ' Aeolic ' was also spoken in the ' Aeolic ' colonies, such as Cumae in Italy.

Let us suppose that the *Lesbians* had wished to express: 'The women remain, having sent to them messengers from the sacred city that, on behalf of that city, they might destroy a a wild beast': they would have said:—

μένοισι (*μένουσι*) *στέλλαισαι αὔτοισι* (*στείλᾶσαι αὐτοῖς*) *ἀγγέλοις πὰρ τᾶς ἴρᾶς πόλιος* (*ἀγγέλους παρὰ τῆς ἱέρᾶς πόλεως*) *ὥς κε* [*ὥς κε* = *ἵνα*] *ὔπερ κήνᾶς* (*ὑπὲρ κείνης*) *φῆρα ἄπυ-φθέρρωσι* (*θῆρα ἀποφθείρωσιν*).

Notice here, among other things,

1. *ελλ*, *ερρ* (*ειλ*, *ειρ*): cp. Latin velle, ferre (from -ls-, -rs-);

2. the Accent thrown back towards the beginning of the word, as near as the Greek Law of Accents allowed: contrast 'Aeolic' *φύγᾱ* and Early Latin fúgā (→ fúgă, ʹ being a mark of Emphasis, not of Note) with Attic and Ionic *φυγή*, and Doric *φυγά*;

3. *-οις* (*-ους*, Acc. Plur., cp. Feminine *-αις* with Attic *-ᾱς*);

4. *πάρ* shows a clipping of the last Vowel: cp. Latin ab (*ἀπό*), sub (*ὑπό*), etc., p. 84;

5. absence of the 'Aspirate': cp. Latin anser, from hanser (*χήν*);

6. *ᾱ* (*η*): cp. Latin paterfamiliās;

7. *ι* (*υ*): cp. to some extent, Latin maxumus and maximus (p. 45);

8. *φ* (*θ*): cp. Latin fera;

9. *υ* (*ο*): cp. Latin agrom → agrum.

It will be convenient to collect some other points here, from other 'Aeolic' Dialects:

10. *-ε* (*-α*) as in *δἰε* (*διά*): cp. Latin pede ? from ped-a;

11. *F* kept till late: cp. *Fῦκῡς* with Latin vīcōs (*οἴκους*);

12. *-ι* (Genitive Singular Ending), as in *Fοίκοι* 'of the house': cp. Latin vīcī;

13. Dative Singular *Fοίκω*: cp. Latin vīcō;

14. *κ-* in *κίς* (*τίς*): cp. Latin quis;

15. *ῡ* (*οι*): cp. *Fῦκῡς* above: for *oi* → Latin ū, cp. oinom → ūnum.

These peculiarities are specially selected from various 'Aeolic' Dialects, such as Thessalian: they are not all to be found in any one Dialect.

As an exercise on the 'Aeolic' of Lesbos, it would be well to turn the beginning of the Iliad into Lesbian (see p. 38).

The following would be another instance of Lesbian (not of very early Lesbian, which would have kept the Digamma, *F*). The Attic forms are put in brackets.

περὶ ὧν (*ὧν*) *οἱ* (*οἱ*) *στρότᾱγοι* (*στρατηγοὶ*) *προτίθεισι προσταξαίσᾱς* (*προσταξάσης*) *τᾶς βόλλᾱς* (*τῆς βούλης*) *καὶ οἱ* (*οἱ*) *πρέσβεις* . . . *ἀπαγγέλλοισι* (*ἀπαγγέλλουσι*) *καὶ δόγμα ἤνῑκαν* (*ἐνίκησαν*) *πὰρ τῶ κοίνω* (*παρὰ τῷ κοινῷ*) *Αἰτώλων περὶ τᾶς οἰκηϊότᾱτος* (Early *Fοικ-*, *τῆς οἰκειότητος*) *καὶ τᾶς φιλιᾶς* (*τῆς φιλίᾱς*), *ὤς κε* (*ὡς*) *διαμένωσι εἰς τὸν πάντα χρόνον καὶ μήδεις μήτε Αἰτώλων μήτε τῶν κατοικήντων* (*κατοικούντωι*) *ἐν Αἰτωλίαι* (*Αἰτωλίᾳ*) . . . *δέδοχθαι τῶ δάμω* (*τῷ δήμῳ*) *ἐπαίνησαι* (*ἐπαινέσαι*) *τὸ κοῖνον τῶν Αἰτώλων καὶ τοὶς προέδροις* (*τοὺς προέδρους*) . . ., *ὄτι* (*ὅτι*) *εὐνόως ἔχοισι* (*ἔχουσι*) *πρὸς τὸν δᾶμον* (*δῆμον*) *τὸν Μυτιληνάων* (*Μυτιληναίων*), *καὶ ἐπιμέλεσθαι* (*ἐπιμελεῖσθαι*) *αὔτων τᾶν βόλλᾶν καὶ τὸν δᾶμον* (*v.* above) *καὶ ταὶς ἄρχαις ταὶς καθισταμέναις* (all in -*ᾱς*) *ὡς* (*ὡς*) *ἅ τε φιλίᾱ* (*ἥ τε*) *καὶ ἀ οἰκηιότᾱς* (*ἡ οἰκειότης*) *ἀ ὐπάρχοισα* (*ἡ ὑπάρχουσα*) *πρὸς Αἰτώλοις* (-*ους*) *διαμένει* (*διαμενεῖ*). . . .

Thessalian expressed *διὰ τὸ χρησιμοὶ εἶναι ἐγένοντο αὐτοῦ τινες ὁποίους ἂν βούληται ἀποστεῖλαι καὶ τὰ ὀνόματα αὐτῶν εἰς στήλᾱς καταθεῖναι* by *διὲ τὸ χρείσιμοι ἔμμεν ἐγένονθο αὔτοι κινες ποίοις κε βέλλειτει ἀπυστέλλειν καὶ τὰ ὀνύματα αὔτουν ἐν στάλλᾱς κατθέμεν.*

Notice here how *ἐγένονθο* was assimilated (p. 67) to *ἐγένεσθε.*

In *Boeotian* we should find *ὁ πάτειρ τίσῑ πέτταρα τοῖσι ἀρχόντεσσι, πὰρ τῦς Βοιτῦς Fύκῡς κεχωρήκων,* not *ὁ πατὴρ τείσει τέσσαρα τοῖς ἄρχουσιν, παρὰ τοὺς Βοιωτοὺς οἴκους κεχωρηκώς.*

To these Dialects we may add :—

(i.) The *North-West* Dialects, i.e. those of the Locrians, Phocians, Acarnanians, Aetolians, etc.; here we find *καλείμενος ἐν Ναύπακτον ἀγώνοις* (*καλούμενος εἰς Ναύπακτον ἀγῶσιν*) ;

(ii.) the *Cross or Mongrel Dialects*, such as that of Elis, which had *Fειζὼς ἔᾱ φάρην* (*εἰδὼς εἴη φέρειν*).

8. 'Homeric' Dialect.

8. *What is Fick's theory about the Homeric Dialect? How far is it likely to have been correct?*

The following nonsense - lines would illustrate some 'Homeric' Dialect-forms, such as Datives in -οισι, Genitives in -οιο, Case-Endings in -θι, 3rd Singulars in -σι, uncontracted Vowels, and other forms, and the sound of the Digamma (*F*) surviving:—

αἴ κέ νιν ὀφθαλμοῖσι ἰδὼν πεδίοιο θέῃσι,
αὐτόθι τεθνηὼς ἔπε' ἐξ ὁρόωντι διδώσει.

The 'Homeric' Dialect was never used in Prose or in conversation: it is made up of the forms of (i.) various Periods (cp. Genitives in -οιο, -οο, and -ου), and (ii.) various Localities (cp. forms in ᾱ or η).

The 'Homeric' Dialect may also be called 'Epic'.

Fick thought that 'Homer' was originally written in the 'Aeolic' Dialect, i.e. in a Dialect like that of Lesbos; the Iliad would then have begun somewhat in this way:—

μᾶνιν ἄειδε, θέᾱ, Πηληϊάδᾱ' Ἀχιλῆος
ὀλλομένᾱν, ᾆ μύρι' Ἀχαίοισ' ἄλγε' ἔθηκε,
πόλλαις δ' ἰφθίμοις ψύχαις Ἄ*F*ιδι προΐαψε
ἠρώων, αὔτοις δὲ *F*ελώρια τεῦχε κύνεσσι
οἰώνοισί τε παῖσι, Δί*F*ος δ' ἐτελήετο βόλλᾱ,
ἐξ ὦ δὴ τὰ πρῶτα διεστάτᾱν ἐρίσαντε
Ἀτρεΐδᾱς τε *F*άναξ ἄνδρων καὶ δῖος Ἀχίλλευς.

This 'Aeolic' (which is well worth learning) was then translated—probably by slow degrees—into Ionic, for Ionic hearers; but 'Aeolic' forms would survive (i.) where the metre excluded the Ionic form (e.g. κύνεσσι), and, sometimes,

(ii.) where Ionic had no exact equivalent in sense, or where the exact sense of the 'Aeolic' word was not clear.

The result would be a kind of Mongrel Dialect ('Aeolic' + Ionic), and later additions in this Mongrel Dialect might have been made, to supplement the original poem or poems.

Still later on, this Mongrel ('Aeolic' + Ionic) Dialect might have become gradually 'Atticised' for Attic readers, in many respects: still, much of the old Dialect would survive, for reasons akin to those already mentioned. Genitives in -οο might sometimes become Attic -ου.

In some words a new form was created, a mixture of the old and the Attic: thus Ιλίοο (πτολίεθρον) might become Ἰλιόου, a mixture of the old Ἰλίοο and the Attic Ἰλίου.

Summary.—If Homer was at first 'Aeolic', and then was (mostly) translated into Ionic, and then sometimes Atticised, and if additions were made in the 'Aeolic'-Ionic Dialect, we should have an explanation of most of the peculiarities of Homer.

To the above it is possible to add a 'Conversational' element: for Homer has many words which seem to have belonged to the Spoken Dialects, and were not to be found in the Literary Dialects. (See Kennedy's *Sources of New Testament Greek*.)

This 'Dialect' ('Homeric' or 'Epic') became the regular Dialect for a Poet to use when he was writing on a Heroic subject: thus Pindar uses many 'Epic' forms when he is telling of the deeds of heroes.

9. Exercises on the Dialects.

9. *Assign the following forms to their respective Dialects, with a few Notes :—*

τόνς, φύγᾱ, ὄκα, ὄκως, πέμπε, λόγοι (Gen.), ἆ (ἥ), κώρᾱ, ἔσπερρε, ἀκούσαις, λόγοισι, βασιλῆς, Fᾱλείοις (Ἠλείοις), μοῦνος, ἐνθαῦτα.

Note.—If you were answering questions about Dialects *in full*, it would be best

(i.) to begin by giving the Attic form ;

(ii.) to mention *all* the points of difference ;

(iii.) to illustrate these from the same Dialects, from other Dialects, and from Latin, etc. ;

(iv.) to give the causes of the peculiarities ;

(v.) *not* to say that one form is '*instead of*' or '*for*' an Attic form : it is far more accurate simply to put the Attic form in brackets. The Dialect form was not 'for' an Attic form : it existed independently, and was not a 'mistake'.

τόνς (τούς) Argive and Cretan, *-ns* being the Early Ending ;

φύγᾱ (φυγή) 'Aeolic' (Doric would have φυγά) : for -ā cp. Early Latin fugā ;

ὄκα (ὅτε) Doric : I think it is doubtful whether κα was not connected with καί rather than with τε ;

ὄκως (ὅπως) Ionic : the Early letter was *q*-, cp. Latin quis ;

πέμπε (πέντε) 'Aeolic' : cp. βελφῖνες (δελφῖνες) for the 'Aeolic' preference for Labials (p. 36) ;

λόγοι (Gen. λόγου) Thessalian : cp. Latin Genitives in -ī, e.g. vīcī from -ko-i ;

ἆ (ἥ) 'Aeolic,' which objected to Aspirates (p. 36) ;

κώρᾱ (κόρη) Doric, from kor-u̯ā, which became Aeolic κόρη, Ionic κούρη ;

ἔσπερρε (ἔσπειρε) 'Aeolic', from *esperset*: for rs → ρρ, cp. Latin ferre (p. 36);

ἀκούσαις (ἀκούσᾱς) 'Aeolic', from -ants: cp. Attic τιθεντς → τιθείς;

λόγοισι (λόγοις) 'Aeolic' and Ionic;

βασιλῆς (βασιλεύς) Arcadian and Cyprian, from -ēus: cp. ϑōus → bōs;

Fᾱλείοις (Ἠλείοις) Dialect of Elis, which might have had -ρ instead of -ς;

μοῦνος (μόνος) Ionic, from monuos → Doric μῶνος, 'Aeolic' μόννος;

ἐνθαῦτα (ἐνταῦθα) Ionic, cp. ἐνθεῦτεν, κιθών (χιτών).

10. Evidences for, and interest of, Greek Dialects.

10. (a) *What are our chief evidences for the different Dialects?*

The chief Evidences for the Dialects are:—

(i.) *Inscriptions,* which are best, because least liable to alteration; they give treaties, laws, honours decreed to people, epitaphs, etc. Their language is mostly the 'official' and not the conversational Dialect;

(ii.) *Writers*—

(*a*) of the Locality itself,

(*b*) of other Localities, who used the Dialect for Literary purposes (cp. the Doric used by Pindar for his Choral Hymns to the gods), or for parody (cp. Aristophanes' Megarian in the 'Acharnians').

But the MSS. are liable to be Modernised and Atticised.

(iii.) *Grammarians,* who wrote notes on obscure words and constructions: cp. to some extent, the great Dialect Dictionaries. Here again the MSS. are liable to be altered.

(iv.) Relics are also found in

(*a*) *names* of people (thus cp. Rūfus, a Sabellian or Oscan form),

(*b*) names of places (cp. English towns in -caster, -don, etc.),

(*c*) names of animals (thus cp. lupus and bōs, Dialect-forms, and possibly ἵππος (p. 88) rather than ? ἔππος),

(*d*) borrowed words generally (pp. 85, 88, 90),

(*e*) Poetry and other Literature which tends to preserve what has elsewhere disappeared (cp. the -υ- of αἰσυμνήτης, a trace of 'Aeolic').

10. (b) *Say why the study of the Dialects should be interesting and useful.*

(i.) As to *Philology*, Dialects often preserve Early and even Māter-forms, which would be hard to get from other sources: thus Doric ἇϝως and ἵστᾱτι were nearer to the Māter-forms *āusōs* and *sist(h)āti* than Attic ἕως and ἵστησι were, and Argive and Cretan τόνς was a Māter-form (*tons*).

(ii.) For *History*, the Dialect-Inscriptions and Names of persons and places, etc., are often first-rate Evidence, not only as to the intercourse and connexion of one people with another (by trade, conquest, etc.), but also as to the life and religion and character of the *smaller States* of Greece, of which we hear so little, and as to the huge number of these States, and the influence of Geography in isolating them from one another. We are too apt to regard Greek History as merely the history of Athens, Sparta, and a few other large States.

(iii.) *Geography* becomes a more interesting study if we know even only a little about some of the out-of-the-way places.

(iv.) *Science-principles*, such as the Survival of the Fittest, and Fossilisation (p. 219), are well illustrated by the disappearances and survivals of Dialect-forms.

For *Research-work* on the Dialects, I should suggest the following subjects:—

(i.) the connexion of Latin and the Italic Dialects with the various Greek Dialects, especially the 'Aeolic' of Thessaly;

(ii.) the inter-connexion of the various Greek Dialects, and the light that this might throw on Migrations, conquests, commerce, communication, etc.;

(iii.) the characteristics of various peoples as shown by their Dialects.

11. Latin Inscriptions. Classical Forms turned into Early Latin.

11. *In what forms might the following words be found on an Early Latin Inscription? Write a few Notes.*

(*a*) *dabunt malum Metelli Naevio poetae;*

(*b*) *Philippus maximi aestimavit;*

(*c*) *Lucius Gnaeo natus, cuius fama virtuti parissima fuit, cum Romae adesset, aedem Iunoni posuit;*

(*d*) *ut facillime figi possit.*

(*a*) (dabunt) *dabont*, malum (*ma-lom* or *-lo*), Metellī (*Metel-ei* or *-ē* or *-ī*), Naeviō (*Cnaiuiōi* or *Gn-*), poētae (*poētāi*).

1. Early Latin had a *choice* of forms, e.g. *-ei* or *-ē* or *-ī*, and sometimes two forms will occur side by side in the same Inscription;

2. the *Early Vowels* here are often like the Greek Vowels: e.g. cp. -o- (Classical -u-) with Greek -ο-, in τρέμοντι (p. 20);

3. for final *-m* weakly pronounced, in malo (malum), cp. the elision of -m in Latin Verses, and Latin frātrem → French frère by loss of the nasal;

4. Early Latin wrote single Consonants, e.g. -l- (-ll-);

5. C, the third letter of the Alphabet, once stood for G (cp. ΑΒΓ), as well as for C: *vide* p. 212.

6. Early Latin had its *Diphthongs* (as well as its Vowels) nearer to those of the Māter-Language, e.g. *-ei* (Classical *-ī*) from *-oi*, cp. Greek λόγοι; *-ōi*, which was rare, (Classical *-ō*) from *-ōi*, cp. Greek λόγωι or λόγῳ; and *-ai* (Classical *-ae*) from *-ai*, cp. Early Latin aidem (aedem) with Greek αἴθω.

Note on ei, ē, ī.—Early Latin *ei* had several origins (p. 164), and was pronounced as an *e*-sound, followed by an *i*-sound; hence it became a sound sometimes nearer to *ē* and sometimes nearer to *ī*, and was written sometimes as *ei*, sometimes as *e*, sometimes as *i*. Still later on, we find the signs *ei*, *e*, and *i*, actually used for one another, so that even the *e*-sound of imp*e*rium is found written as *ei*. In Classical times *i* was the regular way of writing the sound.

(*b*) (Philippus) *Pili-pos* or *-po* (maximī) *maxsum-ei* or *-ē* or *-ī* (aestimāvit) *aistumāu-eit* or *-ēt* or *-īt*.

In addition to some of the above features, we notice

6. Final *-s* weakly pronounced: cp. the Early Latin Scansion of confectu*s* quiescit, at the end of a Hexameter;

7. *ph-* written as *p-* in words borrowed from Greek: Greek pronounced φ as in up-hill, not as in our word Philip (where ph has the f-sound). Early Latin dropped the Aspirate here in writing;

8. *x* was written as *xs ;*

9. *-u-* in maxs*u*mei and aistumāveit had a sound not unlike that of *u* in *u*ne pl*u*me, or of German *ü* : see further p. 210.

For the -eit of the 'Perfect', see p. 140.

(*c*) (Lūcius) *Loucī-os* or *-o* (Gnaeō) *Cn-* or *Gn-aivōd* (nātus) *gnāt-os* or *-o* (cuius) *qu-* or *q-oius* (fāma) *fāmā* (virtūtī) *uirtūt--ei* or *-ē* or *-ī* (parissima) *parisumā* (fuit) *fu*[*u*]*-eit* or *-ēt* or *-īt* (cum) *qu-* or *q-om* (Rōmae) *Rōmăi* (adesset) *adesēt* (aedem) *aid-e* or *-em* (Iūnōnī) *Iūnōn-ei* or *-ē* or *-ī* (posuit) *poseiu-eit* or *-ēt* or *-īt*.

Notice here, besides many of the above features of Early Latin,—

the Diphthong *ou* from *eu* (cp. λευκός and the old form *Leucesie*); also the Diphthong *oi* in quoius (Classical *ū*), cp. 6 above;

10. *ī* in *Loucīos* (Classical *-ĭ*), cp. illīus and illĭus;

11. *-d* in *Gnaivōd*, a trace of the old Ablative or *from-Case* (p. 120);

12. -ā in fāmā (cp. Aeolic φάμᾱ) Nom. Sing., Classical -ă : the -ā → -ă

(i.) in Iambic words like *fŭgā*, where it was hard to pronounce a Short Vowel with Emphasis and then to pronounce a Long Vowel without Emphasis—hence *fúgă ;*

(ii.) in the Accusative fāmām, because Long Vowels were regularly shortened before Final *-m*, -r, or -t : cp. adesēt (adesset);

13. *qu-*, *q-*, and *c-* (cp. quom, qum, cum) were often interchanged in Early Latin spelling : cp. pequnia or pecunia.

Note.—Besides these peculiarities, we may notice e.g. the *-u-* of *Gnaivōd* (Gnaeō).

(*d*) (ut) *utei* (facillimē) *facilumēd* (fīgī) *fei-* or *fī-* *-gei* or *-gī* or *-gier* (possit) *potis sit* (Earlier *siēt* or *siēd*).

Notice—

14. the Archaic Infinitive in *-ier* (p. 148) ;

15. the Optative *siēd* or *siēt* (p. 121) ;

16. the longer form potis sit, not yet 'syncopated' into possit.

It will be found a good exercise to turn the above Classical Latin forms into Early Latin, and the following Inscription might be added ; for the 'Answer', see below.

hunc unum plurimi consentiunt Romae (or Romani)
bonorum optimum fuisse virum virorum
Lucium Scipionem : filius Barbati
consul censor aedilis hic fuit apud vos :
hic cepit Corsicam Aleriamque urbem (pugnando),
dedit Tempestatibus aedem merito votam.

N.B.—Mark the Long Vowels before attempting this.

The following exercises might be added. Turn the *italicised* words into Early Latin forms, putting alternative forms in brackets :—

1. *aequitiae ;*
2. *Curae ;*
3. *si qui essent qui adversum ea fecissent* quam *supra scriptum est ;*
4. *maximi feceris ;*
5. *publico iudicio ;*
6. *si* quis *magistratus multam* irrogare volet, *qui* volet (dum minoris

partis familiae taxat) liceto, eique omnium rerum siremps *lex esto quasi si* is *hac lege pecuniam exegisset ;*

7. de *praetoris senatusque sententia ;*

8. magnam sapientiam *aetate cum parva possidet hoc saxum ;*

9. . . . atque, *ut hoc in tabulam incideretis*, ita senatus *aequom censuit, utque* eam *figi* iubeatis *ubi facillime nosci possit ;* atque ut ea *bacchanalia si* qua sunt (*extra* quam *si* quid *ibi sacri* est, ita *ut* supra *scriptum* est) in diebus x quibus vobis *tabellae datae* erunt faciatis *ut dimota sint ;*

10. *cui vita* defecit *non honor honori.*

First mark the Long V́owels.

Answers :—

N.B.—* means -om or -o or -um or -u ; † means -ei or -ē or -ī.

1. *aiqetiai* (or *-c-*) ; some genitives have -ās, cp. paterfamiliās (χώρᾱς).

2. *coerai ;*

3. *sei quei esent quei aruorso(m)* * *eād fēcisent* quam *sup(e)rād scripto(m)* * *(e)st ;*

4. *maxsumei* † *faxseis ;*

5. *poplicōd ioudiciōd ;*

6. *sei* quis *magist(e)rātus moltā̆m* inrogāre uolē̆t, *quei* uolet (dum minōris *partus fameliās* [or *familiai*] *taxsāt) licētōd, eeique* omnium rērum sīremps *lēxs estōd quasei sei* is *hāce leege* (later form) *peqūniā̆m* (or *-c-*) *exēgisē̆t ;*

7. dē *praitōris senātuosque* (or *-tei-†-que*) *sententiād ;*

8. magnā̆m sapientiā̆m *aitāte qum paruād* (?) *posidēt hōce saxso(m)* * *;*

9. atque, *utei hōce en tabolā̆m inceiderētis*, ita senātus *ai(s)quom cēnsueit*†, *uteique* eā̆m *feig-ei* (or *-ier*) iubeātis *ubei facilumēd gnōsc-ei* (or *-ier*) *potis sit* (or *siē̆-t* or *-d*) ; atque utei ea *bācānālia sei* qua sunt (*exstrād* quam *sei* quid *ibei sacrei* † *siē̆-t* or *-d*, ita *utei sup(e)rād scripto(m)* * (e)st) in diēbus x quibus uōbīs *tabelai datai* erunt faciātis *utei dismōta sient ;*

10. *quoiei uītā dēfēceit* † *noen-o* (or *-u*) *honōs honōrei* †.

12. Latin Inscriptions with Notes.

12. *Explain and comment on any peculiar forms in the following Latin Inscriptions* :—

(*a*) *Manios med fhefhaked Numasioi, etc.*, κ.τ.λ.

A good *Method* of answering this Question would be as follows :—

(*a*) write down the Inscription-forms ;

(*b*) marking the *Long Vowels ;*

(*c*) under each word write the Classical word ;

(*d*) *mention all the points of contrast*, putting the Inscription letters first, the Classical letters next, and then the Instance ;

(*e*) explain these peculiarities ;

(*f*) *Illustrate* them, as far as possible, from Early Latin, Greek, etc.

The following Rhyme sums up the Method :—

Write down each form (Long Vowels show),
then *Normal* forms 'neath each should go ;
note points of *Contrast*, give the *Cause*,
and *Illustrate* Phonetic Laws.

N.B.—The following Answers will only touch on a few points, for most of them have been already discussed.

For details, see Allen's *Remnants of Early Latin*, Lindsay's *Handbook of Latin Inscriptions*, and, for more elaborate writers, Wordsworth's *Specimens of Early Latin*, or Egbert's *Introduction to the Study of Latin Inscriptions.*

(*a*) *Mānios mēd fhefhakēd Numasiōi*
Mānius mē fēcit Numeriō.

This was possibly as early as the 5th Century B.C.

Besides *-o-* (or -u-, p. 44), Dative *-ōi* (-ō, p. 118), notice

(i.) *-d* in the Accusative of Pronouns, as well as in the Ablative (cp. Gnaivōd, p. 118);

(ii.) *fh-* to give the Early sound which the Greek writing of the time gave by the Digamma followed by H: later on the sound was denoted by F alone;

(iii.) for the Reduplicated Perfect, cp. pepigī (from pepagai), and notice that the Latin Accent has not yet reduced the *-a-* to *-i-* (cp. réddatus → rédditus, Númasiōi → Numeriō);

(iv.) for the *-ē-*, from the 'Middle' *-ai*, see p. 45;

(v.) the Final *-d* is found especially in the 'Historic' Tenses and in the Optative;

(vi.) *-s-* between Vowels has not yet become *-r-* (cp. ploisumos → plūrimus).

(*b*) IO VEI SAT DEIVOS QOI MED MITAT NEI TED ENDO COSMIS VIRCO SIED ASTED NOISI OPE TOITESIAI PAKARI VOIS DVENOS MED FECED EN MANOM EINOM DVENOI NE MED MALO STATOD.

For this Inscription, which may be nearly as early as the preceding, I adopt in the main the readings and explanations of Professor R. S. Conway (*American Journal of Philology*) which may be consulted for the details.

The meaning is very obscure; the following might suggest a rough idea of it:—

'(I pray to) the gods, Jove, Vejove, and Saturn, let not Proserpine, to whom they (the gods) will let me be sent, be kind to you unless you are willing to make expiation to Ops Tuteria. Duenos (Bonus) made me as-a-curse-against Manus, and let not harm come to Duenos owing-to-me.'

The Inscription-forms would be:—

Iouos (Old Nom., Iūppiter) or *Iouem* (sc. obsecro), *Vēiouos* or *Veiouem*, *Sāturnos* or Sāturno(m) (Sātūrnus or Sāturnum), *deiuōs* (Old Nom. Plural, as in the Italic Dialects, dīvī, or Acc. Plur. dīvōs) *qōi* (Dat. Sing., cp. λόγωι Numasiōi, p. 118,

? surviving in quō 'whither') *mēd* (Acc., mē) *mitāt* (3rd Plur. Subj., mittant: for the single *t* see p. 44, for -n- weakly pronounced cp. cosentiont, dedat), *nei* (either -ei represented the -ē of nē, p. 45, or more probably nei, later nī, was used here with the meaning of nē, i.e. nī had not yet come to be set apart to denote 'unless': cp. some Italic Dialect uses) *tēd* (tē, see above; it was governed by endo, cp. in te, εἰς σε) *endo* (indu-, as in induperator, in Lucretius, or ? indum like ἔνδον, with -m not written) *cosmis* (cōmis) *uircō* (virgō: for c with the sound of g, see p. 212) *siēd* (sit: Optative, cp. [ε]ἴη, and see p. 121), *asted* (either ast in a corrective sense, 'that is to say', in which case -ed may have been an Ablative Ending, or adstet, 'let not Proserpine be kind to you and stand by you') *noisī̆* (nisi, but the first half would rather become nei- and then nī) *Opē̆* (either opem Acc., cp. aide with aedem, p. 44, or opī Dat.: for -ē, see p. 45. The Acc. would have depended on 'to pacify', the Dative on 'to make expiation to') *Toitesiā̆i* (Tūteriae: for -oi, cp. oino and ūnum, for -s- cp. Numasiōi and Numeriō, for ā̆i, Gen. or Dat., cp. Rōmai and Rōmae: the Gen. would mean 'the Ops of Tuteria', the Dative 'to Ops-Tuteria') *pākārī̆* (pācārī, with Active Sense, cp. some of the 'Deponents' in Plautus, or pācāre: for k in Early Latin, cp. Kaeso) *uois* (vīs, old Diphthong): *Duenos* (Bonus, cp. duellum and bellum) *mēd* (mē) *fēcē̆d* (fēcit: for -ē- from -ei-, see p. 45, for -ĕ- cp. Aorists like ἔθηκε) *en* (in, cp. ἐν) *Mānom* (Mānum), *einom* ('and', would have become īnum, but did not survive) *Duenōi* (Bonō, see above) *nē mēd* (mē, Ablative, p. 118) *malo* (malum) *statōd* (statō).

13. Exercises in Early Latin.

13. *Write down the Classical forms for the following Early Latin Inscription forms, as far as possible without Notes.*

(*a*) *enos Lases invate . . . etc.*, κ.τ.λ.

It will be admirable practice, for Early Latin Inscriptions, to write out *all* the peculiarities in the following forms, and to write Notes on them. Most of them have been treated already:—

(*a*) *enōs* (nōs) *Lasēs* (Larēs) *iuvāte*
nēue lue (luem) *rue* (ruem) *Marmar* (Mar-s, but reduplicated) *sins* (Old Imperative, like δό-ς, or ? sine) *incurrere in pleōrīs* (plūrēs, Acc.)
satur ('satisfied') *fu* ('be') *fere Mars līmen salī stā* (? transitive 'put a stop to, stay') *berber* (verber)
sēmunīs (sēmonēs, 'half-men' or 'sowers') *alternei* (alternī) *advocapit* (advocābit) *conctos* (cunctus)
triumpe (triumphe).

(*b*) *sancus* ('holy') *Iānis* ('Iānus') *es, duonus* (bonus) *Cerus* ('Ceres') *es, duonus Iānusque [pu]meliōsum* (? meliōrum) *rēcum* (rēgum)

(*c*) *quomne* (cp. the -ne- of dōnec) *tonās, Leucesie* (Lūcerī), *prai* (prae) *tēt* (tē) *tremonti* (tremunt).

(*d*) *pīlumnoe* (pīlumnī) *poploe* (populī).

(*e*) *Belōlai* (Bellōnae) *pōcolom* (pōculum): cp. *Lauernai* (Lavernae), *Saeturnī* (Sāturnī), *Salūtes* (Salūtis), *Aisclāpī* (Aesculāpī).

(*f*) *Venos* (Venus) *Diovem* (Iovem) *Prosepnăi* (Proserpinae).

Mirqurios (Mercurius) *Alixentrom* (Alexandrum).

Polōces (Pollux) *Losna* (Lūna) *Amuces* (Amyces).

Iūnō (Iunō, ? Iūnō[nī]) *Iovei* (Iovī) *Hercelē* (Hercul-em or -ī).

Canumēdē (Ganymēdēs) *Diēspatēr* (cp. Iūppiter) *Cupīdō Menerua* (Minerva).

(*g*) *Dindiā Macolniā fīleai* (Dindia Magulnia fīliae) *dedit*.

(*h*) *Nouios Plautios* (Novius Plautius) *mēd Rōmăi fēcid* (mē Rōmae fēcit).

(*i*) *ferī porōd* (porrō), *cofēcī* (confēcī), *made[?t]* (madet) *mī rēciē* (rēgiē 'splendidly'), *misc* (misce, ? old Verb beside miscē) *sānē* ('yes'), *asom* (assum, from arsum 'to burn') *ferō*, *confice piscim* (piscem).

(*j*) *Diānā* (Diānae) *M. Līvio* (Līvius) *M. f.* (Marcī fīlius) *praitŏr* (praetor) *dedit*.

(*k*) *M. Mindios L. fī.* (Mindius Lūcī fīlius) *P. Condetios* (Condetius) *Va. fī.* (Valerī fīlius) *aidīlēs* (aedilēs) *vīcēsmă* (vicēsimam) *parti* (partem) *Apolōnes* (Apollinis, but -ōn- owed its Long Vowel to the Nom. Apollō) *dedēri* (dedēre).

(*l*) . . . *quaistōrēs* (quaestōrēs) *aire* (aere) *moltāticōd* (multāticō) *dederont* (dederunt).

(*m*) . . . *dē praidād* (dē praedā) *Maurtē* (Martī) *dedĕt* (dedit).

(*n*) . . . *dat lubs* (lubens) *mertō* (meritō) . . . *āra* (āram) *Salūtus* (Salutis, but from a Genitive in -os, cp. ἐδήτυος and senātu-os: see p. 54).

(*o*) *L. Cornēlio* (Cornēlius) *L. f. Scīpiō aidiles* (aedīlis) *cosol* (consul) *cēsōr* (cēnsor).

L. Cornelius Scipio was Consul in 259 B.C.: but the Inscription may have belonged to a much later date.

(*p*) *honc oino* (hunc ūnum) *ploirumē* (plūrimī) *cosentiont* (consentiunt) *Rōmāi* (Rōmae) or *Rōmānē* (Rōmānī) *duonōro* (bonōrum) *optumo* (optimum) *fuise* (fuisse) *uiro uirōro* (virum virōrum),

Lūcīom Scīpiōne (Lūcium Scīpiōnem): *fīlios* (fīlius) *Barbātī*

consol (consul) *cēnsōr* (cēnsor) *aidīlis* (aedīlis) *hic fuĕt* (fuit) *apud uōs ;*

hec (hic) *cēpit Corsicā* (Corsicam) *Aleriāque* (Aleriamque) *urbe* (urbem) [? *pucnandōd* (pugnandō)],

dedet (dedit) *Tempestātebus* (Tempestātibus) *aide* (aedem) *meretōd* (meritō) [*uōtām* (vōtam)].

Note.—This is called the *Saturnian* Metre: a good instance of it would be

dabunt malum Metellī Naeviō poētae.

(*q*) *Cornēlius Lūcīus* (Lūcius) Scīpiō Barbātus,

Gnaivōd (Gnaeō) *patre prognātus* (pro-nātus) *fortis vir sapiensque*,

quoius (cuius) *formā* (forma) *virtūtei* (virtūtī) *parisumā fŭit* (? parissima fuit):

consol cēnsōr aidīlis (consul cēnsor aedīlis) *quei* (quī) *fuīt* (*fuĭt*) *apud uōs :*

Taurasiā (Taurasiam) *Cisaunā* (Cisaunam) *Samnio* (Samnium, or Samniō from Samniōd) *cēpit*

subigit (? subēgit) *omne* (omnem) *Loucānam* (Lūcāniam) *opsidēsque* (obsidēsque) *abdoucit* (abdūcit).

(*r*) *honce loucom* (hunc lūcum) *nē quis uiolātōd* (violātō) *neque exvehitō* (ēvehitō) *neque exfertō* (effertō) *quod loucī* (lūcūs) *siēt* (sit) *neque cēditō* (caeditō) *nesei* (nisi) *quo diē rēs deina* (dīvīna) *anua* (annua) *fīet : eōd* (eō) *diē*, *quod rēī dīnae* (dīvīnae) *causā* (caussā) *fiăt*, *sine dolō cēdere* (caedere) *licētōd* (licētō): *seiquis* (sīquis) *uiolāsit* (violassit or violārit) *dolō malō Iouei* (Iovī) *bouīd* (bove) *piāclum* (piāculum) *datōd* (*datō*), *et a CCC moltai* (mulctae) *suntōd* (suntō); *eius piāclī* (piāculī) *moltaique* (mulctaeque) *dicātōrē* (dic[t]ātōrī) *exactiō estōd* (estō).

(*s*) *Iūnōnē rē*[*gin-ā* or -*ăi*] (Iūnonī rēgīnae) *mātrōnā Pisaurēsēs* (mātrōnae Pisaurensēs) *dōno dedrot* (dōnum dederunt).

(*t*) *Mātrē Mātūtā* (Matrī ·Mātūtae) *dōno dedro* (dōnum dederunt) *mātrōnā* (mātrōnae), *M' Cūria Pōla* (Paulla) *Līuia deda* (?dedant—this form disappeared in Latin).

(*u*) . . . *nouem castreis* (castrīs) *exfociont* (effugiunt — a false Archaism, as the -u- was original: cp. φυγεῖν), *Macelamque* (Macellamque) [vī] *pucnandōd* (pugnandō) *cēpit, enque* (inque) *eōdem macistrātūd* (magistrātū) [*bene*] *rem nāuebos* (navibus) *marīd* (marī) *consol* (consul) *prīmos* (prīmus) [gessit], *clasēsque* (classēsque) *nāvālēs prīmos ornāvēt* (prīmus ornāvit) . . .

Duilius won a naval victory over the Carthaginians in 260 B.C., and dedicated the beaks of the Carthaginian ships—hence the Columna Rostrata. This Inscription is a restoration made at the time of Claudius (the Emperor), and contains some false Archaisms: it is somewhat as if an Englishman were to try to make English words look Archaic by adding -e, and were to add -e not only to words which once ended in -om, but also to words like '*that*' (from tod, which did not end in -*e*).

For later Inscriptions, the best (small) collection is that by Lindsay, which should be carefully studied.

(*v*) *heisce magistreis* (hī magistrī) *Uenerus* (Veneris, -us being from -os, cp. πατρός) *mūrum aedificandum coirāuērunt* (cūrāvērunt) *ped.* CC⊥XX (270) *et loidōs* (lūdōs) fēcērunt . . .

Note.—Always mark all the *Long Vowels* before treating any question about forms, whether the forms be Latin or Greek. Long Vowels should be marked either as *ā* or as *aa ;* in Greek we have special Long Vowel signs, viz. η (and ει), ω (and ου), and Circumflexes, but here also *ee, oo, aa* might be used.

13. Useful Early Latin forms, and Italic Dialects.

13 (*a*) *What were the chief peculiarities of Early Latin forms? Give instances.*

See above, p. 44, foll., for the various peculiarities: the following words would help to recall many of them. They are not all in Saturnian metre.

honc(e) oino ploirumei cosentiont Rōmāi
duonōro maxsumēd op(i)tumo Pilipom:
Cnaiuōd prognāto(s) meretōd Veneres aistumaueit
aide, qōi Leucesie touam noenu neglexsit:
deiuās senātuosque fāmā ap cēnsōre auctā.

Notice the variety of forms.

(*b*) *Mention a few forms from the Italic Dialects, with Latin renderings.*

1. In *Umbrian*, for which the *Eugubine Tables* give the best evidence, we find such forms as *faŝia* (faciat), *ar* (ad, cp. arbiter, p. 137), *pis* (quis, p. 161), *beniest* (veniet), *bēnust* (vēnerit, cp. p. 141), *āsā* (ārā, p. 205), *āsāf* (ārās, from -ns, p. 119), *tūtās* or *tūtār* (Gen. Sing. cp. paterfamiliās, χώρας), *āferum* (Acc. Inf., cp. dictūrum, p. 142), *subocau* (subvocō).

For Umbrian and Oscan, see further King & Cookson's *Sounds and Inflections* (pp. 31-32), and Conway's *Italic Dialects*, which is very expensive but will long remain the standard authority on the subject. He gives a good list of Reference Books.

2. In *Oscan* we have the *Tabula Bantina*, giving the Roman Laws for the town of Bantina: Oscan, unlike Umbrian, distinguished D and T, G and K, and Double Consonants, and has Claudius' sign Ⱶ (p. 210). In Oscan we find *pam* (quam, p. 161), *kumbēned* (convēnit, cp. p. 93), *ezum* (Acc. Inf., esse, see p. 136), *deicum* (dīcere), *suvād* (suā, pp. 86, 117), *estud* (estō, p. 117), *ehtrād* (extrā), *viu* (via), *didest* (*S*-future, dabit); here also we have Genitives in *-ās* (cp. above).

14. Use and Interest of Latin Inscriptions.

14. *What is the chief use and interest of Latin Inscriptions?*

With this Answer cp. the Greek Dialects (p. 42).

(i.) In *Philology*, the Inscriptions give a large number of Early and even Māter-Language forms, e.g. *estōd*, *tremonti*, *oino(m)*, *duenos*, *qōi*, *endo(m)*, *Gnaiuōd*, *siēd*.

They also tell us something of the *Spoken and Popular Language*, e.g. the weak Final -m (p. 44), and the expanding and 'telescoping' of words (pp. 52, 175).

(ii.) In *History*, Inscriptions give a great deal of evidence: in fact, Mommsen has been able to re-write a good deal of the history of the Provinces by the light of Inscriptions. They also tell us a very great deal about the customs, religion, law, local government, etc., of other people beside those who lived in Rome.

(iii.) For Geography, and (iv.) for Science, Inscriptions have a value very like that of the Greek Dialects (p. 43).

15. Abbreviations in Latin Inscriptions.

15. *What were the words for which the following Abbreviations stood in Latin Inscriptions?*

A. . . .

For hundreds of other instances, see Egbert's *Introduction to the Study of Latin Inscriptions*: there are over forty closely printed pages of Abbreviations, D alone standing for over twenty-five different words!

A. (annō, Aulus, absolvō, antīquō)
A.A.A.F.F. (aurō argentō aerē [p. 45] flandō feriundō)
ABN. (abnepōs)
A.D.A (agrīs dandīs adsīgnandīs)
ADF. (adfuērunt)
A.V.C. (annō urbis conditae)

Aed(īlis). App(ius). Aug(ustus).

B. (M.) (bovem marem)
C. (Gaius, condemnō)
Ɔ.L. (Gaiae lībertus = 'a freedman manumitted by a woman')
CN. (Gnaeus)
COS(S) (consul[ēs])
III VIR CAP. (triumvir capitālis)
D. (Decimus, dedit)
D.D. (dōnō dedit)
D.D.D: (dat, dicat, dēdicat)
DES. ([consul] dēsīgnātus)
DIS PVB · P · R · Q. (dīs publicīs populī Rōmānī Quirītium)
D · O · M. (Deō optimō maximō)

D · S · F · (dē suō fēcit)
D · S · P · D · D · (dē suā pecūniā dedit dēdicāvit)
D · V · I · D. duumvirī iurē [p. 45] dīcundō)
D · V · V · A · S · P · P · (duumvirī vōtīs Augustālibus sacrīs publicē faciundīs)
EQ. R. EQ. P. (eques Rōmānus equō publicō)
EX D · D · (ex dēcrētō decuriōnum)
EX H · L · (ex hāc lēge)
F. (fīlius)
F · C · (faciendum cūrāvit)
F · F · F · (fēlīx faustum fortūnātum)
H . C . (honōrīs caussā)
H · C · S · E · (hīc conditus situs est)
H · M · H · N · S. (hōc monumentum hērēdēs nōn sequitur)
HS · N · L · (50 sesterces [nummum, gen. plur.])
I · D · (iurē [p. 45] dīcundō)
IMP · (imperātor)
I · O · M · (Iovī optimō maximō)
K · (Kaesō)
L. (Lūcius, lībertus)
M. (Marcus)
M'. (Mānius)
M̄. (modius)
MAM. (Mamercus)
MIL. (mīles)
M · P · (mille or millia passuum)
M · P · C · (monumentum pōnendum cūrāvit)
N. (Numerius, nepōs)
OB · (obiit)
P · (Publius, pedēs). *N.B.*—Saluti P. (publicae)
P · C · (patrēs conscriptī, pondō centum)
P · D · S. (posuērunt dē suō)
P · H · C · (provincia Hispānia Citerior)
P · M · (pontifex maximus)
P · P · (pater patriae)
P . R . (populus Rōmānus)

PR. (praetor)
PRAEF. (praefectus)
PROC. (prōcūrātor)
PRON. (pronepōs)
P·V·S·L·L·M. (posuit votum solvens libens laetus meritō)
Q. (Quintus, quaestor)
QVIR. (Quirītēs)
Q·E·D. (quod eō diē)
R·P· (rēs publica)
S. (Sextus, servos)
S·C· (senatūs consultum)
S·F· (sacrīs faciundīs)
SP. (Spurius)
S·P·D· (salūtem plūrimam dat)
S·P·Q·R· (Senatus populusque Rōmānus)
S·S·E· (suprā scriptum est)
STIP·(stīpendiōrum)
STL·IVDIC· (stlītibus iūdicandīs)
T. (Tītus)
TI(B). (Tiberius)
TR·PL. (tribunus plēbis)
V. (vixit)
V·S·L·M (vōtum solvit libens meritō)
V·V· (legiō Ulpiae Victrīcis)

Calendar:—
(*a*) Weeks of eight days had their days marked by the letters A to H:
(*b*) Ides were EID·
(*c*) F. fastus; N. nefastus; C. comitialis; NP. nefastus hilarior.

Notes on Numerals:—

CIƆ (not unlike the ꟿ of MILLE) or M . . . 1,000
IƆ (half of this and not unlike D) or D . . . 500
— over a Numeral . . . . × 1,000
e.g. $\overline{V}$ = 5,000
C·CIƆƆ (= CIƆ × 10) 10,000

IↃↃ (= IↃ × 10)	5,000
Ψ (Greek ψ) ⊥, later ⊥ or L	50
X (Greek χ)	10
XXC (= C − XX)	80

Some say that C (100) was from Θ. See further Gow, p. 14.

16. Relation of English to Greek and Latin.

16. *What is the relation of English to Greek and Latin?*

The plan (p. 11) will show that English belonged chiefly to the Teutonic group of Languages, which were next to the Baltic and Slavonic group on one side, and to the Celtic group on the other: next to Celtic was Italic, and next to Italic Greek. Teutonic, Italic, and Greek, were therefore sister-Languages, being once sister-Dialects, from the Māter-Language.

As Latin was one Dialect of Italic, and Attic was one Dialect of Greek, so Low German (from which English came) was one Dialect of Teutonic, the other being High German, from which Modern German came. Thus Early English was a cousin of Latin and Greek: but

1. English has other elements besides the Low German—for it has 'borrowed' words from various other Languages (e.g. from French, from Latin, and from Greek, it has borrowed words like *reason*, *elation*, and *astronomy*);

2. English has split up into Dialects (e.g. the Dialects of Cornwall, Wiltshire, Yorkshire, etc.);

3. Literary English has spread widely, and is gradually assimilating to itself not only the Dialects, but also the Colloquial Language, which, however, will last for centuries yet.

17. Grimm's Law.

17. (a) *State Grimm's Law (in reference to English only), with a few instances.*

(b) *What are the chief exceptions to it, and how are they to be accounted for?*

I. Grimm saw that πάτερ and pater, from a Māter-Language form *PəTer* (p. 175), corresponded to English *father;* in other words he saw that *here* the Māter-Language *p* → English *f*, and *t* → *th:* looking for other instances, he found *pro* (πρό pro-) → English *fro*, *pod- ped-* (πόδα pedem) → English *foot feet*, *to-* (τό-ν is-tu-m) → English *the*, and so on. Hence he laid down a *Law* that

1. *p* of the Māter-Language *always* → English *f*,
2. *t* „ „ „ „ *th*.

Looking at κεῖνος (hi)ce from the Māter-Language *ke-*, beside English *he*, he said that

3. *k* of the Māter-Language *always* → English *h*.

Looking at τύρβη turba, from *turbā*, beside *thorp*, he said that

4. *b* of the Māter-Language *always* → English *p ;*

Looking at πόδα pedem, from *pod- ped-*, beside *foot feet*, he said that

5. *d* of the Māter-Language *always* → English *t ;*

ἀγρόν agrum, from *agrom*, beside *acre*, gave him

6. *g* of the Māter-Language *always* → English *c* (*k*).

Similiarly, φέρω ferō, from *bherō*, beside *bear :* ἔθηκε fēcit, from *dhē-*, beside *deed :* χόρτος hortus, from *ghortos*, beside *garth* (Old English), gave him

7. *bh* → *b ;* 8. *dh* → *d ;* 9. *gh* → *g*.

II. But *Verner* pointed out that these Laws did not apply to all instances: he saw that *t* → *th* at the beginning of a

word and under certain conditions (cp. *th*e fa*th*er), but ἑκατόν and centum, from -tóm, gave not hun*th*(red) but hun*d*red. So he said that, at the beginning of a word, or when the Māter-Language showed an *Accent* following the *t*, then *t′* → *d*, not *th* : cp. θετά and dee*d*. It is Greek that shows this Early Accent very clearly.

In order to remember Grimm's Law and Verner's Law, it is best to start with *instances*, which can be collected in a Hexameter: under each word write the Greek word, then the Māter-Language Consonants, then the English word with the Consonant in capitals or thick type. *The Laws can easily be gathered from the Instances, and can then be applied to other Instances* :—

Lat.	turba	pedes	in agris	centum	fert	facta	et	in hortis
Gk.	τύρβη	πόδας	(ἐν) ἀγροῖς	[ἑ]κατόν	[ἔ]φερε(τ)	θετά	(ἔτι)	(ἐν) χόρτοις
Eng.	THorP	FeeT	(in) aCres	HunD(red)	BeareTH	DeeD		GarTH (Old Eng.)

To sum up Grimm's Law and Verner's Law for English :—

(i.) the Hard Consonants or 'Tenuēs' of the Māter-Language → Aspirates, etc., in English—

q and *k* (Guttural) → *h*
t (Dental) → *th* [*t′* → *d*]
p (Labial) → *f* ;

(ii.) the Soft Consonants or 'Mediae' → Hard—

ǵ and *g* → *c* (*k*)
d → *t*
b (rare) → *p* ;

(iii.) the 'Aspirated' Consonants → Soft—

ǵh and *gh* → *g*
dh → *d*
bh → *b*

III. Again, if *p* → *f* (cp. πάτερ pater with *father*), why do we have *paternal* and not *fathernal*? Here the reason was that 'paternal' was not an Anglo-Saxon word, but a Latin word transported onto English soil—*a borrowed word*, which had obeyed the 'Laws' of its own country.

18. Exercises on Grimm's Law.

18. (*a*) *In the following English words, give the Māter-Language forms for the italicised Consonants, and mention one or two Greek and Latin words which were akin.*

1, *b*ro*th*er; 2, wa*t*er; 3, un*t*ame*d*; 4, *b*o*tt*om; 5, *d*ust; 6, *h*ar*d*; 7, *f*ull; 8, *d*au*gh*ter; 9, roo*t*; 10, swee*t*; 11, *d*oor; 12, *t*ear; 13, se*t*; 14, *f*ea*th*er; 15, *h*ave; 16, *k*now; 17, *th*irst; 18, *h*ear*t*; 19, *h*ale; 20, *t*wen*t*y.

Answers: (the Māter-forms are in brackets).

1. *b*ro*th*er: (*bh t*) φράτηρ frāter;
2. wa*t*er: (*d*) ὕδωρ unda;
3. un*t*ame*d*: (*d t*) ἀδάματος indomitus;
4. *b*o*tt*om: (*bh dh*) πυθμήν (from φ-, p. 177) fundus;
5. *d*ust: (*dh*) θυμός fūmus;
6. *h*ar*d*: (*k t'*) κρατύς;
7. *f*ull: (*p*) πλήρης plēnus;
8. *d*au*gh*ter: (*dh g*) θυγατήρ;
9. roo*t*: (*d*) ῥίζα [from ῥιδ-ια, p. 162] rādīx;
10. swee*t*: (*d*) ἡδύ suādeō;
11. *d*oor: (*dh*) θύρα forēs;
12. *t*ear: (*d*) δάκρυ lacruma [from d-];
13. se*t*: (*d*) ἕδος sedeō;
14. *f*ea*th*er: (*p t*) πέτομαι petō (cp. petsna → penna);
15. *h*ave: (*k*) capiō;
16. *k*now: (*ǵ*) γνῶναι nōscō [from gnōscō];
17. *th*irst: (*t*) τέρσομαι terra ('dry land');
18. *h*ear*t*: (*k d*) καρδία cordis;

19. *hale* : (*k*) καλεῖν calendae ;
20. *twenty*—from *-tig* (*d d k*) δύο δέκα duo decem.

18. (*b*) *Give English words which were connected with the following words, putting the Māter-Language Consonant in brackets :—*

(i.) tenuis ; (ii.) ἰδεῖν ; (iii.) κυών ; (iv.) quod ; (v.) πραΰς ; (vi.) fāgus ; (vii.) θάρσος ; (viii.) βαίνω ; (ix.) δρῦς ; (x.) dentem ; (xi.) γυνή ; (xii.) genus ; (xiii.) vehō ; (xiv.) hostis ; (xv.) paucus ; (xvi.) trahō ; (xvii.) ἀντί ; (xviii.) κύκλος ; (xix.) δέκα ; (xx.) κλυτός.

(i.) tenuis : (*t*) thin [τείνω] ;
(ii.) ἰδεῖν from Ϝιδεῖν : (*d*) wit [vidēre] ;
(iii.) κυών : (*k*) hound [canis] ;
(iv.) quod : (*q d*) what, from hwat, [ποδ-απός] ;
(v.) πραΰς : (*p*) friend ;
(vi.) fāgus : (*bh*) beech [φῆγος] ;
(vii.) θάρσος : (*dh*) dare [ferōx] ;
(viii.) βαίνω : (ǥ) come [veniō] ;
(ix.) δρῦς : (*d*) tree ;
(x.) dentem : (*d t*) tooth [ὀδόντα] ;
(xi.) γυνή : (ǥ) queen ;
(xii.) genus : (ǥ) kin [γένος] ;
(xiii.) vehō : (*gh*) waggon [ὄχος] ;
(xiv.) hostis : (*gh*) guest ;
(xv.) paucus : (*p*) few [παῦρος] ;
(xvi.) trahō : (*t*) drag ;
(xvii.) ἀντί : (*t'*) and [ante] ;
(xviii.) κύκλος : (*k k*) wheel, from hweohl ;
(xix.) δέκα : (*d k*) ten from tehun [decem] ;
(xx.) κλυτός : (*k*) loud from hl- [in-clutus].

19. Some Principles of Philology: Phonetic Laws, 'Analogy' (Association), 'Contamination' (Blending), Differences of Condition.

19. *Explain the following expressions, and give instances:—*

(*a*) '*Phonetic Laws*' (*Laws about Sound-Changes*).

We have already seen what Grimm's Law meant (p. 63): he took πάτερ and pater, from the Māter-form *p*——, and then, comparing this with English *father*, he laid down a Law that *p* in the Māter-Language *always* became *f* in English: he compared *pro* (πρό pro-) with English *fro*: from πάτερ pater and father he also got the Law that *t* in the Māter-Language *always* became *th* in English.

But Verner (p. 63) pointed out that ἑκατόν cen*t*um and hun*d*red did not come under this Law: for here *t'* in the Māter-Language became English *d*.

Again, we have in English a word paternal, not fathernal.

This being so, we must either

(i.) say that there are certain *exceptions* to Grimm's Law, *or*

(ii.) *state the Law differently.*

(ii.) is preferable.

We have seen that the Accent after *t'* made a difference in producing hun*d*red (not hun*th*-), and that the life of *p* and *t* in another country made a difference in producing *pat*ernal (not *fath*ernal): hence Philologists say that 'any Law, which holds good for *one* instance, must hold good for *all* instances *if the conditions are the same*'.

But the conditions never are the same: no two men and

no two words have ever had precisely the same conditions (see below), though the conditions may have been *very similar.*

Hence we must *emend* the statement: 'Any Law, which holds good for *one* instance, must hold good for *all* instances *if the conditions are similar enough*' (or, '*if the similar conditions outweigh the different conditions*'). This is vague, but vagueness here is more *accurate* than definiteness.

A Law formulated in this way will have no exceptions: for any apparent exception will be due to some (known or unknown) differences of condition. For a list, see below (p. 70).

Let us apply this to *oi* in the Māter-Language: Greek οἶος 'alone' preserved the Māter-Language *oi-*, and so did Early Latin *oi(nom)*: but then this became *oenom* and then *ūnum*: here *oi* → Latin *ū*, and *oi* must *always* → Latin *ū*, if the conditions are similar enough to those which influenced *oinom* → ūnum: thus cp. *ploi-* → *plū-* in plūrimus.

But, if *oi*nom → *ū*num, why did not *u̯oikoi* (cp. οἶκοι) → vūcū? Obviously, because the conditions were not similar enough: for here

α. the *neighbourhood* of the *u*-sound changed *o* into *e*, and we get vei- and then vī-;

β. the Latin *Accent*, falling on the first Syllable, weakened the -oi to -ei (*u̯oíkoi* → véicei → vī́cī).

(*b*) '*Analogy*' (*Association*): see Wheeler's Essay on 'Analogy'.

When a man is with certain other men, as a member of the same group, he is liable to influence them, and they are liable to influence him: he may become more like them, or they may become more like him. So, when a word is with certain other words, as a member of the same group, this word may become more like them, or they may become more like it. In both these cases much will depend on how many there are in the group: the individual may resist the influence of two or three, but may fail to resist the influence of twenty.

Groups of men are easy to understand: thus men form a

group when they work together. But how can words form a group?

Let us take the word *asparagus*: to what groups does it belong in our minds?

(i.) As a Substantive it belongs to the group of Substantives;

(ii.) as a word denoting 'greenish produce', it belongs to the group of 'greenish produce'-words, including *grass*;

(iii.) it also belongs to the various groups of words which sound something like asparagus, e.g. sparrow, grass, and even (owing to its ending -us) omnibus.

In other words, it belongs to groups according to

(i.) its function,

(ii.) its meaning,

(iii.) its form and its sound.

Owing to (ii.) and (iii.), asparagus has become associated, in the minds of some people, with the words sparrow (sound) and grass (sound and meaning): hence it has sometimes come to be like these words, and is called *sparrow-grass*.

Notice here that both 'sparrow' and 'grass' are *more familiar* words than 'asparagus'.

In every language the *Numerals* must form a group of words, and a group of words in a certain order: change this order, and the meanings will soon have to change also: thus 800 came between 700 and 900, so that Greek ὀκτω-κόσιοι, coming between ἑπτα-κόσιοι and ἐννεα-κόσιοι, became assimilated to them, and changed to ὀκτακόσιοι.

The words for *months* and for *seasons* also form groups: thus between September and November there once (for a brief period) was a new form Oct*em*ber: it seems that *l'été* (cp. aestātem) has become Masculine, e.g. because of *le* printemps (prīmum tempus).

Different forms of the same *Verb* (the same *Mood,* the same *Tense*, the same *Person*, the same *Number*), are liable to change by Association, for they are members of the same group: thus, though we have λέλοιπα beside λείπω, we have, beside φεύγω, not πέφουγα but πέφευγα: we have beside ἐστί and ἐστέ, not εἰμέν (Homeric, cp. the 1st Sing. εἰμί) but ἐσμέν: we have, beside ἴστε, not ἴδμεν and ἴδᾱσι (cp. ἰδεῖν) but ἴσμεν and ἴσᾱσι. And see pp. 37, 132.

So also forms of the same *Noun* (the various Cases of it) are liable to change by Association, because they are members of the same group: thus we have Latin paterem (cp. πατέρα) becoming patrem by Association with patris, etc. (cp. πατρός).

Then, again, words with similiar *functions* (if we may use the expression loosely) are associated together: e.g. all *Plurals* of Nouns form a group in the mind, so that, instead of having book beek (like foot feet), we have book books, by association with the very large group of Plurals in *-s*.

Lastly, even likeness of form or sound alone is enough to bind words in a group: the old woman said she suffered from 'haricot veins', because in her mind 'varicose' had grouped itself with the more familiar (and therefore more powerful) word 'haricot;' and 'haricot beans' and 'varicose veins' had a similar rhythm.

'*Proportional Analogy*' is a term given to the power which we all have of making *inferences*: 'If *long* has a Superlative *longest*, then *good* must have a Superlative *goodest*' would be the conscious or nearly unconscious process in the mind of the child who says 'goodest': in other words

long : longest = good : x, and therefore x = goodest. Cp. also mouse : mice = house : x, and x = hice.

In Greek we have three forms

legō legor legere: beside these we have

amābō amābor x. The x will be *amābere*, a new 2nd Person Singular Passive, like legere.

(*c*) '*Contamination*' (*Blending*):

Another result of this is that two members of a group may blend together and produce a mongrel form: this mongrel form may or may not come into general use.

The meal which serves as both breakfast and lunch, and comes between these two meals, has been called 'Brunch': but 'Contamination' is not usually applied to this kind of word.

A man once wrote, in a letter, ' Give my best respembrances to your wife ': he was thinking of ' respects ' and ' remembrances,' they came ' into his mind ' together, and the result was a Blending; such a slip-of-the-tongue as ' macinproof' (macintosh + waterproof) will also illustrate the general principle, which is this :

' *Two forms with similar meanings blend together into a new form, which often defies analysis* '.

Thus ' he didn't do anything ' + ' he did nothing ' may have blended into ' he didn't do nothing ' (? cp. Greek οὐκ ἐποίησεν οὐδέν).

Again,

1. ' he did not fail more than he could not help ' (where ' help ' = ' avoid '), i.e. ' he did not fail more than was unavoidable ' +

2. ' he did not fail if he could help ', → a Blend-form,

3. ' he did not fail more than he could help ' (where to paraphrase ' help ' by ' avoid ' would make nonsense).

' They follow(ed) ' might have been expressed, in Early Latin, by *sequonto* (suggested by ἕποντο) ; but there was also another form *sequur* meaning ' they follow(ed) ': for we find a 3rd Plural in *-r* (in Sanskrit, the Italic Dialects, and Celtic). These two forms, *sequonto* and *sequur*, both meaning ' they follow(ed) ', were Blended into a new form *sequontur* ' they follow '. See also p. 145.

(*d*) *Give a few instances of sounds which have different developments under different conditions.*

On p. 62 we have already seen that

(i.) pəter → Latin *p*ater, English *f*ather : here the difference of condition was the *different country* (with its different Geography, etc.) in which the words developed ; ' paternal ' was brought up on different soil and then transplanted. Many instances will be found in English.

(ii.) English *paternal* was a borrowed word (p. 63) ;

(iii.) in *father* we also see *t* → English *th :* but in past participles, etc., we find *-tó-* (cp. θετός) → *-d* (cp. dee*d*): here the difference of condition was the Accent (cp. p. 63);

(iv.) on p. 67 we saw that, although *oinom* → *ūnum*, *u̯oikoi* did not → *vūkū*, but → *vīcī*: here the differences of condition were the Accent and *the neighbourhood of a certain letter* (*u̯*); so also we find *was* but *were*, for here -s- came between vowels (p. 205);

(v.) beside *est*, in Early Latin we find *st*, as in English we find he'*s* beside he *is*, but we do not find *rat* beside *erat*: here the difference of condition was that the word *est* was *used so frequently* that it came to be abbreviated;

(vi.) ὀκτωκόσιοι (cp. ὀκτώ) became ὀκτακόσιοι: the difference of condition here was that ὀκτωκοσιοι came between ἑπτακόσιοι and ἐννεακόσιοι, and was *associated with these words in a group*: see further p. 67 foll. For the influence of a neighbouring word in a Sentence-group, see ἄττα (p. 125).

20. 'Accent' and Vowel-Stages.

20. *What do you know about the Early and later 'Accent' (in its widest sense)? Give examples of its effects.*

For further details, see under the Greek Accent (p. 193, foll.): and also Giles' *Manual*.

Imagine yourself listening to various people, first to one and then to another: they will frequently say the word 'I'!

Now if you write down their conversation you will always write simple 'I': the writing does not show that one 'I' differed from another; and yet there would be real differences. What would they be?

In the following remarks I shall not discuss (*a*) the *timbre*, i.e. the difference of sound like that between the note of a violin and the same note of a piano or a trumpet; nor

(*b*) the pause after the sound.

We shall notice

1. a difference of *length:* one 'I' will only last a tiny fraction of a second, while another may last say for a whole second: this is what is meant by a Long Vowel, i.e. a Vowel on which one dwells for a longer time (e.g. two or three times longer);

2. a difference of *loudness* or *stress;*

3. a difference of *note:* thus, say the words 'I came here yesterday, but I didn't find you, did I?' and observe how the *note or pitch* of 'I' changes: besides the mere note, we may have the rising tone (´) or the descending tone (`), or the tone rising and then descending (^), or vice versâ;

4. last of all, when we hear a man say, not 'I', but *oi*, we say he has a terrible 'Accent'.

Let us now consider these four differences in more detail.

1. As to *Length*, which we might denote by repeating the letter (e.g. *oo*, cp. Greek ω, or *ooo* ; cp. Latin AARA, LEEGE), and which we sometimes denote by *ō* or *ā*, or in Greek by a separate letter (η), but which most writers prefer to leave unmarked, we find it of great importance in λέγωμεν λέγητε, ποιμήν, λόγω, where it now denotes (though it need not have originally denoted) a Future or Subjunctive meaning, a Nominative meaning (the Subject), and a Dual meaning (a pair, or two).

2. *Loudness*, which may to some extent be considered with *Stress* or *Emphasis*, has a certain amount of influence in English : thus contrást is a Verb, cóntrast is a Substantive (cp. compact, contract). In Early Latin, Stress fell on the first Syllable of every ordinary word, and the effect often was to 'weaken' the Vowel which followed, or even to destroy it altogether: thus cp. réddatus → rédditus (but dátus), ápo → ap (ab), éti → et, etc. (p. 175).

3. *Note* or *Tone :* a difference of Note or Tone makes often a difference of meaning in such Languages as Chinese : and in Greek also we find νόμος and βίος (for here ′ denotes a rising tone), distinguished in meaning from νομός and βιός.

But it is not only in *single words* that a Note or Tone can be so important: in many *Sentences* (not in Questions) we find a tendency to go down in pitch, so that the first word is on a higher Note than the middle word, and the middle word than the end word. Thus in a sentence like 'I came here yesterday, but I didn't find you', the first 'I' will be on a higher Note than 'yesterday', and 'yesterday' than the second 'I', and the second 'I' than 'you'. Thus the Note of a word depended partly upon its place in the Sentence : *the same word could have several Notes.*

For instance, supposing the Māter-Language had wished to say

'(to) *go* there is pleasant,'

then 'go' would have been on a higher Note; but, in

'I (to) *go* there enjoy',

'go' would be on a lower Note; and, in

'I often there *go*',

'go' would be on a still lower Note. Thus the words for 'go' might have been pronounced in at least three different ways.

4. These different Notes are said to have been the cause of the different *Vowel-Stages* which we get: it is said that

I. the High Note often → the Vowel *e*;

II. the Middle Note often → the Vowel *o*;

III. the Low Note often weakened the Vowel, and made it disappear. But see *N.B.* 2 (below).

Therefore, if we were asked why it is that the Root for 'go', in the Māter-Language, had three forms

I. with *e*	II. with *o*	III. with no *e* or *o*
εἶ-μι	οἶ-μος	ἴ-μεν,

we should say that *one* origin was the difference of Note (due e.g. to position in the Sentence), and that these three forms may have once been as follows:—

I. with High Note; II. with Middle Note; III. with Low Note.

This applies not only to Roots, but also to Suffixes (cp. πάτερ, εὐπάτορες, πατρός), and to Endings (cp. O. L. Apolōn-es and senātu-os).

It must be remembered that the Classical Greek Accent (ʹ) was a sign of Note, so that πατέρα πατρός would be interesting in this connection.

N.B.—1. How can a difference of Note become a difference of Vowel? Mark the cat's cry, and see how, almost *attached to* the Notes, as it were, there come the Vowel Sounds of ? ī(y)ā ū (mee-yah-oo).

2. There may have been *other causes* at work. Thus, if Length or a longer dwelling on the Vowel (p. 73 above) could make the *e* of *pəter* into *pəteer or pətēr* (πατήρ), then the reverse, a shorter dwelling on the Vowel, might have helped to weaken *e* or to make it disappear (*pətr-*).

3. Besides the (I.) *e*, (II.) *o*, (III.) * Series, which was the commonest, we also find other Series, such as

a *o* * ;

and also the Long Vowel Series, in which we shall find I. as *ē* or *ā* or *ō*, and II. as *ō*, and III. often as a short Vowel. For these, see p. 174.

Summary.—Taking 'Accent' in its widest sense, then, it would include differences of

(1) length (contrast *ē ō* with *e o*);

(2) loudness and stress (contrast rébel and rebél);

(3) note or pitch (contrast the 'I' in 'I did' and 'did I?' and *νόμος νομός*);

(4) vowel-differences (especially that which is seen in (I.) *e* (II.) *o* (III.) *): this may have been partly the result of Note-difference.

21. Exercises in the Vowel-Stages.

21. (*a*) *In the following words, give the other forms of the Roots wherever they survive : treat the Root as having only one Syllable) :—*

fides, toga, terminus, δρακών, διφρός, εἶμι, ἐρρύη, μάτις, μέρος, μία, μολοῦμαι, μόνος, νόμος, ὁδός, ὀπᾱδός, πελταστής, πέμπω, πένθος, πτέσθαι, σπείρω, σχεῖν, τέταται, φθείρω, χέω.

N.B.—It is most essential to have practice in working out the three Vowel-Stages of Roots, etc., so that, immediately one is given, the others may be known.

Other names for this Vowel-variation are Vowel-gradation, Vowel-stages, Ablaut, etc.

	I.	II.	III.
fidēs :	fidēs	foedus (from -oi-)	feidō (O.L.)
	πιθεῖν	πέποιθα	πείθω
toga :	tegō	toga	
	στέγω		
terminus :	terminus		tr-āns
	τέρμα	? τορός	? τρητός
δρακών :	δέρκομαι	δέδορκα	δρακών (from dṛ-)
διφρός :	φέρω	φόρος	διφρός
	ferō		furtum (from -ṛ-)
εἶμι :	εἶμι	οἶμος	ἴμεν
	eō (from ei-)	? ūtī (from oi-)	iter
ἐρρύη :	ῥέω (from -εϜ-)	ῥόος	ἐρρύη
	corruō (from -eu̯-)		obrutus

	I.	II.	III.
μάτις :	μένος	μέμονα	μάτις
	Minerva (from Men-)	moneō	mentem (from mṇ-)
μέρος :	μέρος	μόρα	ἄμβροτος (from -mr-, p. 124)
			mortem (from mṛ-)
μία :	ἕν (from sem)	ὁμοῦ	μία ἅμα (from sṃ-)
	semel		
μολοῦμαι :	μέλλω	μολοῦμαι	βλώσκω (from ml-)
μόνος :	μένω	μόνος	μίμνω
	maneō (cp. p. 142)		
νόμος :	νέμω	νόμος	
		numerus	
ὁδός :	ἕδος	ὁδός	ἵζω (from si- sd-ō)
	sedeō	solidus	sīdō (87)
ὀπᾱδός :	ἕπομαι	ὀπᾱδός	σπέσθαι
	sequor	socius	
πελταστής :	πελταστής		παλτός (from pḷ-)
		pepuli (from -ol-)	pulsus (89)
πέμπω :	πέμπω	πομπός	
πένθος :	πένθος	πέπονθα	παθεῖν (from pṇ-)
πτέσθαι :	πέτομαι	ποτᾶσθαι	πτέσθαι πίπτω πτερόν
	petō		
σπείρω :	σπείρω (from speri̯ō)	σπορά	σπαρτός
			sportula (from spṛ-)
σχεῖν :	ἔχω (from segh-)	ὄχος (p. 132)	σχεῖν
			sciō
τέταται :	τείνω from teni̯ō	τέτονα	τέταται
	tendo		tentus (from tṇ-)
φθείρω :	φθείρω (from -er-i̯ō)	φθορά	ἔφθαρται (from -ṛ-)
χέω :	χέω (from -εϝ-)	χοή	κέχυται

(*b*) *Say where you may often look for one particular form of the Root.*

Looking at

I.	II.	III.
λείπω ἔλειπον λείψω ἔλειψα	λέλοιπα	λιπεῖν
λέγω	λόγος	
πελταστής		παλτός (from *pḷtós*, p. 89)
φεύγω		φυγή
μένω	μόνος	μίμνω
φέρω	φορῶ	
μένος	μέμονα	μάτις (from *mṇtís*)

we should say that

I. would be often found in the 'Present', Imperfect, Future, and s-Aorist; II. in the Perfect, and in some Substantives and Adjectives, and in Verbs derived from Substantives (cp. φορῶ); III. in the 2nd Aorist, in Participles in *-to-*, in some Substantives in *-ā* and *-ti-*, and in some Reduplicated 'Presents'.

As to the Vowel-variation in *Suffixes* :

with λέγομεν (II.), cp. λέγετε (I.) ;

with λόγος (II.), cp λόγε (I.) ;

with πάτερ (I.), cp. εὐπάτορες (II.), πατρός (III.) ;

with γένος (II.), εὐγενές (I.) ;

with ἔμμεν-αι (I.), ὄνο-μα, from -mṇ (III.).

As to *Endings*, notice

Genitives like Apolōn-*es* (I.), senātu-*os* (II.), ? nox 'at night,' from noct-*s* (III.) ;

? Dative -*ai*, cp. patr-ī from -ai (I.), Locative -*i*, cp. πατρ-ί (III.) ;

λέγομες, Doric (I.), legom*os* → legimus, Latin (II.).

22. (*a*) *Classify the different kinds of Compound Words in English, Greek, and Latin, giving instances and notes.*

The following Sentence will be useful to remember, as it contains many types of Compounds :—

'The lady's-maid, thunderstruck, uprose unseen by the cut-throats and by the twenty-one blackbirds and redbreasts in the vineyard '.

There are some Compound words which can be interpreted in more than one way, and so may fall into more than one Class : here, as elsewhere, there is much *Neutral-ground between Classes :* for instance, ' self-cure ' might be interpreted as ' curing of self ' or ' curing by self '.

(i.) *Twenty-one.* Here, somewhat as in 21, the two figures are put side by side, and the relation between the two (at first infused by common-sense, but later on definitely attached to the words) is that of ' and ' or + : cp. δώδεκα duodecim.

With this Class, often called Copulatives, cp. νυχθήμερον ἱππαλεκτρύων, suovetaurīlia (sacrifice of a sūs, + an ovis, + a taurus).

In δισχίλιοι we have an instance of (ii.), for δισ- qualified (or ' multiplied ') the 'χίλιοι'

(ii.) (*a*) '*vineyard*', '*football*', '*Nature-Cure*', '*thunderstruck*'. *Vineyard* shows a Substantive, serving as a Genitive or Adjective to qualify a second Noun (' yard of vines ', ' yard for vines ') : we might often represent this relation by an *Adjective* or by such *Prepositions* as '*of*', '*for*', '*by*', (' Cure by Nature '), '*with*', '*in, on*', or by a *Direct Object :* for the latter compare ἱστοδόκη with ὃ ἱστὸν δέχεται.

Greek and Latin instances would be *οἰνόπεδον*, *αἰπόλος*, *θεόδμᾱτος*, caprifīcus, pāricīda, terrigena, manceps, vēlivolum.

Notice here that *the first Substantive is a Stem, and is not in any Case*: we have *οἰνόπεδον*, not *οἰνούπεδον*.

(ii.) (*b*) *lady's-maid*. Here, as in Διόσδοτος, κηρεσσιφορήτους, χαμαιλέων, we have a Case-Ending in the first Substantive: most of these Compounds are generally supposed to belong to a later period than those with the simple Stem [(ii.) (*a*)].

(ii.) (*c*) *ill-will*. Here, if we count 'ill' as an Adjective, we have an Adjective qualifying a Substantive: many instances are on the neutral ground of (ii.) (*a*) and (ii.) (*c*). In Greek and Latin cp. ὠμογέρων, κακογείτων, sacriportus.

(iii.) *blackbird, Longshanks*. The first part is an Adjective (though it might also be regarded as a Substantive in the Genitive): cp. Μεγαλόπολις.

Notice that, in Μεγαλόπολις and ἀκρόπολις, the first part does not agree in form with the Feminine πόλις.

The difference between this and (ii.) (*c*) is that the word cannot be used of *any* black bird, but is *specialised*, i.e. is confined to one special kind of blackbird: in Longshanks and Μεγαλόπολις we have a word confined, still further, to one special Great City, viz. Megalopolis in Arcadia. See p. 222.

(iv.) (*a*) *bloodred*, (*b*) *redbreast*, (*c*) *Bluebeard*. 'Redbreast' was like the previous Class, and has come to be used as a sign or symbol for a special kind of bird of which the red breast was the conspicuous part, just as we might represent the idea of 'war' by a picture of a knife, or 'heat' or 'light' by a drawing of the sun: these Compounds can often be paraphrased by '*having* [a red breast]', and are sometimes called *Attributives*.

In (*a*), *bloodred*, we have a word which can be used of anything which 'has the redness of blood'; cp. ἐννεάπηχυς, anguimanus; cp. here ῥοδοδάκτυλος Ἠώς 'with rosy fingers', 'Rosy-finger' [hence not ῥοδοδακτύλη];

in (*b*), *redbreast*, we have a word confined to a special *class* of animals 'having red breasts';

in (*c*), *Bluebeard,* we have a word confined to a special *person,* i.e. a proper name: cp. Ἐτεοκλέης, Δημοσθενής, Ahenobarbus.

(v.) *uprose, unseen.* These words are not unlike 'vineyard', in so far as the first part qualified and modified the second: but in vineyard the first part was like an Adjective, the second part like a Substantive: in 'uprose' the first part is an Adverb, the second part a Verb. The words 'well-done' would almost lie between the two Classes, for they might be nearer to Adjective + Substantive ('good deed'), or to Adverb + Verb (a thing 'done well'). Cp. ἐπελθεῖν, ἀδάματος, δύσφημος, obīre, indomitus, discors, consulēs.

(vi.) *Cut-throat; obvious.* Cp. τερπικέραυνος ('hurling . . .' connected with torquēre), δακέθῡμος, ἀγέστρατος. Here the first part was like a Noun of Agency, and governed the second part, somewhat as a Participle might (ὁ ἄγων τὸν στράτον). Others, however, interpret some of these as e.g. 'having [or characterised by] the leading of the army'. For the word specialised to be used as a proper name, cp. Lackland.

As an instance of the first part governing the second, as in *obviam* 'facing the way' ('in the way'), we may compare 'an out-of-the-way kind of thing'.

(viii.) *Geology, sociology.* When once a certain number of words have become regular, then other words are formed more or less on their model. φιλό-λογος would be natural, when we compare φίλο-ς and λόγο-ς, but Geology had no γεο- to fall back on: it had γῆ. It seems that Philology, etc., came to be divided as 'Phil-ology', and hence -ology was extended as an Ending: cp. also the wide use of -itis in the diseases. In Greek, cp. ἀληθόμαντις (beside ἀληθες). 'Sociology' was a mongrel word, going back ultimately to Latin and Greek elements.

This list is far from exhaustive: but the main types of shorter Compounds have now been considered. For Sanskrit Instances see Peile's Nala.

(*b*) *What is the chief use and interest of Compound words?*

Compound words are useful and interesting for many reasons. First of all,

(i.) for '*Science*', they serve as illustrations of certain great principles, e.g.

(*a*) *Co-operation:* two words, by frequently co-operating, can come to do something which they could not do by themselves or even by co-operating only occasionally: thus cp. 'hearts-ease' and 'heart's ease';

(*b*) the two words combined begin *a new life*, and may now have different conditions and a different history: they may enter new groups ('heartsease' enters the flower-group), and may influence these groups and be influenced by them (p. 67);

(*c*) 'Science' has its *Fossils*, traces of things which survive under certain conditions even if they have disappeared elsewhere: thus we find Fossils in cliffs and in gum, etc.: so,

(ii.) in *Philology and Syntax*, we often find, in Compounds, traces of old forms and orders of words and constructions which may have (partly or wholly) disappeared elsewhere: e.g. we find an old Genitive form in paterfamiliās (cp. χώρᾱς), and an old Genitive of the Agent in Διόσδοτος.

Compound words may also show survivals of some old meaning of a form, while this meaning may not be often found elsewhere: thus cp. ἔκλογα 'selections' (Latin ēligere), while the Root λέγω usually means 'say'; in fact, Compound Words are very valuable evidence for Etymologies;

(iii.) in *History*, also, Compound words are interesting: e.g. the endings -ham, -caster, -don, throw some light on the sources of English civilisation.

23. Greek and Latin Pairs of Words with Early Forms.

23. *How far were the following pairs of words once identical? Give the parent-forms wherever you can, with a few Notes:*

(*a*) *Sister-forms:* ἀγέτω agito, . . .
(*b*) *Cousin-forms:* ἄγεις agis, . . .

PRELIMINARY NOTE.

The following *general* rules will be found useful for (*a*), the Complete Pairs of Words.

1. Mark all the *Long Vowels.*

2. Pick out all the letters common to the two words, and put them down as Early letters or (possibly) as Māter-letters; leave gaps for the other letters.

3. For doubtful *Consonants, Latin* will sometimes be a safer guide than Greek: thus cp. quoque πότε with the Māter-word *qoqe* (see further p. 99); *English* will occasionally help (see ruddy and rudhrom, p. 87).

4. For doubtful *Vowels, Greek* will generally be a safer guide than Latin, where the Accent altered the Vowels so much: thus cp. λεγόμενοι λεγέμεναι, from the Māter-words *legomenoi legemenai*, with Latin légiminī (p. 91). But there are exceptions: e.g. cp. κλείς clāvis with the Māter-form *klāu̯is*, and see further, p. 99, foll., below.

ἀγέτω *agitō* (O.L. *agitōd*) . . . . . . *agetōd.*

Latin Accent changed ágetōd to ágitōd: final -d was dropped both in Greek, and in Latin after a Long Vowel.

ἀγρός *ager* [*acre*] . . . . *agrós.*

The Latin Accent changed ágros to áger(s): for agro-, cp. Acc. agro-m.

ἀγρῷ (ἀγρωι) *agrō* (O.L. agrōi) . . . . . . *agrōi.*

Greek MSS. wrote the -ι by the side: neither Greek nor Latin pronounced this -ι (-*i*) in Classical times.

ἀλκή *arca* . . . . *alkā, arkā.*

Early l and r were to some extent interchangeable: Early Latin -ā → -ă (i.) partly because of Iambic words [fúgā → fúgă, p. 46); (ii.) partly by Association (p. 69) with the Accusative, where -ām → -ăm.

ἄλλους *aliōs* . . . . *alions (alions).*

Greek *li* → λλ by Assimilation (cp. p. 176); Latin *li* or *li* was pronounced more slowly (cp. glo*ri*ous, usually three syllables, with bi*li*ous, usually two, and see p. 179); -ons → ους -ōs by 'Compensation' (see p. 176): for -ons → -ōs, cp. deci*ens* and deci*ēs*.

ἄμνον *agnum* . . . . *aϑnom.*

ϑ → Greek *β* before certain letters (p. 173): then *ἄβνον* → *ἄμνον* (cp. *σεβ-νόν* → *σεμνόν*) by Assimilation.

ἀμφω *ambō* [*both*] . . . . *ambhō.*

In Latin, as in English, the Aspirate disappeared: cp. ἄλφος albus.

ἄνεμος *animus* . . . . *anemos.*

Latin Accent weakened ánemos into ánimus (cp. Early Latin méretō → mérito); for o → u, see p. 44.

ἄντροις *antrīs* (O.L. -*eis*) . . . . . . *antrois.*

Latin Accent, again, helped to weaken -oi into -ei (later -ī).

ἀπορρέω *abruō* [*off, stream*] . . . . . *apo-sreuō.*

Latin Accent weakened ápo to ap or ab (cp. a*p* templō, a*b* *d*īvō); sr- → rr- in Greek and Latin, and this sometimes → r-

(English made pronunciation easier by the -t-, cp. ἀνρός → ἀνδρός); Accent, again, weakened ábreuō (ábrovō) into ábruō: in Classical Greek the u or *F* between Vowels disappeared, cp. ἐννέ(*F*)α novem: but see p. 38.

N.B.—The change of dḗnovō to dḗnuō becomes easy to understand if we pronounce v not as v but as *w*: see p. 183.

ἀρκεῖτε *arcēte* . . . . *arkēiete.*

In both Greek and Latin, i̯ between Vowel disappeared: it seems that nearly, if not quite, all of the *Contracted* Verbs (cp. φιλεῖν, τιμᾶν, χρυσοῦν, monēre, amāre) once had *-ie-* (*-io-*) between their Long Vowel and the Ending.

ἄρκτοι *ursī* (O.L. *-ei*) . . . . . *r̥k-toi* or *?-soi.*

For *r̥* see p. 164: in Latin, úrcsoi → úrsei → úrsī (p. 84).

βοῦς *bōs* [*cow*] . . . . *ϑōus.*

English *c*ow shows the Early letter to have been a guttural: for *ϑ* → Greek *β*, cp. ἄβνος (above); in Latin, judging from βαίνω and veniō (p. 93), one would expect vōs, but here Latin borrowed from the Dialects, where *ϑ* regularly → *b*: in Greek, *ōu*, followed by a Consonant, → *ŏu*, but in Latin the *u*-sound disappeared (cp. the pronunciation of Bows).

γένει *genere* [*kin*] . . . . *ϑenesi.*

Greek -s- between Vowels first → the rough breathing, and then disappeared; Latin -s- between Vowels → -r-, cp. ἕπεο sequere: Latin final *-i* → *-ĕ*.

δεῖξαι *dīxī* (different meaning) . . . . . *deiksai.*

Latin ei → ī, and *-ai* (unaccented) → -ei (Early Latin), and then -ī: this -ai was perhaps a trace of the Middle (cp. μέμνημαι, meminī).

δείξω O.L. *dīxō* . . . . *deiksō.*

δίς *bis* [*twice*] . . . . *duis.*

Here English is again a help; Greek dropped the *u*-sound:

for Latin *du-* → *b-*, cp. dueslom → bellum, while the 'doublet'-form, duesl̂om (three Syl̂lables) → duellum.

δόμος *domus* [*timber*] . . . . *domos.*

For unaccented -o- → Latin -u-, cp. p. 44.

δοτοὺς *datōs* . . . . *dətốns.*

The I-form of the Root had ō (δῶρον dōnum): the III-form or weak form usually had a Short Vowel, which in Greek corresponded to the Long Vowel (*ō ŏ*), in Latin was usually *ă*: the same applies to the ē- Series, and to the ā- Series:—

I ἔθηκα fēcī. III θετός factus.
I φάμᾱ fāma. III φάμεν fafēor. See p. 174.

δύω *duo* [*two*] . . . . *duō.*

For dŭō → dŭŏ, cp. p. 46.

ἑδρᾱ́ν *sellam* [*seat*] . . . . . . *sedrām, sedlām.*

For r and l, cp. ἄλκη arca (p. 84): in Latin the *d* became Assimilated to the following *l*, and -ām → -ăm. For Greek s- → ', cp. ἕπεο sequere.

εἰδείην *vīderim* [*wit*] . . . . . . *ueidesiēm.*

In Classical Greek, u- disappeared, but cp. the Homeric scansion of αὐτὰρ ἔπειτα (Ϝ)ιδών; for -s- between Vowels, cp. γένει genere (above). In Latin, *-iēm* → *-iĕm* → -īm → -ĭm, for Long Vowels were shortened before final -m: but -ī- may have been partly due to Association (p. 68) with the plural -īmus.

ἔννεπε (Aeolic) *insece* . . . . *enseqe.*

For Aeolic -ns- → νν, cp. ἔμενσα → ἔμεννα (p. 36): for q → π, cp. *qoqe* → πότε quoque. Latin en- → in-.

ἑός (Hom.) *suos* (Early *sovos*) . . . . . *seuos.*

For Greek ς- → ', cp. ἑδρᾱ́ν sellam (above): for Greek *-u-* (Ϝ) between Vowels, cp. ἐννέα novem. In Latin, *eu* regularly → *ou*, and sovos → suos, possibly at first in unemphatic uses where the Accent fell on the previous word: cp. dēnovō → dḗnuō. See p. 163.

ἕπου (ἕπεο) sequere: see p. 110 . . . . . *seqeso,*

ἑπτά *septem* [*seven* from *seb*-] . . . . *septm̥.*

For Greek ϛ- → ʽ, cp. ἑδρᾱ́ν sellam (above): for *m̥*- → Greek α, Latin em, cp. πόδ-α ped-em.

ἐρυθρόν *rubrum* [*ruddy*] . . . . . . *rudhróm.*

Greek ε- was not in the original word: it was more like the e- which helped the 'Vulgar' Latin to pronounce e.g. stella (est- → étoile).

Notice *dh* not *th* (p. 62), English dropping the -*h*-: Latin -dhr- → -br-, cp. ἐλευθερόν liberum; -om → Gk. -ον, Lat. -um.

ἑσπέρᾱ *vespera* . . . . *wesperā.*

uesp- would give Greek ἐσπ-: the *w*- was a stronger sound than *u*-, which disappeared (cp. ἰδεῖν vidēre, above). It used to be held that the ʽ was from the Article (ἡ ἐσπέρᾱ).

For Latin -ā → -ă, see p. 46.

Ζεῦ πάτερ *Iūp*(*p*)*iter* [-*father*] . . . . *dieu pəter.*

di → Greek *ds* and then ζ (cp. ἵζω below): Latin dropped the d-sound, but cp. O.L. Diovos; Latin eu- → ou- → ū (cp. λευκός loumen lūmen); Latin Accent changed Iū́(p)pater into Iūpp*i*ter: for ə see p. 175.

ζυγοῖς *iugīs* (O.L. -*eis*) . . . . . . *yugois.*

i- would → Greek ʽ, as we see in ἧπαρ beside iecur: this y- was a stronger sound; Latin Accent weakened iúgois to iúgeis iugīs.

ἧμα *sēmen* [*seed*] . . . . *sēmn̥.*

For Greek ʽ, see p. 205; for n̥ → Greek α, Latin en, see p. 98.

ἦν [Hom. ἔην] *eram* . . . . *esām.*

-s- disappeared in Greek, but → Latin -r-, cp. ǵenesi → γένει genere; ā → Attic η (then εη contracted into η), but → Latin ă before -m (p. 46); -m → Greek -ν, cp. ζυγόν iugum.

ἵζουσι (Dor. -οντι) *sīdunt* [*sit*] . . . . *sisdonti.*

For Greek ῾, see p. 205: *isd-* here → Greek ιζ, Lat. īd; -onti → Attic -ουσι (but cp. Doric -οντι), Latin -unt (but cp. tremonti).

ἰόν *vīrum* . . . . *uīsom*.

For *u-* in Greek, see p. 162; for *-s-* in Greek and Latin, cp. γένει genere; *-om* → Greek -ον, Latin -um.

ἵππος *equos* . . . . *ekuos*.

In Greek, *ku* → ππ, cp. παντός (below); was the Aspirate due to 'Crasis' with the Article (ὁ ἵππος, cp. an ewt → a newt)? The ι may have been due to the 'Aeolic' Dialect (cp. δίε), from which the word for 'horse' may have been 'borrowed': for Boeotia and Thessaly had the best horses in Greece. Cp. also p. 85.

κλείς (Dor. κλᾱίς) *clāvis* . . . . . . *klāuis*.

ā → Attic η, -u- disappeared (cp. νέος novos); and then κλῆις → κλεις, for Long Vowels were shortened before ι (or υ) if a Consonant followed: cp. νᾱυς (nāvis) → νᾰῦς. Cp. ᾱις → αις (p. 118).

κράνοι *cornī* (O.L. *-ei*) . . . . *kr̥noi*.

For r̥ → ρα or αρ, cp. *kr̥d-* → κραδίη καρδίᾱ cordis: Latin Accent changed córnoi to córnei córnī.

λύκος *lupus* . . . . *luqos*.

In Greek *q* generally → π or τ: but here the neighbourhood of *u* made a difference, cp. *-qol-* in αἰπόλος, but βουκόλος; see p. 173. Latin borrowed its form from the Italic Dialects, where *q* → p, cp. pumpe (cumque).

μέσος (Hom. μέσσος) *medius* [*middle*] . . . *medhios*, ? *medhios*.

Greek *dhi* → θi → σσ, the *i* becoming like *s* in sound; later on -σσ- → -σ-, cp. ποσσί → ποσί: Latin dropped the Aspirate, cp. English; Latin Accent also helped to change médios to médius.

νεούς *novōs* [*new*] . . . . *neuons*.

-u- disappeared in Greek (cp. ἐννέα novem), but in Latin it turned the *-e-* into *-o-*; for -ons → Greek -ους, Latin -ōs, see p. 176.

νίφα nivem [*snow*] . . . . . . *sniǥhm̥.*

Just as Guttural *q* sometimes → a Labial π, so Guttural *ǥh* sometimes → a Labial φ: in Latin it sometimes → v, cp. ἐλαφρός levis; m̥ → Greek α, Latin em, cp. δέκα decem. See p. 173.

N.B.—In the rest of these words, only the most noticeable features will be touched on.

νυός *nurus* (Old Eng. *snoru*) . . . . . . *snusos.*

For *-s-*, cp. γένει genere.

οἴκοι (Dial. οἴκει) *vīcī* . . . . . *uoik-oi* and *-ei.*

For *uo-* → Greek ὀ-, Latin ve-, cp. p. 97.

οἴνη ('the ace') *ūna* (O.L. *oin-*) [*a, an*] . . . *oinā.*

oi → Latin oe- → ū (cp. ποινή poena pūnīre); ā → Greek η, Latin -ă (p. 46).

οἶνον *vīnum* (O.L. *-om*) [wine] . . . . *uoinom.*

Cp. οἶκος vīcus (above).

παλτοῖς *pulsīs* . . . . *p̥ltois.*

For *l̥* → Greek αλ, Latin ul, see p. 96; Latin pul*t*īs → pul*s*īs by Association (p. 67) with other Participles like mis*s*īs, fissīs, etc. (p. 206).

πέμπτος *quin(c)tus* [*fifth*] . . . . . . *penqtos.*

For *q* → Greek π, cp. *qoqe* → πότε quoque; in Latin we have, not penctus → pinctus, but quin(c)tus, the p- becoming Assimilated to the following Guttural: with this cp. *c*octus not p-, Greek πεπτός, from *peqtos.*

πέντε *quinque* [*five*] . . . . *penqe.*

The same will apply to Latin here; in Greek we see *q* → τ, not π, because the following letter was the 'thin' Vowel *e*. See p. 173.

πεπτός *coctus* . . . . *peqtos.*

See above. Latin po*p*īna, not poquīna, or coquīna, was borrowed from the Italic Dialects.

περί *per* . . . . *peri.*

Latin Accent docked off the -*i*, changing péri to pér: cp. ápo → áp (áb), éti → ét. See p. 175.

πῆ (Dor. πᾶ) *quā* [*where*, from *hw*-] . . . . . *qā.*

For *q* → π, cp. *qoqe* → πότε quoque; *ā* → Attic η. Latin quā might possibly have also been from *quād* (Ablative): see p. 83.

ποινήν *poenam* . . . . *poinām.*

oi- → Latin oe, ū (cp. pūnīre); -ām → Attic -ην, Latin -ăm. Some hold that the Early form was *qoi*- → Greek ποι-, and that Latin borrowed its word from Greek or ? from the Italic Dialects (where *q*- → p-, p. 55).

πόσις (Dor. πότις) *potis* . . . . *potis.*

-ti here → Attic -σι, cp. ἵστᾱτι (as in Doric) → ἵστησι.

πότε *quoque* . . . . *qoqe.*

See above, p. 89. This is the best instance for the changes of *q* in Greek: before *o* and some other letters (p. 173) it → π, before *i* and *e* it → τ.

τάτοις *tentīs* [*thin*] . . . . *tn̥tois.*

n̥ → Greek α, Latin en or in, cp. the 'Privative' in ἀ-δάματος indomitus un-tamed.

τεός *tuos* (O.L. *tovos*) . . . . *teu̯os.*

For -*u*- disappearing in Attic, cp. νέος novos: and for tuos cp. abruŏ̯ (p. 84). *N.B.*—Pronounce tovos as tŏ*w*os.

τί *quid* [*whit*, from *hwit*] . . . . *qid.*

For *q* → τ, cp. πότε quoque; Greek -δ disappeared, cp. τό(δ) istu*d*.

τρέμουσι (Dor. τρέμοντι) *tremunt* (O.L. -*onti*) . . *tremonti.*

-onti → Greek οντι (cp. πότις → πόσις) and then → ουσι; Latin Accent changed trémonti to trémunt (cp. éti → ét), though there may have been a Māter-form *tremont* also.

ὑπάγετε *subigite* . . . . *(s)upo-agete.*

In Sanskrit we have *upa*, and Greek ὑ- might have come from *u-*: Latin s- may have been a trace of a Pronoun (?'there'), or of the Preposition (e)x (cp. πιέζω from (ἐ)πι-, p. 132); for súpo → súp (súb), cp. ápo → áb (p. 73); Accent changed súbagete into súbigite.

ὑπέρ *super* [*upper*] . . . . *(s)uper.*

For the Latin s-, cp. above.

φερέμεναι φερόμενοι *ferimini* [*bear*] . . *bheremenai* and *bheromenoi.*

Latin Accent might have changed both these forms into férimini.

The *-menai* form might have been a Dative or 'Infinitive' used with an Imperative meaning (cp. ἀλλ' ἰέναι 'but go'), and the *-menoi* form a Nominative Plural of the Participle used as a Finite Verb (cp. nihil actum 'nothing was done'). See further, my 'Middle Voice' (Macmillan & Bowes).

φῆγος *fāgus* [*beach*] . . . . *bhāgos.*

φράτηρ *frāter* [*brother*] . . . . . . *bhrātēr.*

Latin -ēr → -ĕr, Long Vowels being regularly shortened before -m, -r, -t: see p. 46.

φυγαῖς *fugīs* . . . . *bhugāis.*

In Greek, Long Vowels were shortened before i or u + a Consonant, cp. κλῃις → κλεῖς; would Latin fúgāis → fugīs, or was the -īs due to Association with the 2nd Declension -īs (from -ois)?

ὠά ('*border*') *ōra* . . . . *ōsā.*

For -s-, cp. γένει genere; for Latin -ā → ă, see p. 46.

ᾠόν *ōvom* . . . . *ōuom.*

For Greek -u- or -Ϝ-, cp. νέος novos.

Cousin-Forms.—These, like the above forms, should be tried independently, before the answer is looked at.

(*b*) The following words were not complete Pairs: they only go back *partly* to the same Early forms. It would, of course, be interesting to discuss the Early differences as well as the Early similarities, but there is not enough space: the Early differences, then, will only be considered occasionally.

The full process, of finding how far two words had once corresponded, would be to *get the Early forms of both, and then compare and contrast these Early forms:* e.g.—

ἦθος *suēscō.*

ἦθος from *suēdh-os,*

suēscō from *suēdh-sko:* the common part therefore being

suēdh-

ἄγεις *agis.*

Greek *agesi(s)*, Latin *ages:* to the Stem *age-*, Greek added *-si* and later *-s* (cp. ἦγε-ς), Latin added -s, and áges → ágis.

ἀγρῶν *agrōrum.*

Greek *agro* + *ōm* or *-sōm*, Latin *agro-* + *sōm:* perhaps at first *-sōm* was chiefly in Pronouns, and then extended sometimes to Nouns: for the older -ōm in Latin, cp. Genitives like deum; for -s-, cp. γένες genere; was the -ō- of agrōrum (not agrŏrum) due to Association with agrōs and terrārum.

ἅλος *salis.*

Greek *salos*, Latin *sales:* the Genitive Endings were in different Vowel-Stages (p. 74). For *s*-, cp. ἑδρά sella.

ἀοσσητῆρας *sociōs:* see further, p. 134.

Both had *soq-* and the Acc. Plur. Ending, Greek *-n̥s*, Latin *-ns.*

ἁπλοῦς *simplex.*

Both had had *sm̥-*, and the Nom. Ending *-s;* for *s-* cp. ἑδρά sella; for *m̥*, cp. δέκα decem (undecim).

αὐτόματος *commentus* [mind].

Both had had *mn̥tos:* for *n̥*, cp. τατός tentus.

'Αφροδίτη *imber.*

Both had perhaps had *m̥bhro-*: for *m̥* see above; *bh-* → Greek φ, Latin -b-, cp. ἄμφω ambō; for *ímbros* (?) → ímber, cp. ágros → áger: possibly imber then changed its Declension.

βάσις (Dor. βάτις) *-ventiō* [*come*].

ϑm̥ti-: for *-ϑ* → Greek β, Latin v, cp. βορά vorāre; for *m̥*, cp. δέκα decem; for *-ti* → -σι, cp. ἵστᾱτι ἵστησι.

βαίνει *venit* [*cometh*].

ϑm̥(m)ie-: *m̥* here → Greek αμ → αν, and βανιε → βαίνε-: for the Ending of Greek, cp. ἄγεις, p. 92. Beside βαίνεις there arose βαίνει, cp. ἔβαινες and ἔβαινε.

γένους (Ion. γένεος) *generis.*

ϑenes-: both had the Genitive Ending, but Greek had *-os*, Latin *-es*, i.e. different Vowel-Stages; for -s- cp. ἕπεο sequere.

γέρων *gelidus.*

ger- or *gel-*, *r* and *l* being closely connected together, cp. ἀλκή arca (p. 84).

γίγνονται *gignunt.*

ϑiϑnont-

δική *indicāre.*

dikā: for *-ā* → Attic η, cp. μήτηρ māter.

ἔθηκε *fēcit* [*deed*].

dhēket, Latin -it might also have come from the Middle *-ai-t* (p. 140).

εἴη *sit* (O.L. *siēd* or *siēt*).

-iēd or *-iēt*: Greek had the I-Stage of the Root (*es-*), Latin, the III-Stage (*s-*); -s- disappeared in Greek; for -iēt → -it, see p. 86.

ἑκατόν *centum* [*hundred*].

(d)km̥tom (connected with δέκα, decem, ten): for *m̥*, cp. πόδα pedem; for -om → Greek *-ον*, Latin -um, see p. 44.

ἐλάττω (α) *leviōrem* (β) *leviōra.*

Greek and Latin both had had the Root, but in different

Vowel-Stages: Greek had III *l̥gh-*, Latin had I *legh-*: for *l̥* → Greek λα, see p. 172; *-gh-* here → Latin -h- [some say *-v-*], cp. χόρτος hortus;

Greek and Latin both had had the Comparative Suffix *-ios-* (*-ios-*), cp. mel-ios → mel-ius; for *-s-*, cp. γένει genere; Latin -ō- may have been due to Association with the Nom., which once had the Long Vowel (cp. honōs).

(α) had had *-m̥*, for which cp. δέκα decem; (β) had had *-a* [some say *-ā*], a sign of the Neuter Plural.

ἐννέα *novem.*

Both had had *neun̥*: for *eu-* cp. νέος novos; for *-n̥*, cp. τατός tentus. Possibly Latin -em was due to Association with septem and decem (see p. 67), Greek ἐν- has nothing corresponding to it in novem.

ἕρπετε *serpitis.*

Both had had *serpete*: for *s-*, cp. ἑπτά septem; Latin sér-péte → sérpite; was Latin *-s* due to Association with the 2nd Singular serpis, or had some Early forms this -s? Some Sanskrit forms have -s.

ἔσεσθε *eritis.*

Both had had *ese-*, though Greek ἐσε- may also have come from ἐσσε-, cp. Homeric ἔσσεται: but, supposing ἔσεσθε came from *ese-*, then *-s-* would be preserved by Association with estis, etc.; Latin changed *ése-* into eri-: for *-s-*, cp. γένει genere.

ἔστησα *stārem.*

Both had had *sthās-* (some say *stās-*, but Sanskrit has *sthā-*): for Greek η, cp. μήτηρ māter; to this, Greek had added -m̥ (→ α, cp. δέκα decem), Latin had added the Subjunctive *-ē-* (cp. λέγητε) and -m: then -ēm → -ĕm (p. 46).

εὐῶπα *vōcem.*

Both had had *uōqm̥*: for *u* in Greek, cp. οἶκος vīcus; for *q*, cp. πότε quoque; for m̥, cp. δέκα decem. Vōcem had nothing corresponding to εὐ-.

ἕως (Ion. ἠώς, Dor. ἀϝώς) *aurōra*.

Both had had *ăusōs-* : *ău-* → Greek ηυ-, Latin ău- ; for *-s-* cp. γένει genere ; Greek ἠϝως then → ἠώς, cp. νέος novos. Possibly Greek ' was due to 'Crasis' with the Article (ἡ ἠώς) : cp. an ewt → a newt, and perhaps ἵππος (p. 88) ; Latin added a Feminine Suffix -ā.

ἦ (in ἦ δ' ὅς 'said he') *ait*.

Both had had the Root *āgh* (Latin might have the weak form of the Root) and the Ending *-t* : this → Greek ἠχτ → ἠκ → ἦ, cp. γαλακτ → γάλα. Possibly Greek also had the Augment ἐ-, contracting with this η ; Latin had a (?) Suffix *-e-*, and āghet → āhet → āhit → ait.

ᾔδη '*I knew*' *vīderam*.

Both had had *ueides-* : Greek had the Augment ἐ-, and the Ending *-m̥*, and ἐϝειδεσm̥ → ἐειδεα → ᾔδη : for -u-, cp. νέος novos, for *-s-*, cp. γένει genere, for -m̥, cp. δέκα decem ; Latin had the Suffix *-ā-* and the Ending *-m*, and ām → ăm (p. 46).

ἦθος *suēscō* : see above, p. 92.

Both had had *suēdh-* : for *su-*, cp. ἡδύς suāvis ; Greek ἠθ- then → ἠθ-, cp. ἔχω (ἕξω) → ἔχω (p. 177) ; Latin suēdhscō → suēscō.

ἧπαρ *iecur*.

Both had had *ie-qr̥* : but Greek had had η, Latin ĕ ; for *i-*, cp. ὑάκινθος iuvenis ; for *q*, cp. πότε quoque ; for *r̥*, cp. ἄρκτος ursus.

θεοπρόπῳ *procō* Dat. (O.L. *-ōi*).

Both had had *proqōi* : for *q*, see above ; both Greek and Latin lost the sound of *-i*.

θυμῷ *fūmō* Abl. (O.L. *-ōd*) [*dust*].

Both had had *dhūmo-* for *dh-*, cp. ἔθηκα fēci (deed) ; to this Greek had added the Dative *-ai*, Latin the Abl. *-od*, and possibly fūmō might also have come from the Instrumental *-a* (p. 118).

ἵεμεν *serimus.*

Both had had *sisə-*, to which Greek added *-men*, Latin *-mos*; for *s-*, cp. ἑπτά septem; for *-s-*, cp. γένει genere; for Latin sīse- → seri-, cp. Faliscī and Faleriī.

ἵστημι (Dor. -ᾱμι) *sistō.*

Both had had *sisth-* (or *sist-*, p. 94): for *s-*, cp. ἑπτά septem; Greek had had the *-ā* of the Root (cp. stāre), while Latin had the Root in its III-Stage or weak Stage.

καρδίᾱ (Ion. κραδίη) *cordis* [*heart*].

Both had had *kr̥d-*: for *r̥*, cp. ἧπαρ iecoris.

κλυτῶν *inclutōrum* [*loud* from *hl-*].

Both had had *kluto-*: for the Ending, cp. p. 92.

κοίλου *cavī.*

Both had had *kou̯*: for *-u̯-*, cp. νέος novos; *ou̯* → Latin au, cp. λούω lavō.

λέγητε *legētis.*

Both had had *legēte*: for Latin -s, see p. 94.

μάτις *mentiō* [*mind*].

Both had had *mn̥ti-*: for *-n̥-*, cp. τατός tentus; Greek -τι- was from Doric (cp. Dor. *ἵστᾱτι*, Attic *ἵστησι*).

μητρός (Dor. μᾱτρός) *mātris* [*mother's*].

Both had had *mātr-*: to this Greek added the Genitive *-os* (in the II-Stage), Latin the Genitive *-es* (in the I-Stage) → -is.

μυῖαν *muscam.*

Both had had *mus-*: Greek is generally supposed to have had the Suffix *-ī-*, which might give Acc. *-īi̯m̥* → ιαν (but there might have been a Suffix *-ia-* or *-i̯a-*); Latin had a Suffix *-kā-* + Acc. *-m*.

ὀδόντα *dentem* [*tooth*].

Both had the Present Participle *-nt-*, and the Acc. *-m̥*, cp. δέκα decem; Greek had *od-*, the II-Stage of the Root, and *-o-*, while Latin had *d-*, the III-Stage of the Root, and *-e-*.

οἶδα vīdī.

Both had had *u̯oid-* : for *u̯o-*, cp. οἶκος vīcus; to this, Greek added the 1st Singular *-m̥*, Latin the Middle *-ai*.

παλαί prae.

Both had had the Ending *-ai ;* Greek used the *pl̥-* form of the Root (sometimes written *pl̥l-*), Latin the *pr-* form : for l and r, cp. ἑδρά and sella (p. 86).

παντός cunctus.

Latin had had *kunt-os*, *u* being a Vowel and *n* a Consonant: the *-c-* helped pronunciation; Greek had had *ku̯n̥t-os*, *u̯* being a Consonant and *n̥* a Vowel: for *ku̯* → (π)π, cp. ἵππος (p. 88); for *-n̥-*, cp. ἔλῡσαν (p. 126).

πατράσι patribus.

Both had had *pə-* (p. 175); Greek had had *-tr̥-* → -τρα-, cp. κραδίη cordis; Latin had had *-tr-*, with a Vowel to prevent the r- colliding with the Ending (*? bhos* or *bhi̯os*) : see p. 120.

παχύς pinguis.

Both had had *pn̥ǵhu-* : for *n̥*, cp. Privative ἀ- in-; for *ǵh* not changing near *-u-*, see p. 173. Both had had Nom. *-s*, but Latin had an extra Suffix *-i-*, perhaps at first from the Fem., cp. ἐλαχεῖα : cp. also ἡδύς ἡδεῖα with suāvis.

πείθει fīdit (O.L. *feid-*).

Both had had *bheidhe-* → Greek φειθε- → πειθε (cp. θρίχες → τρίχες); Latin dropped the Aspirate of *-dh-* (p. 88) and added *-t :* for Greek -ει, see p. 92.

πενθερός offendīx [*bind*].

Both had had *bhendh- ;* cp. above.

πηός pāricīda.

Both had had *pāso- ;* for *-s-* cp. γένει genere.

ποδαπούς propinquōs.

Both had had *-n̥qons :* for *-n̥-*, cp. Privative ἀ-, in-; for *-q-*, cp. πότε quoque; for *-ons*, see p. 176.

τέσσαρες (Dial. τέτορες) *quattuor.*

Both had had *qetur̥- :* for *q* → Greek τ, cp. πότε quoque ; *tu̯* → Greek ττ or σσ, Latin -ttu- (cp. Iūpiter → Iūppiter) ; for -r̥-, cp. καρδία cordis.

τόν *istum* [*the*].

Both had *tom :* for *-om* → Greek -ον, Latin *-um*, see p. 44.

ὑάκινθος *iuvenis.*

Both had had *iu(u)n̥- :* for *i̯-*, cp. ἧπαρ iecur ; for *-n̥-*, cp. τατός tentus. The sou̯nd of *i̯uu̯n̥* might be realised (in an exaggerated way) in '*you an*(*d*) me'.

ὑπερφυῶς *superbō.*

Both had had *superbh- :* for the *s-*, see p. 205 ; Greek had had *-u̯ōd*, or possibly *-u̯ōs* [*u̯ōd* would → υως before words like δέ, p. 206] ; Latin had had *-u̯ōd* (one syllable), and *-bhu̯ōd* → *-bō :* cp. fugābam, and see pp. 139, 142.

ὕπνῳ *somnō* (*Dat.*).

Both had had *s-pnōi :* for -ōi, see p. 84 ; Greek had used *sup-* the III-Stage of the Root, and Latin had used *su̯ep-*, the I-Stage of the Root : *ue* → uo (cp. neu̯os → νέος nou̯os), and -pn- → mn, by Assimilation : cp. σεβ-νός → σεμνός.

φέρει *fert* [*beareth*].

Both had had *bher- :* for the Ending -ει, see p. 93.

φημῶν (Dor. φᾱμᾶν) *fāmārum.*

Both had had *bhāmā- :* for *ā*, cp. μήτηρ māter ; Greek had added the Ending *-ōm* and sometimes the Ending *-sōm*, and Latin the Ending *-sōm :* see p. 92.

χαμαί *humī* (cp. χθαμαλός).

Latin had used the II-Stage of the Root, viz. *ghdhom-*, → hum- ; Greek had used the III-Stage, viz. ghdhm̥(m) : for m̥(m), cp. *sm̥*(*m*) → ἅμ-α.

χόρτου *hortī* [*garth*].

Both had had *ghorto- :* but the Early Endings were different.

24. Greek and the Early Vowels, Latin and the Early Consonants.

24. (*a*) '*Greek is nearer to the Māter-Language, than Latin is, with respect to its Vowels.*' *Show, by instances, that this is not always the case.*

Greek λεγόμενοι and λεγέμεναι were certainly nearer to the Māter-Language forms (*legomenoi and legemenai*) than Latin légiminī was: for Latin Vowels were much influenced by the Accent; cp. also ἀπό and ab, from *apo*. (For other instances, see Pairs of Words, p. 83, foll.)

Again, even Accented Diphthongs in Latin were liable to change: cp. οἶος, from *oi*-, with ūnus (p. 113).

But the following points are to be very carefully noticed:—

1. *Early Latin* (p. 44) has Vowels far nearer to those of the Māter-Language: thus we find mér*e*tō (Class. mér*i*tō), *oi*n*o* (Class. ūnum), etc.; if we had Latin of a still Earlier period, we should look for still Earlier Vowel-forms;

2. *Attic Greek* has many of its Vowels different from those of the Māter-Language: thus we have already seen

(i.) [ā → η]: *mātēr* → māter, Attic μήτηρ (Dor. and Aeolic μάτηρ);

(ii.) [Long Vowel → Short Vowel before *i* or *u* + a Consonant]: klāuis → clāvis, Attic κλῃς → κλείς, cp. nāus → ναῦς;

(iii.) [Different Vowel-Stages]: the Māter-Language had the forms *ped*- and *pod*- side by side: neither has been proved older than the other, so, when we find πόδ(α) ped(em), we cannot say that the Greek Vowel was nearer to that of the Māter-Language (see p. 75);

(iv.) [Semi-vowels *ṛ*, *ḷ*, *ṃ*, *ṇ*, p. 172]: *καρδίᾱ*, *παλτός*, *δέκα*, *τατός* had their Vowels *αρ*, *αλ*, *α*, *α* little if at all nearer to the Māter-Vowels (*ṛ*, *ḷ*, *ṃ*, *ṇ*) than Latin co*r*dis, pu*l*sus, dec*em*, t*en*tus had;

(v.) [Greek Dialects, p. 31]: Greek Dialect-forms, however, such as *μάτηρ*, were sometimes nearer to the Māter-forms than Attic Greek forms.

N.B.—The many cases, in which Greek Vowels are Earlier than Latin Vowels, should be worked out as an exercise: some could be collected from the Pairs of Words (p. 83, foll.).

The following Nonsense-Sentence would illustrate the important instances, by which the Rules could easily be remembered:—

(M.) *Ek(s)lege, māter, klāu̯eins pedi (podi) tṇtāi, en dekṃ kṛd- pḷtāns.*
(G.) ἔκλεγε, μῆτερ, κλεῖ(δας) ποδὶ τατῇ, ἐν δέκα καρδ(ίαις) παλτάς.
(L.) ēlige, māter, clāvīs pede tent(ā), in decem cord(ibus) pulsās.

(*b*) ‘*But Latin is nearer to the Māter-Language with respect to its Consonants.*’ *Do the same here.*

Latin *qu*o*qu*e and no*v*o*m* were nearer to the Māter-Language Consonant-forms (*qoqe* and *neuom*): again *s*erpō (from *serpō*) was nearer than ἕρπω, *i*ugum *î*ecur (from *yugom iĕqṛ*) than ζυγόν ἧπαρ, sta*t*iō (from *st(h)əti-*) than στάσις, and so on.

But the Greek Dialects sometimes have older forms, e.g. Doric στάτις.

N.B.—The instances where the Greek and Latin Consonants differ from those of the Māter-Language should be worked out, as a separate exercise, from the Pairs of Words (p. 83, foll.).

PART III.

ANALYSIS OF WORDS.

The Parts of Words.
A few Greek and Latin Words Analysed.
Some Case-Endings, and Suffixes.
Greek Words Analysed.
Latin Words Analysed.
Summary of Data, Methods, and Faults, in Analysing.

25. Parts into which words can be analysed.

25. *Into what parts can words be analysed? Give instances, and say what is the function of each part.*

We have already seen (p. 22) that *aberit* would have its Early form analysed into

apo (Prefix) *es* (Root) *e* (Future Suffix) *ti* (3rd Sing. Ending) or *apo-ese-* (Stem).

In English we say 'he will be away', using four words: *in Latin we have a single word combining something like all these elements in a different order*, 'away-be-will-he', though it is more than doubtful whether *e* at first meant 'will', or *ti* 'he'.

In this word we see all the four elements, Prefix, Root, Suffix, these three forming a Stem, and Ending: these terms can now be better understood.

I. *Every word must have a Root*, and the Root is usually assumed to be one Syllable only (but see p. 105): it was the Root that had the general meaning—here the *verbal* meaning of 'being'.

II. *Anything before the Root is a Prefix*, though a word with a Prefix can generally be treated as a Compound Word (see p. 81). The Prefix usually 'modified' the meaning of Root: thus here the Root 'be' was 'modified' by the Prefix 'away'.

III. *The Ending* sometimes denoted the relation between the word and other words in the same Sentence; in Balbu|s mūru|m aedificāba|t, it was the *-s* that marked out Balbus as the subject, and it was the *-m* that marked out the wall as the 'object': the *-t* denoted that the building was done by a third person, whereas *-m* would have denoted that 'I (Balbus) was building'. So the *-ti* of *apo-es-e-ti* denoted that the 'being away' would refer to 'him'.

IV. *The Suffix came between the Root and the Ending:* here it denoted the idea of Futurity: contrast *apo-es-ti* (→ abest) 'he is away' with *apo-es-e-ti* (→ aberit) 'he will be away'. Other Suffixes denote other relations, and some Suffixes (see p. 108) seem to denote nothing at all.

V. *The Stem was the whole word without the Ending:* thus the Stem of mūrum was *moiro(m)* or mūru-, the Stem of aberit was *apo-ese(ti)* or aberi-.

VI. *NOTE.*—Some words cannot be analysed into anything else but a Root, e.g. *es* 'be thou', and the Particle an (ἄν); other words, such as est (ἐστί), from *es-ti*, would be only Root + Ending; other words, such as abes, from *apo-es*, would be only Prefix + Root; other words, such as genus (γένος), from *ǵen-os*, would be only Root + Suffix; others again, such as genere (γένει), from *ǵen-es-i*, would be only Root + Suffix + (Locative) Ending. But notice that every word had a Root.

26. Roots, Prefixes, Endings, Suffixes.

26. (*a*) *What was the Root of φέρω, φόρος? Give a few words which had this Root, and show why you should write the Root in English letters (not in Greek letters).*

φέρω, φόρος (δι)φρός, ferō, bear all once had the same Root, and this Root we do not put down as φερ-, because Greek was not the parent-language; we want to put down a form which would have been the parent-form, not only of φερ- but also of bear, and so we write *bher-;* the *bh-* was pronounced like the *bh-* of Hobhouse, and → Greek ph (φ), like the ph of top-hat, Latin f-, English b-, which dropped the h-sound. The Root is here given as

(*a*) a Single form,

(*b*) of one Syllable. But

(*a*) bher- would not give us bhor- (cp. φόρος) nor bhr- (cp. δί-φρ-ος), so we write down the Root as having three forms, and not as a single Root; this gives

Root *bher- bhor- bhr-*.

The three forms might all be represented by what I have heard described as an 'omnium-gatherum'—

For the reason why there should have been three forms side by side, see under 'Accent' (p. 74).

(*b*) Some say, however, that certain forms of the Root here originally had two Syllables, and that the Root was not as above, but rather

I. bhere- or bhero- or bher-

II. bhore- or bhoro- or bhor-

III. bhre- or bhro- or bhr-. Moulton and Thorp and other Authorities have done much to prove that many Roots often had two Syllables.

These nine possible forms, which need not all have actually been used, could again be represented by an 'omnium-gatherum' form—

N.B.—1. In analysing a word, try to find the Early form of the Root first: begin by looking for the syllable which once conveyed the main idea; to find out the Early Root is the basis of a correct analysis, and this Early Root should be written in English letters, not in Greek letters.

2. Compound Words (p. 79) had two Roots.

26. (*b*) *Find the Prefix of* ἀπέφερον, *abferēbam*, δέδωκα, *dedī.*

Here again the Early forms must be given, viz. *apo*-, and in Greek (not Latin) -*e*-: *apo* was an Adverb meaning 'away', and → English 'off' (cp. p. 63): possibly it was once a Pronoun ('there'): *e*- was the Root of a Pronoun, and perhaps once meant 'then', or 'that' (carrying): it is the 'Augment' or sign-post of past time. Latin probably seldom, if ever, had an Augment.

δέδωκα and dedī show a Prefix *de*-, being the first letter of the Root *dō*, with *e*: this Prefix was not itself a separate Root, but perhaps arose from an emphatic and energetic pronunciation of the initial part of the Root: it is usually a sign of the Perfect Tense ('I *have* given', etc.).

26. (*c*) *Find the Endings of these words : him who hurteth ; φέρομεν.*

The Ending of him was *-m*, of hurteth *-ti* (cp. ἐσ-τί), of φέρομεν *-men :* the *-m* denoted the object (Accusative Ending), the *-ti* denoted the 3rd Person Singular, and the *-men* the 1st Person Plural ; 'who' had no Ending, the subject being denoted chiefly by the order of words (cp. 'Jack fell down and broke his crown', where 'Jack' is subject, and 'crown' is object).

There was no necessity for an Ending in many words : thus the Nominative often needed no Ending, nor did the Vocative, e.g. ἄνθρωπε, which was a kind of Exclamation, like the Imperative φέρε ; and the Prepositional *ad* needed no Ending. The order of words and the Context were enough to make the meaning clear.

The Ending of a word usually denoted the relation of this word to the rest of the Sentence, e.g. the -μεν of φέρο-μεν denoted that it is *we* who carry, as opposed to the -τε of φέρετε. The most important Endings are those of Person and Case.

It is to remembered that

α. this was not necessarily the original meaning of -μεν (see p. 103) ; for

β. the original meaning may have been entirely lost : thus a Dative-Ending (*-ai*) can actually be used with a Nominative meaning, e.g. (τὸ) λῦσαι ῥᾴδιόν ἐστι.

The original meaning of many Endings, however, is still buried in obscurity, and the question perhaps belongs to Syntax rather than to Philology. See Sayce's *Principles of Philology*.

26. (*d*) *What were the Suffixes of these words : λέγωμεν legātis,* φέρομεν, iter, ποιμένος, manhood.

To get the Suffix, we must find the Root and then the Ending (if there is one) : what remains between the two will be the Suffix ; e.g.

λέγωμεν *leg-ō-men* } (*ō* and *ā* being Suffixes of the Subjunctive
legātis *leg-ā-tes* } Mood) ;

φέρομεν (i) *bher-o-men* (*o* being Suffix of the Verb or of the 'Present' Tense);

(ii) but others regard the Root itself as *bhero-* (p. 105), in which case there would be no Suffix at all.

In looking at an imaginary *bher-o-men*, we cannot help asking what the *-o-* denoted, if indeed it *was* a Suffix: for, if *-men* could denote the 'we' and *bher-* the 'carry', what need was there of a Suffix? This has not yet been satisfactorily answered, viz. why we should have *φέρομεν* rather than *φέρ|μεν* if we have *ἐσ|μεν* rather than *ἔσομεν*. But see p. 106.

iter *i-ter* (*-ter* being Suffix of a Substantive denoting something like Means, 'that by which one goes', or else, like our *-ing*, the Verbal idea of 'going'). This word had no Ending.

Some might connect this -ter with *τέλλω τέλος* terminus, etc., the idea at first being 'accomplishing, bringing to an end'; but later on -ter would merely be a sign of the Instrument or Agent. The same might apply to *ποιμένος*, *poi-men-os*, if *-men-* had been once connected with *μένω* and maneō, or even with mens and mind.

manhood: *hood* (cp. head and caput) was once a Substantive, but then came to be a mere Suffix like -ness in manliness, or the *-tāt-* of vēritātem.

Among the most striking features of Suffixes are

α. their enormous variety of forms (e.g. *-mo-*, *-no-*, *-to-*, *-ro-*, etc.);

β. their enormous range of meanings (e.g. Substantival, Adjectival, Verbal);

γ. their occasional (apparent) freedom from meaning, and therefore

δ. their (apparently) 'unnecessary' character (e.g. dŭc-em had no Suffix, and yet meant 'lead-er' as clearly as duc-tōr-em.

The whole question of the origins of Suffixes, and their Developments, is well worth a careful and sensible investigation.

27. Greek and Latin Words Analysed.

27. '*Analyse these Greek and Latin and English Words*': [Emended Question: '*Analyse the Early forms of these words*'] *and illustrate the chief sound-changes*:—

(*a*) αἰπόλον, ἔδειξα, ἵστησι, λέγου, μεῖζον, μητρός, μόνοις, φημῇ, ἐπιτείνω;

(*b*) *agricola*, *ambire*, *bonos*, *denuo*, *dicturum*, *eritis*, *feci*, *tremunt*, *unum*;

(*c*) *father* (Voc.), *that*, *whit*.

Preliminary Notes:—

1. The words are first *parsed*, for Parsing is a great help towards the finding of the Ending and the Stem: thus, when φημῇ is parsed as '"*Dative*", *cp. Nom.* φήμη,' we expect to find a '*Dative*' *Ending*, added to *the Stem of* φήμη. Parsing is very easy, and at the same time indispensable.

2. Within the Brackets will also be found the forms (especially the Early forms) which throw light on the Early form and on its Analysis: for instance, in Analysing μόνοις, we look at μόνο-ς, with Nominative Ending -ς, and thus we see how much was Ending (-ς), and how much was Stem (μονο-): hence we gather that μόνοις also had Stem μονο-, and the -ις would therefore be the Ending.

3. *The Paper is divided into four columns.*

Prefix.	Root.	Suffix.	Ending.
These three together form the Stem.			

PREFIX. ROOT. SUFFIX. ENDING.

(*a*) *Greek words* :—

αἰπόλον : [Acc. Sing. of Compound Word, cp. αἰπόλο-ς, αἶγ-ος, βου-κόλ-ος, agricola-m]. Stem αἰπολο-

aig
qol (II-Stage) *o* (Agency) *m* (Acc.)

aigqolom → αἰπόλον : for *q*, cp. *qoqe* → quoque πότε ; for *-m*, cp. *uoikom* → vīcum οἶκον.

ἔδειξα : [1st Sing. 1st Aor., cp. δείκ-νῡμι, ἔλῡ-σ-α, dīxī legēba-m]. Stem ἔδειξ- (in 3rd Person, ἔδειξε-).

e (Augment) *deik* (I-Stage) *s* (1st Aorist) *m̥* (1st Sing.)

edeiksm̥ → ἔδειξα : for *-m̥*, cp. *dekm̥* → δέκα decem. For the Aorist -ς-, cp. dīxī. The Augment was perhaps a Pronoun (cp. εἶτα 'them'), being 'a sign-post of past time' (p. 106).

ἵστησι : [3rd Sing. Present, cp. ἵστη-μι, Doric ἵστᾱτι, si-stō, stā-re]. Stem ἱστη-.

si- (Redupl. Pres.) *st(h)ā* (I-Stage) *ti* (3rd Sing.)

sist(h)āti → ἵστησι : for *s-*, cp. *septm̥* → ἑπτά septem ; for *ā-*, cp. bhāmā → φήμη fāma ; for *-ti*, cp. στάσις statiō.

λέγου : [2nd Sing. Imperat. Middle, cp. Ion. λέγεο, ἐλελειπ-σο, legere] : Stem λεγε, and sometimes λεγο-

leg (I-Stage) *e* (Pres.) see p. 105 *so* (2nd Sing. Mid.)

legeso → λεγεο → λέγου : for *-s-*, cp. *ʒenesi* → γένει genere.

μεῖζον : [Nom. and Acc. Neut. of the Comparative, cp. μείζον-ος μέγ-ας, ἥδ-ῑον, Ionic μέζον] : Stem μειζον-.

meg (I-Stage) *ion* (Compar.)

megi̯on → μέζον, cp. ἅγιος and ἅζομαι ; μέζον → μεῖζον by Association with ἀμείνων (p. 124), and ὀλείζων (from ὀλειγ-i̯ων).

μητρός : [Gen. Sing., cp. Doric μᾱτρός, mātr-is, senātu-os] : Stem μητρ-, and sometimes μητερ-.

mā (I-Stage) *tr* (Agency) *os* (Gen.)

PREFIX.	ROOT.	SUFFIX.	ENDING.

μόνοις : ['Dative' Plur., cp. μόνο-ς, μέν-ω]. Stem μονο-, and sometimes μονε-.

	mon (II-Stage)	*o* (Adj., but see p. 105-6)	*is* (Loc. Plur.) *ais* (Dat. Plur.)

monois (Loc.) → μόνοις.
monōis (Dat.) also → μόνοις, cp. νᾱυς → ναῦς (p. 88)

For the Greek 'Dative' being not only Dative (-*ai*), but also Locative (-*i*), and Instrumental, see p. 117.

φήμῃ : ['Dative' Sing., cp. Doric φάμᾱν, δοῦν-αι, ποδ-ί, fā-rī]. Stem *bhāmā*-.

	bhā (I-Stage)	*mā* (Verbal and Abstract Noun.)	*i* (Loc.) *ai* (Dat.)

bhāmāi → φημηι: for *ā*, cp. μήτηρ; for -*i*, see p. 84.

ἐπιτείνω : [1st Sing. Present, cp. ἐπί, τείνο-μεν, ten-dō]. Stem ἐπιτεινο- and sometimes ἐπιτεινε-

epi (Local Adverb)	*ten* (I-Stage)	*i̯o* (Present)	(*o* Lengthened to form 1st Sing.)

epi itself might be Analysed into ? *e* (Root) + *pi* (Suffix), or *ep* (Root) + *i* (Locative Ending).

epi-teni̯ō → ἐπιτείνω: for -*ni*-, cp. *speri̯ō* → σπείρω. For the lengthening of the -*o*, forming a special Person-Ending, see p. 73.

Latin Words.

(*b*) *Latin words.*

agricola : [Nom. Sing. of Compound Word, cp. agricola-m, O.L. fāmā, ἀγρό-ν, ἄγ-ω, col-o, βου-κόλ-ος]. Stem agricolā-

	ag	*ro* (Subst.)	
	qol	*ā* (Agency)	

agroqolā → ágricola: for unaccented -*o*-, cp. legomenoi → λεγόμενοι lég*i*minī; for -*ā*, see p. 46.

ambīre : ['Infinitive', cp. ἀμφί, εἶ-μι, es-se, γενε-ι gener-e]. Stem ambīr-. Cp. p. 136.

PREFIX.	ROOT.	SUFFIX.	ENDING.
ambhi (Local Adverb)	*ei* (I-Stage)	*s* (Verbal Noun)	*i* (Loc.)

ambhi-eisi → ambi-īre → ambīre: for *-bh-*, cp. *albhos* → ἄλφος albus; for *-ei-*, cp. *bheidhō* → πείθω fīdō; for *-s-*, cp. *ǵenesi* → γένει genere.

Note.—The Infinitive was once a Verbal Noun in the Locative (*-i*) and Dative (*-ai*).

bonōs: [Acc. Plur., cp. Dueno-s, and Argive τό-νς]. Stem bono- and sometimes bone-

PREFIX.	ROOT.	SUFFIX.	ENDING.
	?	?	
	due (I-Stage)	*no* (Adj.)	*ns* (Acc. Plur.)
	duen	*o* (Adj., p. 105)	

duenons → bonōs: for *du-*, cp. *dueslom* → bellum; for *ue-*, cp. p. 86; for *-ons* → *-ōs*, cp. deciens and deciēs.

dēnuō: [Prep. + 'Ablative', cp. dē, novō, νέο-ς, Gnaivōd]. Stem novo- and sometime nove-. Cp. p. 140.

PREFIX.	ROOT.	SUFFIX.	ENDING.
dē			
	neu (I-Stage)	*o* (Adj., p. 105)	*od* (Abl.)

dēneuōd → dénovō → dénuō: for *eu-*, cp. *neuṇ* → (ἐν)νέα novem; for *-d*, cp. *legetōd* → λεγέτω legitō(d); for the effect of the Accent, cp. cónflovont (O.L.) → cónfluont.

dīctūrum: [at first perhaps Acc. Sing. of Neuter Verbal Noun, cp. dīctu-m, δείκ-νῡμι, ἐδητύ-ος and Italic Infinitive es-o-m 'being']. Stem dīctūro-.

PREFIX.	ROOT.	SUFFIX.	ENDING.
	deik I-Stage)	*tu* (Verbal Noun)	
	es (I-Stage)	*o* (Verbal Noun, p. 105)	*m* (Acc.)

deiktuesom → dīctūrum: for *ei-*, cp. εἶ-μι ī-re; for *-s-*, cp. *ǵenesi* → γένει genere; for *-o-*, cp. οἶκον vīcum.

Note.—This word was perhaps at first a Substantive, 'being for saying' or 'being about to say': some think that the Early form was *deiktou-*, an old Case meaning 'to or for' (cp. some of Livy's uses of these forms in -tū). In putō tē dīctūrum it seemed to agree with tē (cp. putō tē

PREFIX. ROOT. SUFFIX. ENDING.

dictum), and hence they came to say putō vōs dīctūrōs, rather than dīctūrum. This is Dr. Postgate's theory, modified.

eritis: [2nd Pers. Plur. Future, cp. es-tis, ἐσ-τέ, ἔσ-ε-σθε]. Stem ere- and sometimes ero-.

es (I-Stage) *e* (Fut. and Subj.) *te* (2nd Plur.)

esete → erite: for *-s-*, cp. *ǵenesi* → γένει genere; for *-e-*, cp. λεγέτω legito. For the *-s*, see p. 94.

fēcī: [1st Sing. Perf., cp. τί-θη-μι, ἔ-θη-κ-α, τέθεικα, μέμνη-μαι memin-ī]. Stem *fēc-*, and other forms.

dhē (I-Stage) *k* (Perf. and Aor.) *ai* (Middle)

dhēkai → fēcī: for *dh-*, cp. *dhūmos* → θῦμός fūmus; for *-ai* → -ei → -ī, cp. δοῦναι darī.

Note.—fēcī was once a Perfect Middle.

tremunt (p. 20): [3rd Plur. Pres., cp. O.L. tremo-nti, Doric τρέμοντι, τρόμ-ο-ς]. Stem tremo- and sometimes treme-.

trem (I-Stage) *o* (Present, p.) *nti* (3rd Plur.)

tremonti → trémunt: for unaccented *-o-*, cp. οἶκον vīcum; for *-i*, cp. éti → ἔτι ét. It is possible that there was an Early form *tremont* as well, cp. ἔτρεμον(τ), which would also have become tremunt.

ūnum (p. 52): [Acc. Sing., cp. O.L. oino, οἶο-ς].

oi (II-Stage) *no* (Adj.) *m* (Acc.)

oinom → ūnum: for *oi-*, cp. ποινή pūnīre; for unaccented *-o-*, cp. οἶκον vīcum.

English Words.

(*c*) *English words*.

father: [cp. πάτερ, pater].

pə (III-Stage, p. 174) *ter* (Agency)

pəter → father: for *p-*, cp. πόδα pedem foot; for *t*, cp. τρεῖς trēs three.

PREFIX.	ROOT.	SUFFIX.	ENDING.

that: [cp. τό is-tud].

	to		*d* (Neut. Nom. and Acc. of Pronouns)

tod → that: for *t*-, cp. above; for *d*, cp. edō ἔδομαι eat.

whit: [O.E. hwit, cp. τί, qui-d].

	qi		*d* (cp. above)

qid → hwit (whit): for *q* → h, cp. κεῖνος and he.

28. (i) Endings.

28. (i) *What function does a Case-Ending perform, and how else can this function be performed?*

When we look at forms like 'the man who saw me, the man who*m* I saw, the man who*se* house I was in,' we see that the Case-Ending of a word tells us the connexion between that word and some other word or words in the Sentence: thus the *-s* of *οἶκο-ς* (vīcu-s) tells us that the *οἶκο-* (vīcu-) was Subject of the Sentence: the *-ν* (*m*) of *οἶκο-ν* (vīcum) would tell us that it was perhaps Object of a Verb, e.g. 'he built': *πατρ-ὸς* (patr-is) would tell us that the *οἶκο-* (vīcu-) was connected with the *πατρ-* (patr-), e.g. it was his possession.

1. When we have a Sentence like 'we love our native land', 'native land' is clearly the Object of 'we love': and yet it has no Case-Ending. Here the meaning comes from *the order of the words*, as we shall see if we write 'our native land is dear', where 'native land' is Subject. This will apply to Neuter Nouns, like *γένος* and genus, in Greek and Latin, though here (as sometimes in English)

2. the *Context* is a far greater help than the order of words, which is so apt to depend on Emphasis. In Ἀχαιοὶ *γένος* we have the meaning '*by* race', without any Case-Ending such as *γένει* and genere had: and in Latin we have homo id genus 'a man *of* that kind'; so also in Compound Words we often find a Case-meaning (cp. *οἰνόπεδον* 'a *πέδον for οἶνος*'), but to find a Case-Ending is the exception.

3. *Prepositions* tend to take the place of many of the Case-Endings, one reason being that they often are more definite and clear, and another being that they had *more* meanings (e.g. 'above'). In English we say, with Case-Ending, 'who-m'

(Object, etc.), 'father's' (Genitive), and we say, without Case-Endings, 'Jack beat Jim', 'Jim beat Jack' (Subject and Object), 'Go home' (Goal), 'Give me' ('Indirect' Object), etc.: but for most other Case-meanings we use Prepositions, such as 'of', 'by', 'with', 'from', 'to', 'at'; and there was a tendency to use Prepositions + Cases, rather than simple Cases, in Greek and Latin also, especially in the Spoken Languages, as we see by the Romance Languages (descended from Spoken Latin): thus contrast donner à lui, aller à Rome, with illī dōnāre, Rōmam īre.

28. (ii) Case-Endings.

28. (ii) *What were the chief*

(a) Case-Endings,

(b) Suffixes of Moods, in the Māter-Language?

Give instances, with their Greek and Latin descendants.

The Case-Endings are learnt most easily, and most satisfactorily, from actual instances: we may begin by declining a Māter-Substantive *bhāmā* * (→ fāma and φήμη): the Case-Endings will show that the bhāmā was related in a certain way to some other word or words in the Sentence: the Māter-Language Cases should be thoroughly mastered, viz.

Nominative (Subject),
Vocative (Exclamatory),
Accusative (Direct Object, etc.),
Dative ('to or for'),
Instrumental ('by, with, with respect to'),
Locative ('in, at, on'),
Ablative ('from, than'),
Genitive ('of'),

* The -a is generally assumed to have been -*ā* throughout: but there is not sufficient proof. J. Schmidt held that the -*ā* of the Fem. Sing. was once the same as the -*ă* of the Neut. Plur., repuls*a* being later on differentiated into (i.) Fem. Sing. 'defeat' (abstract), and (ii.) Neut. Plur. 'defeats' (concrete). Cp. arma (Lat. Neut. Plur.) with l'arme (French Fem. Sing.). The theory is ingenious, but only applies to *some* instances of *ă*.

N.B.—The English Prepositions give only a very rough idea of the Early Case-meanings: it is more than probable that the Early meanings were *very much wider.*

It is important to remember the Cases in this order: after the Nom. Voc. and Acc., the five other Cases come in the order of the word D I L A G: of these five Cases,

(1) the *Instr. and Loc.* have amalgamated in both Greek and Latin, but in Greek they have amalgamated with the *Dative* ('to or for'), to form a Case called the '*Dative*', in Latin they have amalgamated with the Ablative ('from'), to form a Case called the '*Ablative*'. In other words,

the Latin 'AbLatIve' was Abl. ('from') } + *Loc. ('in', 'at'),*
the Greek 'Dative' was Dat. ('to' or 'for') } + *Instr. ('by,' 'with');*

(2) the *Genitive* in Greek amalgamated with the Ablative ('from'), but amalgamated to some extent with the Locative ('in', 'at') in Latin: in other words,

the Latin 'Genitive' was Gen. ('of') + Loc. ('in', 'at'),
the Greek 'Genitive' was Gen. ('of') + Abl. ('from').

Now, supposing you were speaking the Māter-Language, and wished to say '*in* speaking', to this *bhāmā-* you would add the Case-Ending for 'in', viz. the Locative-Ending, which was *-i*, and you would therefore say *bhāmāi.* This is quite an incorrect account of the actual process of speech-forming, but it is convenient for the present purpose.

I.		Att. Greek ᾱ → Att. η	Latin
Nom.	*bhāmā* [lengthened or no Ending]	φήμη	fāmă (O.L. fāmā, p. 45)
Voc.	*? bhāmă* [no Ending]	[φῆμα]	fāmă
Acc.	*bhāmā-m*	φήμην	fāmăm (p. 46)
Dat.	*bhāmā-ai (-māi)*	φήμῃ ('Dat.')	? fāmā (O.L., p. 53)
Instr.	*bhāmā -a* or *-e (-mā)*	[φήμῃ, cp. ? πῇ]	fāmā
Loc.	*bhāmā-i*	φήμῃ ('Dat.')	fāmae *
Abl.	*bhāmā-(e)d (-mād)*	[φήμη] ? φήμης before Dentals	fāmā (O.L. fāmād)

Gen. *bhamā-(e)s* (*-mās*) esp. in Pronouns, same as Loc.	φήμης	[fāmās cp. paterfamiliās, p. 47] fāmae *

Plural	Att. Greek	Latin
N.V. *bhāmā-(e)s*	[φήμης]	[fāmās, cp. O.L.]
-i (esp. in Pronouns)	φῆμαι	fāmae
Acc. *bhāmā-ns*	φήμᾱς	fāmās
Dat. *bhāmā-ais* (*-māis*)	φήμαις (p. 88)	?
Loc. *bhāmā-is*	φήμαις (p. 88)	? fāmīs †
-si		
Gen. *bhāmā-ōm*	φημῶν (Dor. φημᾶν)	[fāmum, cp. agricolum]
-sōm (esp. in Pronouns)	Do.	fāmārum

II. (*a*) Stem *u̯oiko-* and sometimes *u̯oike-*: for *o* and *e*, see p. 74.

		Att. Greek	Latin
Nom.	*u̯oiko-s*	οἶκος	vīcus
Voc.	*-ke*	οἶκε	vīce
Acc.	*-ko-m*	οἶκον	vīcum
Dat.	*-ko-ai* (*-kōi*)	οἴκωι (-κῳ)	vīcō (O.L. -cōi, p. 84)
Instr.	*-ko-a* (*-kō*)	[οἴκω cp. ? οὕτω]	vīcō (?multō)
	-ke -a or *e* (-kē)	[οἴκη, cp. ? πάντη]	[vīcē, cp. ? cārē]
Loc.	*-ko-i*	οἴκοι	vīcī } cp. Corinthī
	-ke-i	οἴκει (Dialect)	vīcī } cp. Corinthī
Abl.	*-ko-od* (*-kōd*)	[οἴκω] ?-κως before Dentals, cp. ? οὕτω(ς)	vīcō (O.L. -ōd)
	-ke-ed (*-kēd*)	[οἴκη]	[vīcēd, cp. facilumēd, p. 138]
Gen.	*-ko-si̯o*	οἴκου (cp. Hom. -οιο and -οο)	
	esp. in Pronouns, ? same as Loc.	[οἴκοι Thessalian]	vīcī

* Possibly some Archaic forms like fāmāī were due to Association with the -ī of the 2nd Declension (cp. Corinthī).

† Was this due to Association with 2nd Declension forms, e.g. verbīs? Cp. p. 91.

Plural	Att. Greek	Latin
N.V. *u̯oiko-os(?) (-kōs)*	[οἴκως]	[vīcōs, cp. O.L. deivōs]
esp. in Pronouns *-ko-i*	οἶκοι	vīcī
Acc. *u̯oiko-n̥s*	οἴκους (Argive and Cretan τόνς)	vīcōs
Dat. *u̯oiko-ais (-kōis)*	οἴκοις (p. 88)	[? vīcīs]
Loc. *u̯oiko-is*	οἴκοις	vīcīs
Gen. *u̯oiko-ōm (-kōm)*	οἴκων	[vīcum, cp. O.L. and Poetry]
esp. in Pronouns *-sōm*		vīcōrum (p. 92)

II. (*b*) Neuter Stem, *yugo-:* like the above, except in the Nom., Voc. Acc., which were

Singular		
yuʒo-m	ζυγόν	iugum
Plural		
yuʒ-a (see p. 116)	ζυγά	iuga

III. Stem *nokt-* [there is not space to discuss here the *-υ-* of Greek νύξ]

	Att. Greek	Latin
N.V. *nokt-s*	νύξ	nox
Acc. *nokt-m̥*	νύκτα	noctem
Dat. *nokt-ai*	[νυκται, cp. δοῦναι]	noctī
Instr. *nokt-a* or *-e*	[νυκτα, cp. ? ἅμα]	nocte
Loc. *nokt-i*	νυκτί	nocte
Abl. *nokt-?ed*	[νυκτε]	? nocte
Gen. *nokt-es*		noctis
-os	νυκτός	[cp. O.L. Venerus]
?-s		[?cp. O.L. nox 'at night']
Plural		
N.V. *nokt-es*	νύκτες	[O.L. noctēs, noctēs by Assoc. with ovēs, etc., p. 139]
Acc. *nokt-n̥s*	νύκτας	noctēs
Loc. *nokt-si*	νυξί	
Gen. *nokt-ōm*	νυκτῶν	noctum
? *nokt-(ə)-bhios* or *-b̥hos*		noctibus

IV. Stem *pətér-*, *pətr-* ': when the Accent (p. 74) fell on the *é*, *e* was preserved, when the Accent fell on the Case-Ending, *é* was dropped: but the forms have been harmonised into a uniform system, Latin paterem, for instance, become patrem by Association with patris and patrī.

Only the Māter-forms are given here, except, e.g. for the Greek Dative Plural.

Nom. *pətēr* (Vowel Lengthened)
Voc. *pə̀ter* (Accent on first Syllable, probably in all Vocatives)
Acc. *pətér-m̥*
Dat. *pətr-aí*
Instr. *pətr-á* or *-e*
Loc. *? pətér-i*
Abl. *? pətr-éd*
Gen. *pətr-és*
-ós

Plural

N.V. *pətér-es*
Acc. *? pəter-n̥s* (πατέρας, patrēs, see above)
Loc. *pətr̥-si* (πατράσι, cp. p. 134)
? *pətr-(ə) -bhos or -bhios* (patribus). Celtic had-bos.

The following *Verses* summarise the chief Case-Endings: in the Analysis of Words these Endings recur so constantly that it saves trouble to master them once for all.

The first Case has no sign, or Vowel long, or else an -S,
Accusative from hi-*m* and who-*m* as -M (or -*m̥*) you guess,
DAtIve A-I in δοῦν-αι, InstrumEntAl A or E,
LocatÍval I in ποδ-ί, Ablatives in OD, ED, D;
Then Genitives in OS, ES, S, or I, or S-I-O.
Nóminative Plural ES, I, A, from πόδ-ες οἶκο-ι know,
Th' Accusative in -n̥s or else in N-S (as in τό-νς),
The Genitive in ŌM or SŌM (mensārum here belongs);
DAtIve A-I-S, LocatIval I-S or S-I;
The Latin Case in BHOS or bhios is still a mystery.

28. (ii) (*b*) Suffixes of Moods.

28 (ii) (*b*)

As to the Suffixes of Moods,

I. The *Optative* Suffixes can be seen in δο-ίη-ν δο-ῖ-μεν λέγο-ι-μι:

(α) -*iē*- or -*iḗ*- in the Singular, where at first the Accent fell on the -*ḗ*-: cp. O.L. s-iē-d or s-iē-t (→ sit, pp. 93, 86);

(β) -*ī*- in the Plural, where the Accent fell on the Ending, as in εἶ-μι ἰ-μέν (later ἴμεν): cp. sīmus;

(γ) -*i*- in Verbs like λεγο-.

II. The *Subjunctive* Suffixes can be seen in leg-ā-tis, λέγ-ω-μεν λέγ-η-τε leg-ē-tis, ἴ-ο-μεν (Homeric 'let us go'): these suggest

(α) -*ā*- (leg-ā-tis, and *? some* Attic Subjunctives like λέγητε: but see (β));

(β) a Long -*ō*- or -*ē*-, where the Indicative had a short Vowel* (λέγ-ω-μεν λέγ-ο-μεν, λέγητε legētis λέγετε legete-s → légitis); this Suffix has been largely extended in Greek (cp. ἴωμεν);

(γ) a Short -*o*- or -*e*-, where the Indicative had no Vowel* (ἴ-ο-μεν ἴ-μεν, ἔσ-ε-σθε ér-i-tis, ἐσ-τέ éstis).

III. The *Imperative* Suffix can hardly be separated from the Ending: e.g. cp. λεγέτω legitō (p. 83).

IV. The *Participle*, in so far as it was a Mood, had among its Suffixes those which are seen in λέγο-ντ-α, lege-nt-em, τα-τό-ς ten-tu-s, εἰδ-Fός λελυκ-F-ια, etc. For dīctūrum, see p. 112. These give us, e.g.

(α) -*nt*- (cp. also ὀδό-ντ-α de-nt-em);

(β) -*uos* in the II-Stage, and -*us* in the III-Stage (εἰδ-Fός → εἰδός, λελυκ-υ-ῖα).

V. The *Infinitive*, in so far as it was a Mood, had Suffixes which were once Suffixes of Verbal Nouns: leg-ī had no Suffix. Instances would be λέγε-ιν, λέγε-σθ-αι, ἔμ-μεν and ἔμ-μεν-αι (Homeric), leg-er-e and es-s-e. These suggest

* For this 'Thematic' Vowel, -*o*- or -*e*-, see p. 105.

(α) *-uen-* or *-sen-* (λεγε-ιν: for *-u-* and *-s-*, see pp. 162, 161);

(β) *-(s)dh-*, possibly from -s- —see (d) below— + *-dh-*, or starting in Dentals Stems, where ἐσκιδ-θαι → ἐσκιδ(ς)θαι → ἐσκίσθαι. Sanskrit has a form in *-dhy-;*

(γ) *-men-* (cp. nō-men and the Datives λεγέ-μεν-αι legi-min-ī, p. 91);

(δ) *-es-* and *-s-* (with legere cp. genere, from *genesi* → γένει).

VI. *The Indicative.*

The Suffixes here are rather those of the various Tenses, e.g.

(α) The *'Presents'* δείκ-νῡ-μι δείκ-νυ-μεν, λέγ-ο-μεν λέγ-ε-τε, σπερ-ιο-μεν (→ σπείρομεν) σπερ-ιε-τε, etc., suggest *-nū-* and *-nu-*, *-o-* and *-e-* (p. 105), *-io-* and *-ie-*; and there are various others;

(β) The *'Perfects'* amā-vī, ἔθη-κ-α and τέθει-κ-α, suggest *-u-*, *-k-* (the latter also Aorist, cp. fēcī);

(γ) The *Future:* for both Greek and Latin, cp. the Subjunctive above, and, for the Latin *-b-* future, cp. p. 142 below;

(δ) The *1st Aorist,* besides *-k-* (see above), has *-s-*, suggested by ἔδεικ-σ-α (ἔδειξα) and dīc-s-ī (dīxī);

(ε) for the Pluperfect, see ᾔδη and vīderam (p. 95).

29. Greek Words Analysed.

29. *Analyse [the Early forms of] the following Greek words, with a few notes :—*

N.B.—Here, as on p. 109, foll., the words will be parsed ; and then will be put, in Brackets, the forms which throw light on the Early forms or on the Analysis: *far more important than the Answer itself is the Method of arriving at the Answer.* The learner should not merely wish to know the Analysis of any one word : he should wish also to know *how he may Analyse any given word for himself and by himself, if possible in the light of what he already knows.*

It will be a capital exercise to **illustrate all the Sound-changes in these words** : wherever any hard sound-change occurs, I add an explanation—elsewhere I leave the illustrations to be gathered from the preceding pages.

The reader should try every word for himself before he looks at the Answer.

PREFIX.	ROOT.	SUFFIX.	ENDING.

ἀλόχων :

[Gen. Plur., cp. ἄλοχο-ς, λέχ-ος, ἅ-θροος sim-ul, ποδῶν.] Stem ἀλοχο-.

sm̥ (III) *logh* (II) *-o-* (Nominal) *-ōm* (Gen. Plur.)
sm̥loghōm → ἁλόχων → ἀλόχων : *sm̥-* was connected with sem- (ἕν) and som- (ὁμοῦ) ; for the Greek objection to the double Aspirates in certain positions, cp. ἅθροος → ἄθροος, θριχ-ός → τριχ-ός (p. 177). This change is called '*Grassmann's Law*'.

PREFIX. ROOT. SUFFIX. ENDING.

ἀμβρότῳ :

[' Dative ' Sing., cp. ἄμβροτο-ς, βροτό-ς, im-mortalis, δοῦν-αι dar-ī.] Stem ἀμβροτο-.

n̥ (Negative) *smr* (III) *o* (Verbal, see p. 105) *ai* (Dative).
tó (Participle)

n̥-smrotōi → ἀμβρότωι: for -s-, see p. 205; for *n̥-* → ἀμ-, cp. *g̑m̥iō* → βαν-ιω (→ βαίνω); for *-mr-* → -μβρ-, cp, μεσημ(β)ρίᾱ with ἡμέρᾱ, chambre with camera, ἀν(δ)ρός with ἄνερ.

ἀμείνων :

[Nom. Sing. of Comparative, cp. ἄμεινον, ἥδ-ῑον, ? μέν-ος or μένω.] Stem ἀμεινον-.

men (I) *ion* -*o*- lengthened to form Nom. (p. 73)

meniōn → ἀ-μείνων: for ' Prothetic ' ἀ- in Greek, cp. ? ἀ-λείφω λίπα, and see p. 180.

ἀμφιέννῡμι :

[1st Sing. Present, cp. ἀμφί, ves-tis, δείκ-νῡ-μι.] Stem ἀμφιεννῡ-.

ambhi (Local Adverb) *wes* (I) *nū* or *neu* (Pres.) *mi* (1st Sing.)

ambhi 'on both sides' might be itself Analysed, thus:

am or *an* (I) *bhi* (Case-Ending)

ambhi-wesnūmi → ἀμφιέννῡμι: for -esn- → -εννv-, perhaps at first in 'Aeolic', cp. φαεσ-νό-ς → φάεννος (Att. φαεινός).

ἀνομίᾳ :

[' Dative ' Sing., cp. ἀνομίᾱ-ν, ἀ-δάματος in-domitus, νέμ-ω, δοῦν-αι, ποδ-ί.] Stem ἀνομιᾱ-.

n̥ (Negative) *nom* (II) *iā* (Abstract Subst.) *ai* (Dat.)
i (Loc.)

n̥nomiāi → ἀνομιᾳ.

Note.—It would be good practice to do this next word and a few others before trying a Question on Analysis: for the others see p. 134.

PREFIX. ROOT. SUFFIX. ENDING.

ἀοσσητῆρας (Homer):

This is a very hard word indeed, but it illustrates so many common changes that it is worth thoroughly mastering. [Acc. Plur. of word meaning 'companions', 'followers': cp. ἀοσσητῆρ, ἅ-θροος, ἅμ-α, soc-iōs, πα-τέρ-ας, τό-νς.]

sm̥ (Adverbial) *soq* (II) *iā* or *iē* (Verbal Noun) *n̥s* (Acc. Plur.)
ter (Agency)

sm̥-soqiēterns → ἀ-οσσητέρας. This illustrates *s*- → Greek ', -*s*- between Vowels disappearing (p. 205), *m̥* → α, -qi- → -τι- (cp. quis τίς) → σσ (p. 162); *n̥* → α. In 'Aeolic', ἁ- → ἀ- (cp. ἡρώων, p. 36); the -η- was due to Association with the Nom Sing. in -τηρ (see p. 69).

ἀσπουδεί:

[Locative Adverb, cp. ἀ-δάματος in-domitus, σπεύδ-ω, ποδ-ί.] Stem ἀσπουδε-.

n̥ (Negative) *spoud* (II) *e* (p. 105) *i* (*Loc.*)

n̥spoudei → ἀσπουδεί.

ἅττα ('some'):

[Neut. Plur., cp. qui-s τι-ς, ζυγ-ά iug-a.]

qi *a* (Neut. Plur.)

qia → τια → ττα, cp. μελιτια → μέλισσα; ττα was an Enclitic, and πόσα ττα πράγματα became divided as ποσ' ἅττα πράγματα, like πόσ' ἄλλα πράγματα (cp. a norange → an orange, like an apple): hence came a new word ἅττα. This can be called Changed Division.

βουλῡτόνδε:

[Acc. + Postpositional -δε, cp. βού-ς cow, λύ-ω, λυ-τό-ς, οἶκο-ν-δέ.] Stem βουλυτο-.

ǥou
leu or *lū* (I) *to* (Verbal Noun) *m* (Acc.) *de* (Post-
or *lu* (II) positional)

ǥoulŭtomde → βουλυτόνδε: was the ῠ lengthened so as to make the word scan?

PREFIX. ROOT. SUFFIX. ENDING.

γέγαμεν:

[1st Plur. Perf., cp. γί-γν-ο-μαι, γέν-ος.] Stem γεγα- etc.

ǵe (Perf. Redupl.) *ǵn̥* (III) *men* (1st Plur.)

ǵeǵn̥men → γέγαμεν.

γενεῆφιν:

[φι-Case of γενέη, cp. γενεᾱ γέν-ος εὐ-γεν-ές.] Stem γενεᾱ-.

ǵen (I) *es* (Abstract Noun) *bhi* (Greek -ν)

ā (do.)

ǵenesābhi → γενεῆφι(ν): -φι had a very wide range of meanings.

δεσπότης:

[Nom. Sing., cp. dom-inus, δέμ-ω, πό-τι-ς po-ti-s, κρι-τή-ς.] Stem δεσποτᾱ-.

dem (I) *s* (Gen.)

po *tā* (Agency, etc.) *s* (Nom.)

demspotās → δεσπότης: for *ems-* (followed by a Consonant) → ες-, cp. en-s → ἐς (before Consonants, at first).

δυσμενής:

[Nom. Sing., cp. δυσμενές, μέν-ος.] Stem δυσμενές-.

dus *men* (I) *es* (Adj.) Long Vowel to form Nom.

ἐγέλασσαν (Hom.):

[3rd Plur. 1st Aor., cp. ἐγέλασσ-α, ridēba-nt, γέρ-ας, ἔ-λῡ-σ-αν.] Stem ἐγελασσ-.

e (Augment, p. 110) *gel* (I) *as* (Verbal Noun) *n̥t* (3rd Plur.)

s (1st Aorist)

egelassn̥t → ἐγέλασσαν → ἐγέλασαν: cp. ἐτέλεσσαν with εὐ-τελ-ές. For *n̥-* → -αν, cp. *n̥-* → ἄμ(βροτος), p. 124.

εἰδώς:

[Nom. Sing. Perf. Partic., cp. εἶδ-ός, vīd-ī, εἰδυῖα.] Stem εἰδος-.

u̯eid (I) *u̯os* (Perf. Part.) Vowel Long to form Nom.

u̯eidu̯os → εἰδός: for *du̯*, cp. *du̯is* → δίς bis. (p. 73)

PREFIX. ROOT. SUFFIX. ENDING.

εἵμαρται:

[3rd Sing. Perf. Pass., cp. δέ-δο-ται, μέρ-ος, smart.] Stem εἵμαρ-.

se (Perf. Redupl.) *smr̥* (III) *tai* (3rd Sing. Middle)

sesmr̥tai → εἵμαρται: for *esm-* → εἰμ-, cp. esmi → εἰμί.

ἔλιπον (3rd Plur.):

[3rd Plur. 2nd Aor., cp. λείπ-ω, lic-tus legēbā-nt.] Stem ἐλιπο- and ἐλιπε-

e (Augment) *liq* (III) *o* (p. 105) *nt* (3rd Plur.)

eliqont → ἔλιπον.

ἔλπις:

[Nom. Sing., cp. ἐλπίδ-ος voluptās.] Stem ἐλπιδ-.

u̯el or *u̯elp-* (I) *pid-* or *id-* (Abstract Noun) *s* (Nom.)

u̯elpids → ἔλπις, cp. mīlets → mīles.

ἐλύθη:

[3rd Sing. 1st Aor. Pass., cp. λύ-ω, ἐλύ-θη-ς, luēba-t.] Stem ἐλυθη-.

e (Augment) *lu* (III) *ē* (Aor. Pass.) *t* (3rd Sing.)

Possibly the -θ- started with a 2nd Sing. in -θης; for Sanskrit has the *-th-* in this Person only, as well as in the Imperative (cp. -θι). For extension of a letter through a Tense, see below.

eluthēt → ἐλύθη.

ἐλύσατε:

[2nd Plur., 1st Aor., cp. λύ-ω, ἔ-λῡ-σ-α, δό-τε.] Stem ἐλῡσα- and ἐλῡσ-.

e (Augment) *lū* or *leu* (I) *s* (1st Aor.) *te* (2nd Plur.)

The -α- started in the 1st Pers. Sing. and the 3rd Pers. Plur., where *elūsm̥* → ἔλῡσα, and *elūsn̥t* → ἔλῡσαν: it was then extended to the other Persons, owing to the Tense forms being Associated in a group (p. 68): hence

elūste → ἐλύσ(α)τε.

PREFIX. ROOT. SUFFIX. ENDING.

ἔμεινε:

[3rd Sing. of the 1st Aor., cp. μέν-ω, ἔ-λῡ-σα, mansi-t.] Stem ἐμεινε- and ἐμειν-.

e (Augment) *men* (I) *se* (1st Aor.) *t*

emenset → ἔμεινε: for *-ens-*, cp. *etensm̥* → ἔτεινα.

ἕνη καὶ νέᾱ ('the old day and the new'):

[Nom. Sing. Fem., cp. sen-ex, sen-ā-tus, nova-m, new.] Stems ἑνη· κα- νεᾱ-.

sen (I) *ā* (Fem. Adj.)

ka *i* (Loc.).

neu (I) *ā* (Fem. Adj.)

senā kai neuā → ἕνη καὶ νέᾱ (ἡμέρᾱ).

ἑστήκᾱσι:

[3rd Plur. Perf., cp. δε-δώ-κᾱσι, stā-re, O.L. tremo-nti.] Stem ἑστηκ-.

se (Perf. Redupl.) *st*(*h*)*ā* (I) *k* (Perf.) *n̥ti* (3rd Plur.)

sest(h)ākn̥ti → ἑστήκᾱσι: *-n̥ti* → -ανσι (cp. ἵστᾱτι and ἵστησι); for -ανσι → ᾱσι, cp. γίγαν(τ)σι → γίγᾱσι.

ἐπῆεν:

[3rd Sing. Imperf., cp. ἐπί, ἔ-λεγ-ε, er-ā-s er-a-t, ἐσ-τί.] Stem ἐπηε- etc.

epi (Local Adverb)

e (Augment) *es* (I) *e* (p. 105) *t* (3rd Sing.)

epiēset → ἐπηε (+ Greek -ν).

εὔαδε 'it pleased':

[3rd Sing. 2nd Aor., cp. ἁδ-ήσομαι, ἐ-δόκει, suād-eō, suāsi-t.] Stem εὔαδε-.

e (Augment) *suəd* (III) *e* (p. 105) *t*

esuədet → εὔαδε ('Aeolic').

εὐρυάγυιαν:

[Acc. Sing., cp. εὐρύ-ς, ? οὐρ-ανός, ἄγυια, ἄγ-ω.] Stem εὐρυαγυῖα-.

PREFIX.	ROOT.	SUFFIX.	ENDING.
	eur- (I)	*u* (Adj.)	
	ag	*us* (Participle)	*m̥* or *m* (Acc.)
		i̯ or *i̯a* (p. 96)	

euruagus-i̯m̥ or *-i̯am* → εὐρυάγυιαν.

ἦ δ' ὅς 'said he'.

[3rd Sing., cp. ἔ-φη, ai-t, ἠχώ; Nom. Sing., cp. ὅ-ν.] Stems ἠ- and ὅ-.

e (Augment)	*āgh* (I)		*t* (3rd Sing.)
	de		
	i̯ or *su̯* (III)	*o* (p. 105)	*s* (Nom.)

The Greek Relative ὅ-ς was originally a Demonstrative: it might have come either from *i̯o-s* or from *su̯o-s*, and perhaps the two streams met and produced ὅ-ς.

e-āght de i̯os (or *su̯os*) → ἦ δ' ὅς: see p. 95.

ᾔει 'he went':

[3rd Sing. 1st Aor., cp. ἔ-βη, εἶ-μι, ἔδεικ-σε dīxi-t.] Stem ᾐει- etc.

e (Augment)	*ei* (I.)	*ese* (1st Aor.)	*t* (3rd Sing.)

ēieset → ἠιεε → ἠιει.

ἥκω:

[1st Sing. Perf. (declined like a Present, because of its meaning: cp. New Testament στήκω), cp. ἧ-κ-α, ἵη-μι iē-cī, sē-vī.] Stem ἡκο- and ἡκε-.

? *e* (Augment)	*i̯ē* (I)	*k* (Perf.)	*m̥* (1st Sing.)
or *i̯e* (Perf. Redupl.)			

i̯ei̯ēkm̥ → ἔηκα → ἧκα; from the Root *sē-* (cp. sē-men), we should have *sesēkm̥* → ἧκα. Then ἧκα became ἥκω, by Association with Presents like μένω. For -ω, see p. 73.

ἴσθι (*a*) 'know', (*b*) 'be':

[2nd Sing. Imperat., cp. (*a*) ἰδ-εῖν, vid-ēre, (*b*) ἐσ-τί, s-it.] Stem ἰσ-, etc.

	(*a*) *u̯id* (III)		*dhi* (Imperat. 2nd Sing.)
	(*b*) *s* (III)		

PREFIX. ROOT. SUFFIX. ENDING.

uid-dhi → *uid-s-dhi* → ἴσθι; in ἴσθι 'be', we perhaps have a 'Prothetic' Vowel, like that of stella → éstella → étoile (p. 180).

ἰοχέαιρα 'arrow-shooter':

[Nom. Sing. Fem., cp. ἰό-ν, χέω χεύ-σομαι. σπείρω from σπεριω.] Stem ἰοχέαιρα-.

īs or *eis* (I) *o* (Subst., see p. 105)
gheu (I) *r* (Agency)
ī or *ia* (p. 96)

īso-gheuria → ἰοχέαιρα: for *-u-* disappeared (p. 162), and *-ria* → *-αρια* → *-αιρα*.

κορή:

[Nom. Sing., cp. Ionic κουρή-ν, 'Aeolic' κόρρᾱν, Doric κωράν.] Stem κορη-.

kor (II) *uā* (Subst. and Adj.)

korua → Attic κορή.

κρείττους:

[Nom. and Acc. Plur. cp. Ionic κρέσσον, κράτ-ος, mel-ius, πατέρ-ες, πατέρ-ας.] For the two Comparative Stems, cp. p. 124.

kret (I) *ios* (Comparative) *es* (Nom.)

kretioses → κρεσσοες → κρέσσους; κρείσσους was due to Association with ἀμείνους and ὀλείζους (p. 110); the Acc. κρείσσοας would → κρείσσως, and perhaps the Nom. form was extended to the Acc., because Nom. and Acc. were alike in the Neuter.

λέγῃ (2nd Sing. Subj. Middle):

[Cp. λέγ-ω, λέγ-η-ται, γεγραπ-σαι.] Stem λεγη- and λεγω-.

leg (I) *ē* (Subj.) *sai* (2nd Sing. Middle)

legēsai → λέγηι.

λιλαίεται:

[3rd Sing. Present Middle, cp. lascīvos, δί-δο-ται.] Stems λιλαιε- and λιλαιο-.

li (Present Redupl.) *las* *ie* (Present) *tai* (3rd Sing. Middle)

lilasietai → λιλαίεται.

PREFIX.	ROOT.	SUFFIX.	ENDING.

λῦσαι :

[(*a*) Dative Singular of Verbal Noun, cp. ἔ-λῡ-σ- , δοῦν-αι ; (*b*) 2nd. Sing. 1st Aor. Middle Imperative.] Stem λῡσ-

(*a*)	*lū* or *leu* (I)	*s* (Verbal Noun)	*ai* (Dat.)
(*b*)		*s* (1st Aor.)	*ai* (Middle)

lūsai or *leusai* → λῦσαι.

μεμάτω :

[Perf. or 2nd Aor. Imperat., cp. *μέ-μν-η-μαι*, *μά-τις* men-tiō, *λέγε-τω* legitōd.] Stem *μεμα-*, etc.

me Perf. or 2nd Aor. (Redupl.)	*mn̥* (III)		*tōd* (Imperative 2nd and 3rd Sing.)

memn̥tōd → *μεμάτω*: *tōd* might be Analysed into

	to (Pronoun)		*od* (Abl.)

meaning, at first, 'from or after this', i.e. 'henceforth' or 'afterwards'.

μέμβλωκα :

[1st Sing. Perf., cp. *δέ-δω-κ-α*, *μολ-εῖν*.] Stem *μεμβλωκ-*.

me (Perf. Redupl.)	*ml* (III)	*ō* (Verbal) *k* (Perf.)	*m̥* (1st Sing.)

memlōkm̥ → *μέμβλωκα*, cp. *ἄμβροτος* (p. 124).

Μοῦσαι :

[Nom. Plur., cp. *μοῦσα-ν*, mon-eō, *λέγ-ουσα λέγοντ-ος*.] Stem *μοῦσα-*.

	mon (II)	*ti̯a* (Subst., see p. 96)	*i* (Nom. Plur.)

monti̯ai → *μονσσαι* → *μοῦσαι*.

οἰνοπέδου :

[Gen. Sing., cp. *οἶνο-ν* vīnu-m, *πέδο-ν*, Homeric *οἰνοπέδο-ιο*.] Stem οἰνοπεδο-

	u̯oin- or	*o-* (Subst., p. 105)	
	u̯oi (II)	*-no-* (Subst.)	
	ped (I)	*-o-* (Subst.)	*si̯o* (Gen.)

u̯oinopedosi̯o → οἰνοπεδοιο → οἰνοπεδ-οο (cp. trei̯es → *τρεες* → *τρεῖς*) → οἰνοπέδου.

PREFIX. ROOT. SUFFIX. ENDING.

ὄχεσφι :

[φι- Case, cp. ὄχ-ος, ἔχ-ω ἕξω σχ-εῖν, veh-ō.] Stem ὀχοσ- and ὀχεσ-

uogh (II) *es* (Verbal Noun) *bhi* (Case with wide
ŝogh (II) meaning)

uoghesbhi → ὄχεσφι.
soghesbhi → ὄχεσφι → ὄχεσφι : cp. θριχός → τριχός.

παρέμιμνεν :

[3rd Sing. Imperf., cp. παρά, ἔ-μεν-ε si-stō manēba-t.] Stem παρεμιμνε- and -νο-.
pṛ(r)a (Local Adverb)
e (Augment) *mn* (III) *e* (Present, and see p. 105) *t* (3rd Sing.)
mi (Present Redupl.)
pṛ(r)emimnet → παρέμιμνε, + Greek -ν

πέπομφα :

[1st Sing. Perf., cp. δέ-δω-κ-α, πέμπ-ω.] Stem πέπομφ-, etc.
pe- (Perf. Redupl.) *pomp* (II) *m̥* (1st Sing.)
pepompm̥ → πέπομπα : the -φ- was from Association with πέπομφ-θε and Imperative πεπόμφ-θω, where π → φ by Assimilation.

πεφευγοίην :

[1st. Sing. Perf. Opt., cp. δέ-δω-κα, φεύγ-ω, δο-ίη-ν, O.L. siem.] Stem πεφευγοιη-.
bhe (Perf. Redupl.) *bheug* (I) *o* (Verb) *iē* (Opt.) *m* (1st Sing.)
bhebheugoiēm → πεφευγοίην. It is probable that we have πέφευγα, not πέφουγα (cp. λείπω λέλοιπα), through Association with φεύγω.

πιέζω :

[1st Pers. Sing. Pres., cp. ἐπί, sed-eō.] Stem πιεζο- and πιεζε-
pi (Local Adverb, cp. ἐπί) *sed* (I) *i̯o* (Present) Long Vowel to form 1st Sing. (73)

PREFIX. ROOT. SUFFIX. ENDING.

pisediō → πιέζω, cp. *dieu* → Ζεῦ.

πρίν:

[Comparative Adverb, cp. πρ-ό, ἥδ-ῑον.]

pr (III) *in* (III) (Comparative :-*ion* was II)

στῆναι:

[Dat. Sing. of Verbal Noun, cp. Old Greek δοϝεναι, stā-re.]

st(h)ā (I) *uen* (Verbal Noun) *ai* (Dat.)

st(h)āuenai → στῆναι.

σχές:

[2nd Sing. Imperat. of 2nd Aor., cp. ἔχ-ω, ἕξω, δό-ς.] Stem σχε- and σχο-.

sgh (III) *e* (Verbal) *s* (2nd Sing.)

sghes → σχές. Such forms in Sanskrit are used with wide meanings, e.g. as a Past Tense and in Commands. See p. 51.

τετράφαται:

[3rd Plur. Perf. Pass., cp. τρέπ-ω, torqueō, λέγο-νται.] Stem τετραφ-, etc.

te (Perf. Redupl.) *tr̥p* (III) *n̥tai* (3rd Plur. Middle)

tetr̥pn̥tai → τετράπαται: for the -φ-, see above, p. 132.

τράπεζα ('a four-footed thing, a table'):

[Nom. Sing. Fem., cp. τετρα-, ped-em.] Stem τραπεζα-.

qet (I) *ur̥*

or *qt* (III)

ped (I) *ī* or *ia* (p. 96)

qetr̥pedia → τετραπεζα → τράπεζα: cp. ἀμφιφορευς → ἀμφορεύς venēnificium → venēficium, εἰδωλολάτρεια and idolatry: p. 179.

qtr̥pedia → (π)τράπεζα.

τριχός:

[Gen. Sing., cp. θρί-, ποδ-ός.]

dhrigh (III) *os* (Gen.)

dhrighos → θριχός → τριχός (p. 177)

PREFIX.	ROOT.	SUFFIX.	ENDING.

ὑπόδρα ('askance'):

[Aor., cp. ὑπό, δέρκ-ομαι δρακ-ών.]

upo or *supo* (Loc. Adv., p. 91)	*dṛk* (III)		

(*s*)*upodṛk* → ὑποδρα(κ).

φαεννοῖς (from 'Aeolic'):

['Dative' Plur., cp. φαεννό-ς, φάος.] Stem φαεννο-.

	bhə (III)	*u̯es* (Abstract Subst.) *no* (Adj.)	*is* (Loc.) *ais* (Dat.)

bhəu̯esnois and *-nōis* → φαέννοις in 'Aeolic', φαεινοῖς in Attic: cp. p. 36.

φαίνοισα ('Aeolic'):

[Nom. Sing. Fem., cp. φαίνο-μεν, φαιν-ο-ντ-α.] Stem φαινοισα-.

	bhə (III) + *n*	*i̯o* (Present) *n̥t* (Partic.) *i̯a* or *ī* (Fem., p. 96)	

bhəni̯ontia → φαινονσσα → φαίνοισα in 'Aeolic' (p. 36), φαίνουσα in Attic. *bhən-* might be called a 'Secondary' Root.

φρασίν (Pindar):

[Dat. Plur., cp. φρέν-ες, γαλακ-σι.] Stem φρεν-, etc.

	bhrṇ (III)		*si* (Loc. Plur.)

bhrṇsi → φρασί, φρεσί owing its ε to Association with φρένες, etc.

An Exercise in hard Greek Words.

Analyse the Early forms of the following words:—

μητρός ἀοσσητῆρας ἔχων λίπεν αἰπόλος οἶκον.
ἄττ' ἔσπειρεν ὁμοῦ ἠῶι πέφῡκεν ἀμείνω.
τέσσερας ἀλλ' ἐσιδών ἑκατὸν βοῦς ἕζετ' ἀληθῶς.

Answer: for details see the Instances above.

	mā (I)	*tr*	*os*
sṃ (III)	*soq̯* (II)	*ie* or *ia* *ter* (p. 125)	*ṇs*

PREFIX.	ROOT.	SUFFIX.	ENDING.
	segh (I)	*o* (p. 105) *nt*	Long Vowel for Nom.
	liq (III)	*e* (p. 105)	*t* (Greek -*ν*)
	{ *aig* (I)		
	{ *qol* (II)	*o* (p. 105)	*s*
	u̯oi- or *u̯oik*-	*ko*- or *o*-	*m*
	i̯- or *su̯* (III)		*a*
	qi̯		*a*
e	*sper* (I)	*se*	*t* (Greek -*ν*)
	som (II)	*o*	*t si̯o*
	āus (I)	*ōs*	*i*
bhe	*bhū* or *bheu* (I)	*ke*	*t* (Greek -*ν*)
(Greek *α*-	*men* (I)	*i̯os*	*a*
p. 108)	*qet* (I)	*u̯r̥*	*n̥s*
	al	*i̯*	*a*
en-*s*	*u̯id* (III)	*o* (p. 105) *nt*	Long Vowel for Nom.
? *sem* (I)	*dkm̥* (III)	*to*	*m*
	gou		*ns*
	sed (I)	*i̯e*	*to*
n̥	? *lāth* (I)	*os*	? Long Vowel for Adverb.

30. Latin Words Analysed.

30. *Analyse [the Early forms of] the following Latin words, with a few Notes.*

	PREFIX.	ROOT.	SUFFIX.	ENDING.

aevom:

[Nom. and Acc. Neuter, cp. αἰών.] Stem aevo-.

PREFIX.	ROOT.	SUFFIX.	ENDING.
	aiu̯-	*o* (Subst., p. 105)	*m* (Nom. and Acc. Neuter)

aiu̯om → aevom.

amāvī:

[1st Sing. Perf., cp. amā-s, memin-ī μέμνημαι.] Stem amāv-, etc.

PREFIX.	ROOT.	SUFFIX.	ENDING.
	? *m̥(m)* (III)	*ā* (Abstract Sub. and Verb) *u̯* (Perf.)	*ai* Middle, esp. 1st Sing.)

m̥(m)au̯ai → amāvī: for *m̥(m)* cp. p. 93: it is possible that the I-Stage of the Root was *em-* (cp. emō), with a meaning like 'take' or 'choose'; for em- → am-, cp. perhaps μέγας and magnus, ἐρετμός and ratis.

ambīre:

[Locative Sing. of Verbal Noun, cp. es-s-e, genere γένει, ἀμφί, εἶ-μι.] Stem ambīr-.

PREFIX.	ROOT.	SUFFIX.	ENDING.
ambhi (Local Adverb, pp. 84, 132)	*ei* (I)	(*e*)*s* (Verbal Noun)	*i* (Loc.) *a* or *e* (Instr.)

ambhi-ei(*e*)*si*, etc. → ambīre.

anceps:

[Nom. Sing. of word meaning 'two-headed' (in the sense

of 'with two minds'): cp. ἀμφί, cap-ut, κεφάλη, ancipit-em.] Stem ancip(i)t-.

ambhi (Local Adverb) ? *keph* (*ə*)*t* (Subst.) *s* (Nom.)

ambhikeph(*ə*)*ts* → ámbicepts → ánceps: cp. perhaps ántiquairō → ánquīrō, and see p. 178. For ἀμφί 'on both sides', cp. ἀμφιφορεύς → ἀμφορεύς.

arbitrōrum:

[Gen. Plur., cp. ad-, O.L. bītere, ἀπο-τρό-ν.] Stem arbitro-.

ad (Local Adverb) *bi* (III) *tro* (? Agency) *sōm* (Gen. Plur., esp. in Pronouns)

adbitrosōm → arbitrorum: for *d* → r, cp. arcessō, and some Umbrian forms (p. 55); for -ō-, perhaps by Association with arbitrōs and the 1st Declension in -ārum, see p. 92.

arcĕssō:

[1st Sing. Pres., cp. ad, cēdō, arcessi-mus λέγο-μεν.] Stem arcessi-, etc.

ad (Local Adverb) *kēd* (I) or *kəd* (III) *to* (Causal) Vowel Lengthened to form 1st Sing.

adkĕdtō → arcĕssō: for d → r, cp. esp. Umbrian, and also arbiter (above): for *-dt-* → -dst- → -ss-, cp. scid-tos → scissus (p. 206).

aufugiunt:

[3rd Plur. Present, cp. αὖ, φυγ-εῖν, O.L. trem-o-nti.] Stem aufugio-, etc.

au (Local Adverb) *bhuǥ* (III) *io* (Pres.) *nti* / *nt* } (3rd Plur.)

au-bhuǥiont(*i*) → áufugiunt; if *ambhō* → ambō (ἄμφω), one might expect au*b*ugiunt here, but Association with fugiunt (cp. ferunt from *bheront*(*i*)) produced aufugiunt. It is probable that a form from *ápo-* would not have become aú- but áb-.

bene:

['Ablative' Adverb, cp. cārē, O.L. facilumēd, O.L. Dueno-s.] Stem bene-, etc.

PREFIX.	ROOT.	SUFFIX.	ENDING.
	? *duo* (II)	*ne* (Adj.)	*ed* (Abl.)
			a or *e* (Instr.)

duon(ē)d → benē: for *uo* → *ue*, cp. *uoid-* → (οἶδ-α) veid-. For benē → bene̮, owing to the Stress Accent, see p. 46.

brūma:

[Nom. Sing., cp. brūma-m, brevi-s βραχύ-ς, πρό-μος sup-mos → summus.] Stem brūma.

	ROOT.	SUFFIX.
	breʒh (I)	*u* (Adj.) ? *i* (Fem.)
		mā (Superl. Fem.)

breʒhu(i)mā → brehu(i)mā → breu(i)mā → broumā → brūma. For -h- disappearing, cp. bihimus (χιών) → bīmus; for eu, see p. 86; for ā → ă, see p. 46. For the 'Ellipse' of diēs, cp. τῇ ὑστεραίᾳ, and see p. 128.

cerebrum:

[Nom. and Acc. Sing., cp. κέρ-ας, fūnebris from fūnesris, p. 167.] Stem cerebro-, etc.

ROOT.	SUFFIX.	ENDING.
ker (I)	*es* (Abstract Noun)	*m* (Nom. and Acc.
	ro (do.)	Neut.)

keresrom → cerebrum: for *b*, cp. fūnebris, p. 167.

cito:

[Adverb, cp. citu-s, κῖνεῖν.]

ROOT.	SUFFIX.	ENDING.
ki (III)	*to* (Verbal Noun)	*od* (Abl.) or *a* (Instr.)

kitō(d) → citō → citŏ: see bene, above.

citrā:

[Adverb, cp. in-trā, κεῖ-νος, O.L. -trād.] Stem citrā-.

ROOT.	SUFFIX.	ENDING.
ki (III)	*trā* (Suffix of Comparison)	*(e)d* (Abl.)

kitrād → citrā: For the 'Ellipse' of parte, cp. brūma, above; for the Ablative 'from the side' → 'on the side', cp. ex alterā parte.

comitābimur:

[1st Plural Future of Deponent, 'we will go with': cp. com-, i-ter, φύομεν, Doric ἵ-μες.] Stem comita-bi-, etc.

PREFIX.	ROOT.	SUFFIX.	ENDING.
kom (Local Adverb)	*i* (III)	*tā* (Verbal Noun or Agency)	
	bhuo-		*mos* (1st Plur.)

komitā-bhuomos, a Compound word, 'we are [for] going together', → cómitābimus: for -bhu-, cp. super-bō with ὑπερφυῶς, p. 98. For the 'Deponent' *-r*, originating in the old 3rd Plural *sequur*, etc., besides *sequunt*, see p. 145: it was extended to this form by Association.

consulātuī:

[Dat. Sing., consulātu-s, cp. ἐδή-τυ-ος, com-, sed-ēre, δοῦν-αι.] Stem consulātu-.

PREFIX.	ROOT.	SUFFIX.	ENDING.
kom (Local Adv.)	*sod* (II)	*ā* (Verbal Noun)	*ai* (Dat.)
		tu (do.)	

komsodātuai → consulātui: for *d* → l, cp. δακρύ, O.L. dacruma, with lacrima.

contentiōnēs:

[Nom. and Acc. Plur., cp. contentiōn-ís, τα-τός tentus, πόδ-ες τό-νς.] Stem contentiōn-.

PREFIX.	ROOT.	SUFFIX.	ENDING.
kom (Local Adverb)	*tn̥* (III)	*ti* (Verbal Noun	*es* (Nom. Plur.)
		ō̆n (do.)	*n̥s* (Acc. Plur.)

komtn̥tiō̆n- → contentiōn-: was the ō of -ōn- due to Association with the Nom. Sing., which had the Long Vowel? Nom. Plur. *-es* is sometimes found in Old Latin, but → -ēs by Association with *i-* Stems, e.g. turrēs; Acc. *-n̥s* → -ens → ēs, cp. deciēns → deciēs.

cuīcuīmodī:

[Gen. Sing., 'of whatsoever kind', cp. O.L. quei, modu-m.] Stem modu-, etc.

PREFIX.	ROOT.	SUFFIX.	ENDING.
	qo (Indef. Pronoun, II)		*i* (Gen. of Pronouns)
	mod (II)	*o* (Subst., p. 105)	*i* (Gen. from Pronouns)

qoi-qoi-modoi → cuīcuīmodī.

PREFIX.	ROOT.	SUFFIX.	ENDING.

danunt (O.L.):

[3rd Plur., cp. δο-τός da-tus, δῶ-ρον dō-num, τρέμ-ο-ντι trem-o-nti.] Stem dano-, etc.

	də (III, p. 174)	*no* (Pres.)	*nti* (3rd Plur.)
			nt (do.)

dənont(i) → dánunt: cp. p. 113.

dēnuō:

[Adv., from dē novō, O.L. novōd: cp. νέο-ς.] Stem novo-, etc.

dē (Prep.)	*neu* (I)	*o* (Adj., p. 106)	*od* (Abl.)

dēneu̯ōd → dénovō → dénu̯ō (p. 112).

Diēspiter:

[Nom. Sing., cp. Ζεύς Ζηνός πατήρ.] Stem Diēspiter-.

	dieu (I)		*e* Lengthened to form Nom., + Nom. -*s*
	pə (III)	*ter* (Agency)	*e* Lengthened to form Nom.

diēus-pəter → diēspater → Díēspiter. For -*ēus* → -ēs, cp. *ϑōus* → bōs βοῦς.

dīgnōs:

[Acc. Plur., cp. dignu-s, τό-νς, dec-et.] Stem digno-, etc.

	dek (I)	*no* (Adj.)	*ns* (Acc. Plur.)

deknons → dīgnōs, for Latin lengthened Short Vowels before -gn.

ēducāvit:

[3rd Sing. Perf., cp. ἐξ ex, duc-em, ēducāvi-mus, O.L. fueit.] Stem ēducāvī-, etc.

eks (Local Adv.)	*duk* (III)	*ā* (Verbal Noun)	
		u (Perf.)	*t* (3rd Sing.)

eksdukāu- → ēducāv-: the -i̯(t) may have come from the Middle -a̯i, cp. μέμνημαι memimī, or from *e*, cp. ἔθηκε fēcit. The *v* of the Perfect may have started with Verbs which had

PREFIX.	ROOT.	SUFFIX.	ENDING.

a *u*- belonging to the Stem, e.g. statuō statuī (cp. statu-s): others identify it with a Particle *u* (? 'then'). I think it may have started partly from a 3rd Plur. in -ur.

eōrum:

[Gen. Plur., cp. i-s, O.L. eieis.] Stem eo-, etc.

	ei (I)	*o* (Pronoun, see p. 106)	*sōm* (Gen. Plur. of Pronouns)

ei̯osōm → eorum: for -*i̯*- between Vowels, cp. *trei̯es* → trees → τρεῖς trēs; for -ō-, see p. 92.

falsus:

[Nom. Sing., Past Partic. Pass., cp. fallō, σφάλλω, παλ-τό-ς pulsus.] Stem falso-, etc.

	sbhal (I)	*to* (Partic. Pass.)	*s* (Nom. Sing.)

sbhaltos → (s)faltus. It is possible that the Early form was *sbhl̥tos* (which would → f*u*ltus), but that Association with f*a*llō produced f*a*l-; for the -sus, cp. on pulsus, p. 89.

faxit:

[Fut. Perf., or Perf. Subj. or Opt., 3rd Sing., cp. faciō, θε-τός, ἔδω-κ-α, δέδω-κ-α, δείκ-σ-ω, sit from s-iē-d.] Stem faxi-, etc.

	dhə (III)	*k* (Aor. and Perf.) *s* (Aor.) *iē* (Opt.)	*t* (3rd Sing.)

α. *dhəksiēt* → faxiet → faxīt → faxit (but see p. 93). This would make faxit Perfect and Aorist Optative;

β. others say that to *dhək*- was added siēd, Optative of the Verb 'be', so as to form a Compound Verb;

γ. others say that faxit was sometimes *Future or Subjunctive* in origin, from *dhəks-e-t,* and cp. λύσ-ε-τε.

fīdere:

[Infin., i.e. Locative of Verbal Noun, cp. gen-ere γένει, πείθω.] Stem feider-, etc.

	bheidh (I)	*es* (Verbal Noun)	*i* (Loc.)

bheidhesi → fīdere.

PREFIX.	ROOT.	SUFFIX.	ENDING.

findō :

[1st Sing. Pres. Ind., cp. fissus.]

	bhid (III)	*no* (Pres.)	Vowel Lengthened to form 1st Sing.

bhidnō → findō : cp. skid-nō (σκίδνημι) → scindō.

foederis :

[Gen. Sing., cp. foedus, πέ-ποιθ-α, O.L. Ven-er-es.] Stem foeder-, etc.

	bhoidh (III)	*es* (Verbal Noun)	*es* (Gen.)

bhoidheses → foederis.

fugābam :

[1st Sing. Imperf., cp. fug-a, φυγή, φύω, fugābā-s.] Stem fugābā-.

	bhug (III)	*ā* (Verbal Noun)	
	bhu̯ (III)	*ā* (Imperf.)	*m* (1st Sing.)

bhugā-bhu̯ām → fugābam. This was at first a Compound, cp. 'I was fly̯ing'. For the Sound-changes, see p. 98.

futūrum :

[Fut. Inf., cp. φύ-ω, dīc-tu-m, Dialect ezum, an Accusative Infinitive.]

	bhu (I)	*tu* (Verbal Noun)	
	es (I)	*o* (Verbal Noun, see p. 105)	*m* (Acc.)

bhutu-esom 'being (for) becoming', 'being about to become', → futūrum : see p. 112.

gravibus :

[Plural Case, cp. gravi-s, βαρύ-ς.] Stem gravi-.

	ϑre (I)	*u̯* (Adj.) *i* (Fem.)	*bhos* or *bhi̯os* (Plur. Case)

ϑreu̯ibhos → gravibus : for this *e* → a, cp. μέγας magnus, ἐρετμός ratis. For the Plural Case *-bhos* or *-bhi̯os*, Dat. Instr. Loc. and Abl., see p. 120.

igitur :

[Adv., ? cp. agitur, ag-ō ἄγω, ἤγ-ε-το.]

()	*ag* (I)	*e* (Pres.)	*to* (3rd Sing. Middle.)

PREFIX. ROOT. SUFFIX. ENDING.

ageto ('it was done' -> ágito) + agur ('they did it', 'people did it' -> 'it was done') were Contaminated (p. 69-70) into agitur 'it was (or is) done': see p. 145. It is possible that quíd agitur? 'what now?' or 'what then?' -> quíd igitur? (cp. rédagitur -> rédigitur), and that then the words quíd igitur? 'what now?' or 'what then?' were split up into *quid* 'what?' and *igitur* 'now' or 'then': just as the school-boy thought that brum must mean 'a stick', if candēlabrum meant 'a candlestick', and candēla meant 'candle';

(β) others refer to *a Pronoun-Root i* (III), cp. i-ta, i-d: the -gitur is hard to Analyse, though we can compare γε and ἐγώ for the *-ge-*, and τό-τε tu-m for the *-to-;* this gives i-ge-to- -> ígitu-, but leaves the *-r* unexplained. In favour of this derivation from the Pronoun is the use of igitur in Early Latin as the first word of a Clause, e.g. igitur em capitō 'then take him'.

īlicō:

[From in locō, cp. O.L. en ἐν, O.L. stlocus, στέλλω, O.L. Gnaivōd.] Stem loco-, etc.

PREFIX	ROOT	SUFFIX	ENDING
en (Prep.)	*stl* (III)	*o* (Verbal, see p. 105)	*od* (Abl.)
		ko (Subst.)	*a* (Instr.)

en-stlocō(d) -> énlocō -> illicō: for Unaccented *-o-*, cp. légomenoi -> lég*i*minī. For *stl-* -> *sl-* -> l-, cp. stlītibus (surviving in D.S.I., decemvirī stlītibus iūdicandīs) -> lītibus. For two words fusing together under one Accent, cp. dénovō -> dénuō.

impedīmentum:

[Nom. and Acc. Sing., cp. impedī-re, πέδ-η, ἐν, ὄνο-μα nō-men.] Stem impedīmento-, etc.

PREFIX	ROOT	SUFFIX	ENDING
en (Local Adverb)	*ped* (I)	*ī* (Verb)	*m* (Nom. and Acc. Neut.)
		mn̥ (Abstract and Verbal Noun)	
		to (do.)	

enpedīmn̥tom -> impedīmentum.

PREFIX. ROOT. SUFFIX. ENDING.

īmus (2):

[*a.* 1st Plur., cp. εἶ-μι, Doric ἴ-μες;

β. Nom. Sing., Superlative, cp. ἐν, in, πρό-μος, sum-mus.]

a. *ei* (I) *mos* (1st Plur.)

eimos was possibly *imós* at first (cp. ἴ-μες), but → īmus by Association with īs, īre, etc.;

β. *en-s* (Local Adv.) *mo* (Superl.) *s* (Nom. Sing.)

ensmos → insmos → īmus.

inventus:

[Nom. Sing. Passive Partic., cp. τα-τό-ς ten-tu-s, ἐν, βά-σις -ven-tiō come.] Stem invento-, etc.

en (Local Adv.) *ꝺm̥* (III) *to* (Partic. Pass.) *s* (Nom. Sing.)

enꝺm̥tos → inventus: see p. 93.

legendīs:

['Abl.' Plur., cp. legendu-s, leg-ere, ? frigi-du-s, οἴκο-ις.]

leg (I) *e* (Verbal, p. 106) *o* (Adj.) *is* (Loc. Plur.)

lege-ois → lege-īs. About the Suffixes there is much dispute:

a. (*e*)*n* * (Verbal Noun) + *i̯o* (Adj., cp. ἅγ-ιο-ς);

β. (*e*)*n* * (Verbal Noun) + *do* (Adj., cp. frīgi-du-s); *en* would be I, *on* would be II (→ *un* in *-undus*);

γ. *u̯en* (Verbal Noun, cp, αἰϝέν, ? λεγεϝεν → λέγειν) + *do* (see above); *u̯en* would be I, *un* (cp. -undus) would be III;

δ. (*e*)*n̑t* (Pres. Partic.) + some Suffix such as *-no-* (Adj., cp. σεμ-νό-ς).

legeris:

[2nd Sing. Passive, cp. λέγ-εο leg-ere, legi-s.]

leg (I) *e* (Pres., p. 105) *so* (2nd Sing. Mid.)

legeso → legere (p. 110): it is possible that *-s* was added by Association with legi-s, and to distinguish the Indicative from the Imperative legere; others, however, connect the -sis with Middle *-sai* (cp. λέγε(σ)αι λέγεται), and make the *-s* have the above origin.

* See L. Horton-Smith's paper in the *American Journal of Philology*. It is a very excellent piece of work.

PREFIX. ROOT. SUFFIX. ENDING.

legĭtur:

[3rd Sing. Pass., cp. ἐ-λέγ-ε-το, and see p. 143.]

leg (I) *e* (Pres.) *to* (3rd Sing. Mid.)

For *légeto* Contaminated with *legur*, an old 3rd Plural Active ('they choose or chose,' 'people choose or chose'), see p. 70. *This old 3rd Plural Active in -r* is found in Sanskrit, Celtic, and in the Italic Dialects, and perhaps a trace is to be seen in the 3rd Plural of the Latin Perfect (fuēre): but it is not found in Greek. For legu-*r* beside legu-*nt*, cp. (ὕδω)ρ beside ὕδατος from (ὑδ)*n̥t*(os).

leviter:

[Adv., cp. levi-s, ἐλαχ-ύ-ς.] Stem levi-.

leǥh (I) *u* (Adj.) *i* (Fem.)

tro (Adj.) ? *s* (Adv.)

leǥhuitro(s) → léhuitro(s) → léviter(s), cp. *ágros* → áger(s); it used to be derived from leve-iter (for iter, see p. 108), whence, by Association, such forms as ācr-iter, where the meaning of 'journey' has already disappeared.

macte estō:

[α. Vocative, or β. Adverb, cp. ac-tu-s, μέγ-ας mag-nus, O.L. facilumēd; O.L. es-tōd.] Stem macte-.

meg (I) or *te* (Partic. Pass.) ? *ed* (Abl.)

məg (III) ? *a* or *e* (Instr.)

α. *megte* → macte: for *e*, see p. 142; for the Vocative, cp. exspectāte venīs, mātūtīne venī;

β. megtē(d) → mactē, → mácte by Association with bĕnĕ (p. 138): for this Construction of the Adverb, cp. bene est 'it is well'. For *es-tōd*, see pp. 93, 131.

mentiōnibus:

[Plural Case, cp. mentiōn-is, μά-τι-ς.] Stem mentiōn-.

mn̥ (III) *ti* (Abstract Noun) *bhos* or

on (do.) *bhi̯os* (Plur. Case)

mn̥tiŏn(ə)bh(i̯)os → mentionibus: the ō was perhaps by Asso-

PREFIX. ROOT. SUFFIX. ENDING.

ciation with the Nominative, which had the Long Vowel (cp. λέων λέοντ-ος), or else, for the *-ōn-*, cp. ἀγ-ῶν-ος. For *-bh(i̯)*os, see p. 120. For the Vowel *-ə-*, see p. 174.

minister:

[Nom. Sing., of old Comparative, cp. min-us, mag-is, ὕσ-τερο-ς, ministru-m.] Stem ministro-, etc.

PREFIX	ROOT	SUFFIX	ENDING
	min (III)	*is* (Comparative)	
		tro (? do.)	*s* (Nom. Sing.)

ministros → mínister(s), cp. ἀγρός and áger(s).

monērī:

[Dat. of Verbal Noun, cp. mon-eō, γένε-ι gen-er-e, δοῦναι.] Stem monēr-.

PREFIX	ROOT	SUFFIX	ENDING
	mon (II)	*ē* (Verb)	*ai* (Dative)
		e(s) (Verbal Noun)	

monē(e)sai → monērī.

neu:

[Conjunction, cp. nē-ve.]

PREFIX	ROOT	SUFFIX	ENDING
	nē (I)		
	u̯e		

nē-u̯e, of which the second part may have been connected with the *u̯* of aut, → néu, cp. ápo → áp (áb).

prīmus:

[Nom. Sing. Superlative, cp. pr-ius, mag-is, πρό-μο-ς.] Stem prīmo-, etc.

PREFIX	ROOT	SUFFIX	ENDING
	pr (III)	*is* (Comparative)	*s* (Nom. Sing.)
		mo (Superl.)	

prismos → prīmus, cp. audīsne → audīn(e).

regāminī:

[1st Plur. Subj. Pass., cp. reg-ō, reg-ā-mus, λεγό-μενο-ι.]

PREFIX	ROOT	SUFFIX	ENDING
	reg (I)	*ā* (Subj.)	*i* (Nom Plur.)
		meno (Partic. Pass.)	

regāmenoi → regāminī, see p. 91: regāminī was, strictly speaking, a new form modelled on regāmus + regiminī.

PREFIX. ROOT. SUFFIX. ENDING.

rexerit:

[3rd Sing. 'Perfect' Subj. or Opt., cp. rexerīs, εἰδ-ε-ίη vīd-er-it, reg-ō.] Stem rexerī-, etc.

reg (I) *s* (1st Aor.) *es* (do.) *iē* (Opt.) *t* (3rd Sing.)

regsesiēt → rexerit: see further, p. 86, however. It is possible that the -erit started with words like vīderit, and was thence transferred to rexerit, which already had the Aorist -*s*- once. Others derive -rit, from -sit, Optative of the Verb 'be' (p. 141).

The Latin 'Perfect' was Perfect + Aorist, just as the Latin 'Subjunctive' was Subjunctive + Optative.

secundum:

[Neuter Nom. and Acc., cp. sequor ἕπ-ομαι, and see legendus, p. 144.] Stem secundo-, etc.

seq (I) *o* (Verb, p. 105) . . . *o* (Adj.) *m* (Nom. and Acc.)

seqo-om → secu-um: for the possible Suffixes, see p. 144.

superiōrem:

[Acc. Sing., Comparative, cp. ὑπέρ super, mel-ius, πατέρ-α patrem.] Stem superiōr-, etc.

(*k*)*sup* (Local Adv.) *er* (Comparat.) *ios* (do.) *m̥* (Acc.)

(*k*)*superiosm̥* → superiorem: for the s- (from [*e*]*ks*- or *s*-) see p. 91; for -ō-, by Association with the Nominative which (like amōs) had the Long Vowel, see p. 145-6.

tulī:

[1st Sing. 'Perf.' Indic., cp. tol-erāre, μέμνη-μαι memin-ī.] Stem tulī, etc.

tol (II) or *tl̥* (III) *ai* (Middle)

tolai or *tl̥*(*l*)*ai* → tulī. Some hold that this form was a 'telescoped' form of tétulī, perhaps partly due to the Compound Verb rétetulī → rét(t)ulī. But, for an old Perfect without Reduplication, cp. οἶδα, from u̯oid-.

PREFIX.	ROOT.	SUFFIX.	ENDING.

ubi:

[Adverb of Place, cp. O.L. ubei, quā, sī-cubi, κλισίη-φι.]

	u (III)		*bhi* (Case-form)

ubhi → ubī by Association with Locatives like Corinthī. Others derive these *u*- forms in Latin from the *q*- Root which appears in quis, etc.

The arguments in favour of this are

(i) *the meanings:* ubi, like quā, and English 'where' (from *hw*-), is Interrogative ('where?'), Indefinite ('some-where'), and Relative ('the place where . . .');

(ii) *the forms* utrum and πότερον, side by side, together with the Dialect forms like puteruspid. The difficulty lies in the Sound-change: why did cubi → ubi? Some hold that sī-cubi and ne-cubi became differently divided, viz. as sīc-ubi, nec-ubi, and that hence we have ubi by itself; others hold that there was, besides the Stems *qo*- (cp. quod), and *qi*- (cp. quid), a third Stem *qu*-, which might → u- for all that we know to the contrary.

usque:

[Adverb, cp. out.]

	ud (Local Adv.) (III)		*s* (? Case-Ending)

For the -*s*, cp. ἀπ-ς, ἐν-ς, ἐκ-ς, toward-s; the *qe* (cp. ὥσ-τε) made little or no difference to the meaning: or was it *ke* (cp. hon-ce, and the κ- of κεῖνος)?

ūtier:

[Passive Inf., cp. ūtī, O.L. oetier.]

	oi (II)	*t* (? Verbal)	*ai* (Dat.) *i* (Loc.)

oit(a)i → ūtĭ̄, meaning at first 'to or at using': to this was added -*ad* (cp. quō-ad, and Dialectic āsam-ad equivalent to ad āram) meaning 'to' or 'at': -ad then → -er; the change from -*d* to -*r* was either due to Umbrian (whence Ennius borrowed it), or to Association with the Passive -*r*, for which see legitu*r* (p. 145). For -ī- → -ĭ-, cp. nullīus (and see p. 45). Others make the forms in -ier a mixture of ūtī and ūt*er*(*e*).

PREFIX. ROOT. SUFFIX. ENDING.

utrum :

[Neut., cp. πότερον.]

u (III) *tro* (Comparative, etc.) *m* (Neut. Acc.)

For the possibility of u- coming from *qo-* or *qu*, see p. 148 (above).

velīmus :

[1st Plur. Opt., cp. volō, Aeolic βόλ-λā.] Stem velī-, etc.

ϑel (I) *ī* (Opt.) *mos* (1st Plur.)

ϑelīmos → velīmus: for ϑ → β and v, cp. βορā and vorāre, from *ϑorā-*.

An Exercise in hard Latin Words.

Analyse the Early forms of the following words :—

indomitō pede septem ursōs sequere ūnus equum vī;
fende quoque et veniens legitō iuga suāvia pulsīs;
fīde iecur vīnō: tua vōx quā Iūppiter est sit.

N.B.—The Long Vowels and the Early Latin forms are, as usual, of the very greatest importance.

Answer : (for details, see the Instances above).

PREFIX	ROOT	SUFFIX	ENDING
n̥	*dom* (II)	*ə-to*	*od*
	ped (I)		*i* (Loc.), *a* or *e* (Instr.)
	? *sept*, or *sep-* (I)	*m̥* or *tm̥*	
	r̥k (III)	*to* or *so*	*ns*
	seq (I)	*e* (p. 105)	*so*
	oi (II)	*no*	*s*
	ek (p. 88) (I)	*u̯o*	*ōm*
	u̯ī or *u̯ei*		*i* (Loc.), *a* or *e* (Instr.)
	ϑhen (I)	*de*	
	qo (II)	*qe*	
	e (I)	*ti*	
	ϑm̥ (III)	*i̯e- nt*	*s*
	leg (I)	*e* (p. 105)	*tōd* (p. 131)
	yug (III)		*a*
	su̯ād (I)	*u̯ i*	*a*

PREFIX.	ROOT.	SUFFIX.	ENDING.
	pl̥ (III)	*to*	*is*
	bheidh (I)	*e* (p. 105)	
	i̯ĕq (I)	*r̥*	
	u̯oi or *u̯oin-*	*o* (p. 105) or *no*	*ai*
	teu̯ (I)	*ā*	
	u̯oq (II)		*s*, and ? Vowel Long for Nom.
	q (III)	*ā*	*a* (Instr.)
	dieu̯ (I)		
	pə (III)	*ter*	Vowel Long for Nom.
	es (I)		*ti*
	s (III)	*iē*	*d* or *t*

31. Analysis of words: Data, Method, Commonest Mistakes.

31. *Sum up (a) the Data by which we analyse a word in a certain way.*

(b) the Method which you would advise a beginner to use in analysing a word;

(c) the chief mistakes which a beginner is likely to make in trying to analyse a word.

(*a*) Some of *the Data*, for analysing a word in a certain way, will be found on p. 20, foll.: we have

(1) some knowledge about the Indo-European or *Māter-Language* (p. 10, foll.), and about the relation between Greek and Latin (p. 16, foll.), and English (p. 61);

(2) some knowledge about the *Laws or Principles* according to which sounds develope (see p. 66, foll.);

(3) *Old Greek* forms (e.g. from the Dialects and Homer), p. 31, foll.;

(4) *Old Latin* forms (e.g. from Inscriptions, p. 44, foll.);

(5) English forms occasionally (see Grimm's Law, p. 62);

(6) some knowledge about the *Parts* into which words can be divided (p. 103, foll.).

As the student of Philology advances, his Data increase: and to the above List he can add, e.g.

(7) a number of actual *Indo-European or Māter-Language words and parts of words*, with their Greek and Latin and English descendants (p. 158, foll.);

(8) a large number of Laws of Sound-Changes (p. 161, foll.); and so on.

(*b*) *the Method of fully Analysing a word* may be best seen by a full Analysis of tremunt (cp. p. 113):

(1) tremunt;

(2) 3rd Plur. Present;

(3) Cp. O.L. tremonti, Doric τρέμοντι, τρέμο-μεν, τρόμ-ος;

	STEM.			
(4)	PREFIX	ROOT (and its Vowel-Stage)	SUFFIX (OF)	ENDING (OF)
(5) and (6)		*trem* (I)	*o* (Present, see p. 105)	*nti* (3rd Plur.)

(7) *tremonti* → trémunt, by Latin Accent: cp. oínom → ūnum, éti (ἔτι) → ét;

(8) tremunt could also have come from *tremont*, cp. the Unaugmented forms like τρέμον(τ).

The Method of analysing a word may therefore be summed up as follows:—

(1) Write down the word, and Mark Long Vowels;

(2) parse the word;

(3) collect Early forms of the word, and of its various parts, from Greek Dialects, Latin Inscriptions, etc.;

(4) divide the paper into four or five columns, viz.

[STEM =] PREFIX + ROOT (and its Vowel-Stage) + SUFFIX (OF) . . . ENDING (OF) . . .

(5) write, in English letters, the Early form of the *Root* (one Syllable, provisionally, p. 105): mark its Vowel-Stage (I, II, or III); then the *Prefix;* then either the *Stem* (all except the Ending), *or the Ending* (all except the Stem); and lastly the *Suffix;*

(6) say what the Suffix and Ending are the Suffix and Ending of;

(7) *mention and illustrate* the Sound-changes from the Early form to the form which you have before you;

(8) write any Notes which you think may be necessary.

N.B.—This process seems long, and at first it will be very slow:

but by degrees it will get quicker and quicker. Steady and careful *practice in the right way* will soon make the above stages become almost 'automatic'; the initial stages in learning the piano or in learning rowing must at first be slow, but will soon become almost 'automatic' and *unconscious*: *then, and not till then*, it will often be safe to leave out some of these stages, and to proceed straight to the writing down and analysing of the Early form.

To slur over or omit any stage in the above process would be like telling a man to slur over some part of his stroke in rowing: it would be false economy of time.

The following *Verses* will summarise *the process of Analysing a word.*

Write the word down: then (as you've heard)
mark all Long Vowels,* parse the word;
find Earliest forms, which one selects
from Inscriptions and Greek Dialects.

In English letters now restore
the Early form, in columns four—
find Root, then Stem and Termination,
then Suffix, Prefix,† Illustration.
A Compound's two words rolled in one.
Explain Sound-changes. Then 'tis done.

31 (c). Chief Mistakes in Analysing Words.

(*c*) *The Chief Mistakes in Analysing words* will be illustrated (as usual) by a concrete instance, viz. an attempt (by Jones) to '*Analyse μήτηρ*'.

Let us suppose Jones to write down, as his Answer, μη Root, τηρ Ending.

1. He makes a mistake in writing the Early form in *Greek letters*: for the Early form here has to be the parent of both the Greek and the Latin forms. Greek was not the parent of Latin, but the sister or cousin (p. 61).

He now corrects μη-τηρ to *me-ter.*

* Or Long Vowels can be written as Double Vowels, e.g., ē, as ee.

† This is the order in *finding out* the parts: but the order of the columns is PREFIX, ROOT, SUFFIX, ENDING.

2. His second mistake is that his Early form has two short Vowels: μητηρ could not come from *meter*, which would → μετερ. *He ought to have marked the Long Vowels.* Long Vowels and Short Vowels were, and are, very different things.

He corrects now to *mē|tēr*.

3. This would become Attic μήτηρ all right, but it would not become

(*a*) Aeolic and Doric μάτηρ, nor

(*b*) Latin māter.

His Early form here should have been not merely an Attic form in English letters, but a Māter-Language form, developing into the *Aeolic and Doric and Latin as well as the Attic forms*.

The next correction, then, is to *mā* (Root) *tēr* (Ending). This surely must be right, he thinks. But no, for

4. μήτηρ was connected with μῆτερ, etc., and the -τερ- (or -τρ-) runs through the whole word: -tēr- is *not the Ending* of this particular Case, the Nominative, for *-ter-* (or *-tr-*) is found in all the other Cases as well: it must be *part of the Stem*. Jones ought to have 'declined' the word, and to have seen how much of it ran through the word and was part of the Stem.

Jones now corrects to *mā* Root *ter* Suffix.

5. This would only give μῆτερ. In μήτηρ there was no *Case-Ending*, but the Vowel *e* was lengthened to *ē*, and we have μήτηρ.

6. The suggestion of Nominative *-s* (cp. λόγο-ς) would be wrong, because *māter-s* would → μήτειρ: the suggestion would '*violate a Law of Sound-change*'.

The mistakes will then be chiefly due to the fact that Jones

has not marked the *Long Vowels* (both in the form which he has to Analyse, and in the Early form which he restores);

he has written the word in *Greek letters*, instead of in ordinary letters;

his Early form *does not account for the Latin and the Dialect forms* as well as for the Attic form;

it does not take into consideration that the word is *part of a system*, and is connected with other words from the same *Stem*.

A final Hint as to Analysing Words.

He who wishes to be able to Analyse words must be patient in the first stages: he must make his foundations very, very firm. Let him go through the above instances again and again, till he knows every peculiarity *thoroughly*: let him try to collect the Evidences *by himself*, let him try to find these Early forms and to Analyse these Early forms *by himself*, and let him not look at the Answers till then: then let him look at the Answers, and correct his own Answer, and see *where* he has made a mistake and *why* he has made it, *and how he might have avoided it*. Let him note his weak points, and let him work at these, at first with slow and steady concentration, until he has made them his strong points. Hours of work will ultimately be saved if minutes be rightly spent at the outset: there is an Economy which consists of spending a little in the present in order to save great expense in the future.

PART IV.

GENERAL QUESTIONS ON SOUND-CHANGES, ETC., AND TECHNICAL TERMS EXPLAINED.

Māter-Language Sentences.
Some Māter-Language letters → Greek and Latin letters.
Some Greek and Latin letters and the Māter-Language letters.
The Māter-Language Alphabet.
Technical Terms.

32. English Sentences Translated into the Māter-Language.

32. *Turn the following sentences into the Māter-Language, giving alternative forms when necessary and also the Greek and Latin descendants :—*

(*a*) *'O mother bear the yoke : the horse is in the field' ;*
(*b*) *'may the liver of the seven untamed bears be red' ;*
(*c*) *'tell me who it was, father, and what he did' ;*
(*d*) *'in another boat I am coming to the new house' ;*
(*e*) *'he has seen (knows) five wolves' ;*
(*f*) *'in birth he surpasses the brother of those women'.*

Notes on a few features of the Māter-Language.

(*a*) In Principal Sentences the Verb was not accented ;

(*b*) Simple Cases were used in many Constructions where later Language used Prepositions ;

(*c*) the 'Demonstrative' had not yet been developed into an Article.

For Early Latin forms, which are not given here, see p. 44 foll. *Only a few Accents are put in here.* The Greek and Latin forms are not meant to be actual Greek and Latin Constructions.

(*a*) *mā́ter, yugóm bhere :* *ékuos* *agroí esti ;*
Gk. μῆτερ ζυγὸν φέρε ἵππος (p. 88) ἀγροῖ ἐστι,
(Dial. μᾶτερ) (cp. οἴκοι)
Lat. māter iugum fer (cp. p. 73) equos agrī est (cp. p. 73).
(cp. domī)

(*b*)	*i̯ēqṛ*	*sép̣tṃ*	*ṇdomə-*[or *ṇdmə-*]*-tōm*	*ṛktṓm* [or *ṛks-*]	[*e*]*siēd* *estōd*	*rudhróm ;*
Gk.	ἧπαρ	ἑπτά	ἀδαμάτων	ἄρκτων	εἴη ἔστω	ἐρυθρόν,
Lat.	iecur	septem	indomitum (O.L.)	ursum (O.L.)	sit estō	rubrum.

(*c*)	*enseqe moi,*	*qís*	*esāt,*	*pə́ter,*	*qíd qe*	*dhēket ;*
Gk.	ἔννεπέ μοι,	τίς	ἦν (p. 87)	πάτερ	τί τε	θῆκε (Unaug.),
Lat.	insece mī,	quis	erat,	pater,	quidque	fēcit (p. 93) ?

(*d*)	*ali̯āi*	*nāu̯i*	*ǵṃi̯ō*	*néu̯ōi* *neu̯om*	*u̯oīkōi* *u̯oikom*	[or *dómōi*, etc.] ;
Gk.	ἄλλῃ	νηὶ	βαίνω	νέῳ νέον	οἴκῳ οἶκον	[or δόμῳ],
Lat.	aliā [or aliae]	nāve	veniō	novō	vīcō	[or domō] :

N.B.—We find a Dative expressing the Goal, in Early Sanskrit, Persian, Greek, and Latin Poetry.

(*e*)	*pénqe*	*lúqons*	*u̯oídet ;*
Gk.	πέντε	λύκους	οἶδε,
Lat.	quinque (p. 89)	lupōs (p. 88)	vīdit.

(*f*)	*ǵenesi*	*super*	*esti*	*bhrāterṃ*	*tāsōm ;*
Gk.	γένει	ὑπέρ	ἐστι	φρātέρα	τῶν,
Lat.	genere	superest		frātrem	[is]tārum.

33. Māter-Language Letters, and their Greek and Latin Descendants.

33. *What did the following Māter-Language letters become? Give instances.*

(*a*) *in Greek, q, s, i̯, ā, u̯, w, ə, ṃ.*
(*b*) *in Latin, dh, ai̯, eu̯, a, ei, s, ṃ, ṛ, ə.*

(*a*) *Greek:*

The results of these letters are best seen from Greek *instances* as compared with Latin Sister-forms or Cousin-forms (see pp. 83, 92, foll.)

1. *q*: πότε, αἰπόλος βουκόλος agricola, ἅττα (p. 125) quia quoque;

q therefore could →
(i) π (πότε αἰπόλος),
(ii) τ (πότε),
(iii) κ (βουκόλος).
(iv) ττ, from *qi̯* (ἅττα).

Note.—This *q* is sometimes written q_u, the *u* representing a Labial-sound which helped to change q_u to π or τ by bringing it further forward in the mouth. This *u*-sound is sometimes called 'Parasitic': see p. 173.

2. *s*: στῆναι stāre, οἶκος vīcus, ἑπτά septem, ἡδύ suāve, γένει genere, πεδίοιο → πεδίοο → πεδίου;

s therefore could →
(i) σ- (στῆναι), -ς (οἶκος),
(ii) ʽ- (ἑπτά, ἡδύ from *su̯*-),

(iii) ʽ (found in Laconian, p. 32), disappearing later (γένεʽι → γένει, πεδίοο from -*si̯o*): in Greek it is sometimes preserved, as in ἐλῡ-σ-α (by Association with ἔδειξα, etc.).

3. *i̯* was a very hard letter:

ἧπαρ iecur, πεδίοιο, τρεῖς trēs, Ζεύς Diēspiter, Ionic μέζων μέγας, τύπτω, μέλισσα μέλιτος, ἥσσων ἥκιστα, ἄνασσα ἄνακτος, κορύσσω κόρυθες, θάσσων ταχύς, ἄσσων ἄγχι, σπείρω σπέρμα, τείνω tendō, βαίνω veniō, ἄλλος alius;

i̯ therefore could →

(i) ʽ- (ἧπαρ),

(ii) disappearing between Vowels (πεδίοο from -*si̯o*, τρεῖς from *trei̯es*),

(iii) ζ from *di̯* and *gi̯* (Ζεύς, μέζων),

(iv) ττ from *pi̯* (τύπτω),

(v) σσ and ττ from *ti̯*, *ki̯*, (?)*kti̯*, *dhi̯*, *ghi̯*, *ṇghi̯* (μέλισσα, ἥσσων, ἄνασσα, κορύσσω, θάσσων, ἄσσων),

(vi) ιρ, ιν from *ri̯*, *ni̯*, *mi̯* (σπείρω, τείνω, βαίνω),

(vii) λλ from *li̯* (ἄλλος).

This letter creates more difficulties than any other, and needs repeated study.

4. *ā*: μήτηρ μάτηρ māter, χώρᾱ (Att. and Doric), ναῦς nāvis;

ā therefore could →

(i) η (μήτηρ),

(ii) ᾱ (χώρᾱ),

(iii) α (ναῦς p. 88).

5. *u̯*: οἶνον vīnum, νεός novos, ἀμεύομαι moveō, δίς bis twice;

u̯ therefore could →

(i) nothing (οἶνος, see p. 89, νέος),

(ii) υ (ἀμεύομαι),

(iii) β from *du̯* (δίς).

6. *w* (ἑσπέρᾱ vespera) → ʽ. Except at the beginning of a word, it had the same development as *u̯*, both in Greek and Latin: in Aeolic we have βρόδον from ϝροδον.

7. *ꝺ* : βαίνω veniō, ζυγόν iugum, ἀδελφός βρέφος, σεμνός σέβομαι ;

ꝺ could therefore →

(i) β (βαίνω),

(ii) γ (ζυγόν, near *u*, cp. p. 173),

(iii) δ (ἄδελφος, cp. p. 173),

(iv) -μν from -βν- (σεμνός).

8. *m̥* : δέκα decem, ἅμα simul, βαίνω veniō ;

m̥ therefore could →

(i) α (δέκα),

(ii) αμ (ἅμα)

(iii) αν (βανi̯ω → βαίνω).

(*b*) *Latin*.

1. *dh* : fēcī ἔθηκα deed, aedēs αἴθω, rubrum ἐρυθρόν ruddy, Rūfus ;

dh → (i) f (fēcī),

(ii) d (aedēs),

(iii) b (rubrum),

(iv) f (Rūfus, borrowed from Italic Dialect).

2. *ai* : aedēs αἴθω, ínquīrō quaerō (O.L. quaistor), darī δοῦν-αι ;

ai → (i) ae, when Accented (aedēs),

(ii) ī, when Unaccented (ínquīrō, darī).

3. *eu* : * novos νέος, moveō mōtus ? mūtō ἀμεύομαι, dēnuō and dē novō ;

eu could →

(i) ov, when Accented (nóvos, móveō, and see p. 86),

(ii) ō, do. (mōtus),

(iii) ū, do. (mūtō),

(iv) u, when unaccented (dḗnuō). Cp. also tua (p. 150).

4. *a* : agō ἄγω, ἐξάγω exigo, capio áccipiō ácceptus aúcupō, péd-e ? ἄμ-α ;

a could →

* See L. Horton-Smith's excellent pamphlet (Macmillan and Bowes).

(i) a, when Accented (ágō),

(ii) i, e, u, according to the following letters, when unaccented (see above).

5. *ei* : fīdō πείθω, eunt εἶμι, trēs τρεῖς, οἴκει ? domī;
ei could →
(i) ī (fīdō, ? domī),
(ii) e, when a Vowel followed (*ei̯ont*(*i*) → eunt, *trei̯es* → trees → trēs).

6. *s* : septem quaesō quaeris, genere γένει, honor;
s could →
(i) s (septem, quaesō, between Vowels with certain neighbouring letters)
(ii) r, from -s- between Vowels, etc. (quaeris, genere, honor by Association with honōrem, etc.).

7. *m̥* : septem ἑπτά, undecim δέκα, veniō βαίνω;
m̥ could →
(i) em (septem),
(ii) im (úndecim),
(iii) en (veniō).

8. *r̥* : ursus ἄρκτος, cordis καρδίᾱ;
r̥ could →
(i) ur (ursus),
(ii) or (cordis).

9. *g̑* : genus γένος, βαρύς gravis, βαίνω veniō, βοῦς bōs;
g̑ could →
(i) g (genus, gravis),
(ii) v (veniō),
(iii) b (bōs, from Italic, p. 85).

34. Greek and Latin Letters, and their Parent-forms.

34. *From what Indo-European letters do the following letters come? Give instances.*

(*a*) *Greek* α, π, β, η, ει, τ, σσ *and* ττ, ζ, φ, *and the 'Rough Breathing'*;

(*b*) *Latin b, ī, i, d, f, g, h, r, ū, e.*

(*a*) *Greek.*

1. α: ἄγω agō, ἑπτά septem, ἅμα simul, ἀ- in- ('Privative'), παλτός pulsus, καρδίᾱ Ionic κραδίη cordis, πατήρ pater, ναῦς nāvis; α therefore could come from

(i) *a* (ἄγω),

(ii) *m̥* (ἑπτά ἅμα),

(iii) *n̥* (ἀ—),

(iv) *l̥* (παλ-τός),

(v) *r̥* (καρδίᾱ κραδίη),

(vi) *ə* (πατήρ, p. 175),

(vii) *ā* (ναῦς, p. 88).

2. π: πατήρ pater, πείθω fīdō, πότε quoque: from

(i) *p* (πατήρ),

(ii) *bh* (πείθω, p. 97),

(iii) *q* (πότε).

3. β: τύρβη turba, βαίνω veniō, ἄμβροτος immortalis, βλώσκω μολοῦμαι, βρόδον 'Aeolic': from

(i) *b* rare (τύρβη),

(ii) *ℊ* (βαίνω),

(iii) *mr* (ἄμβροτος),

(iv) *ml* (βλώσκω),
(v) *u̯* or *w* (βρόδον).

4. η: ἡμι- sēmi-, φήμη fāma; from
(i) *ē* (ἡμι-),
(ii) *ā* (φήμη).

5. ει: πείθω fīdō, κλείς clāvis, ἐποίει Ionic ἐποίεε, εἰς ἐν-ς, τιθείς τιθέντ-ος, εἶναι ἐστι; from
(i) *ei* (πείθω),
(ii) *āi* (κλείς, p. 88),
(iii) *ee* (ἐποίει),
(iv) *ens*, *ents* (εἰς, τιθείς),
(v) *esn* (εἶναι).

There were two kinds of ει, (α) one the Early ει, as in πείθω, (β) the other the later form resulting from Contractions, etc., as in ἐποίει. These are distinguished on Early Inscriptions, (α) appearing as E I, (β) as E: see p. 183.

6. τ: πατήρ pater, τριχός θρίξ, πότε quoque, τύπτω; from
(i) *t* (πατήρ),
(ii) *dh* (τριχός, p. 133),
(iii) *q* (πότε),
(iv) *i̯* (τύπτω from τυπι̯ω).

7. σσ and ττ: ἐγέλασσα (Hom.), ποσσί (Hom.), μέσσος (Hom.), μέλισσα μέλιτος, ἧσσων ἥκιστα, ἅττα quia, κορύσσω κόρυθες, θάσσων τάχιστα, ἄσσων ἄγχι; from
(i) *ss* (ἐγέλασσα),
(ii) *ds* (ποσσί),
(iii) *dhi̯* (μέσσος, p. 88),
(iv) *ti̯*, *ki̯*, *qi̯*, *dhi̯*, *ghi̯*, *nghi̯* (μέλισσα ἧσσων, ἅττα, p. 125, κορύσσω, θάσσων, ἄσσων),

8. ζ: Ἀθηνᾶζε Ἀθηνάσδε, Ζεύς Διός, Ionic μέζων, ζυγόν iugum; from
(i) *sd* (Ἀθηνᾶζε),
(ii) *di̯* (Ζεύς),
(iii) *ϑi̯* (μέζων),
(iv) *y* (ζυγόν, p. 87).

9. φ: φέρω ferō, φόνος θείνω fendō, τετράφαται τρέπω; from
(i) *bh* (φέρω),
(ii) *ϑh* (φόνος, p. 173),
(iii) *p* (τετράφαται, p. 133).

10. *The 'Rough Breathing'*: ἑπτά septem, ἡδύς suāvis, ἧπαρ iecur, ἑσπέρā vespera, ἕως aurōra, ἵππος equos, ὕδωρ unda; from
(i) *s* (ἑπτά),
(ii) *su* (ἡδύς),
(iii) *i̯* (ἧπαρ),
(iv) *w̯* (ἑσπέρā),
(v) ? 'Crasis' with the Article (ἕως, p. 95, ? ἵππος, p. 88),
(vi) initial υ regularly had the 'Rough Breathing' (ὕδωρ). See Darbishire's Relliquiae Philologicae.

(*b*) *Latin.*

1. *b*: turba τύρβη, ἄμφω ambō, amābō φύω, rubrum ἐρυθρόν ruddy, bōs βοῦς, bis δίς twice, fūnebris fūnere (from *-esi*), ab ἀπό; from
(i) *b*, rare (turba),
(ii) *-bh-* (ambō),
(iii) *bhu̯* (amābō, cp. p. 142),
(iv) *-dh-* (rubrum),
(v) *ϑ* (bōs, from Italic, p. 85),
(vi) *du̯* (bis, p. 85),
(vii) *sr̂* (fūnebris),
(viii) *p* (ab)

2. *ī*: vīs ῑ-φι, fīdō πείθω, vīcī οἶκοι, darī δοῦναι, īnquīro quaerō, ovīs, audīn audīsne, prīmus, sīs siēs; from
(i) *ī* (vīs),
(ii) *ei* (fīdō),
(iii) *oi* after *u*, or when unaccented (vīcī),
(iv) *ai*, when unaccented (darī, ínquīrō),
(v) *in(s)* (ovīs),
(vi) *īsn ism* (audīn, prīmus),
(vii) *iē* (sīs).

3. *i* : fidēs πιθεῖν, éxigō ágō, rédditus dátus, patribus, légiminī λεγόμενοι λεγέμεναι, sim siem (from siēm); from
(i) *i* (fidēs),
(ii) *a* when unaccented (éxigō),
(iii) *ə* when unaccented, p. (rédditus, patribus),
(iv) and (v) *o* and *e*, when unaccented (légiminī),
(vi) *iē* (sim, p. 93).

4. *d* : δυο duo, aedes αἴθω; from
(i) *d* (duo),
(ii) *dh* (aedēs).

5. *f* : ferō φέρω bear, fēcī ἔθηκα deed, Rūfus ἐρυθρόν ruddy, fendō φόνος θείνω, effert ἐκ, afficit ad, frīgus (s)ρῖγος; from
(i) *bh* (ferō),
(ii) *dh* (fēcī, Rūfus from Italic),
(iii) *ɡh* (fendō, p. 173),
(iv) *k*, *d*, Assimilated (effert, afficit),
(v) *sr* (frīgus).

6. *g* : agō ἄγω, genus γένος, gravis βαρύς, unguis ὄνυχος from
(i) *g* (agō),
(ii) *ɡ* (genus, gravis),
(iii) *ɡh* after n (unguis).

7. *h* : hiems χιών, honus onus (late); from
(i) *gh* (hiems),
(ii) nothing (honus).

8. *r* : pater πατήρ, arca ἀλκή, arbiter ad, genere γένει; from
(i) *r* (pater),
(ii) *r* or *l* (arca),
(iii) *d*, p. 137 (arbiter),
(iv) *s*, p. 205 (genere).

9. *ū* : sūs ὗς, lūmen λευκός, ūnum oinom; from
(i) *ū* (sūs),
(ii) *eu* (lūmen),
(iii) *oi* (ūnum).

10. *e*: et ἔτι, ácceptus cápiō, éffectus faciō θετός, iste τό-ν, rédditus dátus δοτός, suāve suāvis, decem δέκα, tentus τατός; from

(i) *e* (et),

(ii) unaccented *a*, *ə*, *o*, *i* (see above),

(iii) *m̥ n̥* (decem, tentus).

35. The Māter-Language Alphabet, with Notes.

35. *Give the Māter-Language Alphabet, with a few brief Notes on it.*

There is a great variety of opinion as to the Indo-European Alphabet: for details, and for other views, see Giles' *Manual* (throughout), and Fennell's excellent work on the *Indo-Germanic Sonants and Consonants.*

Vowels e, o, a, ə (p. 174), *ē, ō, ā,*

Semi-vowels—

*i, u, ṛ,** *ḷ,** *ṃ,** *ṇ* † (and some add *k, z,* etc.) as Vowels.

i̯, u̯, r, l, m, n (do. *k̇, ż,* etc.) as Consonants.

Diphthongs: the above Vowels + *i* or *u* (or *i̯* or *u̯*).

Consonants	*Gutturals* (p. 173)		*Dentals*	*Labials*
	Velar	*Palatal.*		
Sharp ‡	*q*	*k*	*t*	*p*
Soft §	*ᵹ*	*g*	*d*	*b* (rare)
'*Aspirated*'	*ᵹh*	*gh*	*dh*	*bh*
	qh (rare)	*kh* (rare)	*th*	*ph* (rare)
Spirant		*y*	*s, z*	*w*

This is a very imperfect list: among the letters that are most subject to controversy may be mentioned the Gutturals (p. 173), and the Semi-vowels, especially the long Semi-vowels (p. 172). There were also two kinds of *t* (cp. Sanskrit *t* and *ṭ*).

* Some hold that these Vowels also had Long forms (*r̥̄*, etc., p. 172).

† This *ṇ* here includes the Guttural *n*, as in build*ing*.

‡ Also called Tenues or Thin, Mute Explosives, etc.;

§ Also called Mediae, Soft, Voiced Mutes, etc.

36. Technical Terms Explained.

36. *Explain the following terms with Instances :—*

(*a*) *Semi-vowels*, (*b*) *Gutturals*, (*c*) *the Indeterminate Vowel*, (*d*) *Anaptyctic Vowel*, (*e*) *Anastrophe*, (*f*) *Apocope*, (*g*) *Aspiration*, (*h*) *Assimilation*, (*i*) *Changed Division*, (*j*) *Compensation*, (*k*) *Crasis*, (*l*) *Deaspiration*, (*m*) *Dissimilation*, (*n*) *Doublets*, (*o*) *Enclisis*, (*p*) *Epenthesis*, (*q*) *Loss of Letters and Syncope*, (*r*) *Metathesis*, (*s*) *Metrical Convenience*, (*t*) *Prothesis*, (*u*) *Rhotacism.*

(*a*) *Semi-vowels.*

If we consider the word LUMINAREO (or the words *inlue Roma*) we shall see that *l*, *m*, *n*, *r* are used as Consonants, and *u*, *i*, *a*, *e*, *o* as Vowels : so also *Cumberland* gives us *m*, *r*, *n* as Consonants, supported by *u*, *e*, *a* as Vowels. Such are the ordinary uses of these letters.

But, suppose we had spelt Cumberland as Kmbrlnd, then we should have *m*, *r*, *n* *unsupported* by Vowels : they themselves would be Vowels : to mark this unfamiliar Vowel-power we write them as *m̥*, *r̥*, *n̥* : and so we might write Nūn*m̥*, Girt*n̥*, bet*r̥*, and met*l̥*, rather than Newnham, Girton, better, and mettle.

Again, take the Latin word *iūs* (yooce), where ū was a Vowel : here i was a Consonant (y), and might be written *i̯* ; in *uīs* (weece), where ī was Vowel, u was a Consonant (w), and might be written *u̯*. See p. 84.

As LUMINAREO would illustrate the ordinary use of

these letters, so their extraordinary use would be illustrated by 'Cumberland'll win yet', if we spelt it *kṃbṛlṇd ḷ u̯in iet.*

To sum up, these letters (to which some would add *k̑* and *z*) were Consonants when they were supported by Vowels, as in *Girton,* but Vowels when they were not supported by Vowels but themselves had to support Consonants or to form a Syllable, as in *Gṛtṇ.*

Some of the Greek and Latin descendants would be illustrated by these Māter-Language words:—

dekṃ	tṇta	pḷta	kṛd(a)
δέκα	τατά	παλτά	καρδίᾱ κραδίη
decem	tenta	pulsa	corda:

		Greek	Latin
ṃ	→	αμ α	em im
ṇ	→	αν α	en in
ḷ		αλ λα	ol ul
ṛ		αρ ρα	or ur

Notes—

1. There are some who suggest that στρωτός strātus went back to Long *ṝ;* and they suggest other Long Semi-vowels; e.g. see King and Cookson's *Comparative Grammar,* p. 46;

2. *ṃ* and *ṇ* are sometimes called Sonant Nasals, *ḷ* and *ṛ* Sonant Liquids;

3. for *i̯* see pp. 85, 162; for *u̯* see p. 162;

4. The letters *ṃ, ṇ, ḷ, ṛ, i̯, u̯* will soon cease to be hard to pronounce, after a little practice, though at first sight a form like *ϑṃi̯ō* is terrifying: once I even saw a suggestion that ἀάατος was originally *ṇ-sṃ-su̯ṇ-to-s !*

On this subject, see further Fennell's *Indo-Germanic Sonants and Consonants.*

(*b*) *Gutturals.* For these, see further Giles, § 136 foll.

In the Māter-Language there were at least two sets of Gutturals, the second set being formed *further back in the mouth* than the first set, and being *more liable to change in*

Greek and the Italic Dialects: an instance of the second set, which are called *Velars* (from the velum palati at the back of the mouth) would be seen in *colony* (*c* before *o*), the first set, which are called *Palatals*, in *king* (*k* before *i*).

I. The *Palatals*, further forward in the mouth:

(*Sharp*)	δέκα	decem	from *k*,
(*Soft*)	ἄγω	agō	from *g*,
(*Aspirated*)	χιών	hiems	from *gh* [Latin dropped the *g*-sound].

II. The *Velars*, further back in the mouth, are more puzzling, and the symbols for them are also more puzzling, viz. *q*, *ɡ*, *ɡh*.*

(*Sharp*)	βουκόλος, αἰπόλος	agricola	from *q*
	τίς	quis	
	πότε	quoque	
(*Soft*)	γύαλον	vola	from *ɡ*
	βαίνω	veniō	
	βαρύς	gravis	
(*Arcadian*)	βαλεῖν, ἐσδέλλοντες	volāre	
(*Aspirated*)	ὄνυχος	unguis	from *ɡh*
	φόνος, θείνω	fendō	

The statistics seem to be that, in Greek, these Changeable *Velars*, *q*, *ɡ*, *ɡh*,

(i) near *u* became κ, γ, χ (Gutturals), e.g. βουκόλος;

(ii) before ο, τ, θ, σ, Nasals, or Liquids, e.g. αἰπόλος, πότε; became π, β, φ (*Labials*).

These letters could be remembered by *O* and the Consonants of *solemn truth*;

(iii) before ι, ε, became τ, δ, θ, (*Dentals*), e.g. πότε, τίς.

But there have been many changes owing to *Association*: thus we have ἕπεται, like ἕπομαι (sequor), not ἕτεται.

* Authorities are not agreed as to the Symbols: thus we sometimes find these *Velars* as q_u, etc., sometimes as k^u, sometimes as *k*, etc.

(*Sharp*)	σκῦτος	scūtum	from *q*
(*Soft*)	γένος	genus	from ǥ
('*Aspirated*')	χανδάνω	(pre)hendō	from ǥ*h* [Latin dropped the
	κόγχος	congius	ǥ-sound and the *h*-sound respectively].

The learner will naturally ask, 'What is the difference between I and II? So far no difference has appeared in Greek or Latin, but

(*a*) Languages like Sanskrit show a difference, and

(*b*) the changeable forms, which we shall now consider, show a great difference in Greek.

For these changes, "πότε quoque" is far the best instance by which to remember that *qo-* → πο-, *qe* → τε. Notice Ionic κότερος, not πότερος, Thessalian κίς not τίς.

As to the Cause of these changes, of which the change to Labials is seen in the Italic Dialects (see bōs, p. 85):

(α) some say that there sometimes 'grew up' a '*Parasitic*' *u*-sound attached to the *q*, ǥ, ǥ*h*, and that this might alter the pronunciation of the Greek Guttural, and change it to a Dental or Labial;

(β) others say that between (I) the Palatals and (II) Velars came another Class, an intermediate Class, the *Palatal-Velars*.

(*c*) *The Indeterminate Vowel.*

1. In *patribus* we saw a Vowel ə inserted between the the Stem patr- and the Ending -bus: see further the 'Anaptyctic Vowel' (below);

2. We have often had the *ĕ-Series of Vowel-Stages*, e.g. (p. 74).

I	II	III
ei (εἶμι, īre) E	*oi* (οἶμος) O	*i* (ἴμεν, iter); —

Sometimes, however, the I-Stage had a Long Vowel: in that case the II-Stage had *ō*, and the III-Stage often had ə: for instance,

ē (ἔθηκα fēcī)	*ō* (θωμός 'a heap')	ə (θετός factus),
(ἵημι ? sēvī)	(ἀφεώνται)	(ἵεμεν satus);
ā (φάμᾱ Dor., fāma)	*ō* (φώνη)	ə (φαμέν fateor),
ō (δῶρον dōnum)	*ō* (δέδωκα)	ə (δοτός datus).

Sometimes the III-Stage does not show any Vowel at all, but, where it does show traces of ə, this ə appears as follows:—

in Sanskrit as *i*, e.g. πατήρ, pater, pitā,

in Greek as a Short Vowel corresponding to the Long Vowel in the I-Series, e.g. θετός ἔθηκα, φαμέν φᾱμᾱ, δοτός δῶρον,

in Latin as *a*, or whatever *a* would become (see p. 73), e.g. factus, fateor, datus, éffectus, cónfiteor, rédditus.

(*d*) *Anaptyctic Vowel.*

When Latin adopted words like μνᾶ and Ἀσκληπιός, the pronunciation was made easier by inserted Vowels (called by the name 'Anaptyctic'), viz. m*i*na and Aesc*u*lapius: we find also pōc*u*lum beside pōclum, and perhaps in Greek ἤλυθον beside ἦλθον.

We might regard the -β- of μεσημ(β)ρίᾱ (cp. ἦμαρ), the -b- of cham(b)re (cp. camera), and the -δ- of ἀν(δ)ρός (cp. ἀνέρες), as *Consonants* which had a somewhat similar origin.

(*e*) *Anastrophe.*

ἔπι and ἄπο were thus accented when they came after the Case they governed (ἔπι also when it was equivalent to ἔπεστι, cp. ἄνα 'arise'); this is a trace of an Early Accent (cp. Sanskrit), and in other positions ἐπὶ τοῦτο, ἀπὸ τούτου, the Acute Accent is lost: for a Grave Accent meant no Acute Accent.

(*f*) *Apocope.*

In Latin we find ápo → áp (áb), súpo → súp (súb), éti → ét, ésti → ést, víros → vír, etc.; and in Greek we also find, especially in the Dialects, such forms as κάββαλε (κατα-), κάππεσε (κατα-). Cp. p. 36.

(*g*) *Aspiration.*

For the origins of the Greek Aspirate (ʽ), e.g. *s*- in ἑπτά (septem), see p. 167.

For the Latin Aspirate, see p. 168, and for the 'Vulgar' Latin Aspirate, cp. Catullus' poem on Arrius (p. 177).

See further on Deaspiration (below, p. 177).

The *h*-sound was apparently not present, or not common, in the Māter-Language, except after Consonants, as in *bh-* (*bherō* → φέρω ferō bear): Sanskrit is very fond of such sounds—cp. *Buddha*. The *h*-sound was made by breathing with more 'emphasis', as we can realise when we hear a dog out of breath and panting: the puff-puff of an engine is not far off the *h*-sound.

(*h*) *Assimilation.*

Besides individual letters there were also intermediate letters, stepping-stones from letter to letter, which are not often represented in actual writing: thus, in σεβ-νός (cp. σέβομαι), there was the β-sound, then a half-sound (μ) in passing from β to ν, then the ν-sound: hence by degrees arose σεμ-νός: cp. also adficiō → afficiō, etc. This might be called 'Anticipating [or Progressive] Assimilation', as opposed to 'Recollecting [or Retrogessive] Assimilation' which is found in *alios* → ἄλλος, ferse (cp. esse) → ferre, and see 'Aeolic', p. 36, and Early Latin Doublets like ap templō, ab dīvō. See also p. 88.

(*i*) *Changed Division.*

In English we have *an ewt* (cp. ὕδωρ) → a newt, *a norange* → an orange, and cp. ἡ ἠώς → ἕως (p. 95): we have also seen πόσα ττα → πόσ' ἄττα (p. 125). In Compound Words the process is very common: thus, on p. 81 we saw that *Philo-logy* became divided as Phil-ology, whence Ge-ology, and 'the other -ologies'.

(*j*) *Compensation.*

We have seen that τόνς → τούς ('Aeolic' τοῖς), and (is)tōs: so deciens → deciēs, is-dem → īdem, prismus → prīmus, and so on: it seemed at first as if Language had lost or dropped a letter and had then put in another letter or lengthened its Vowel to compensate for this loss. But as a matter of fact the change was very gradual—in τονς, for instance, side by side with the weakening of the ν-sound went the lengthening of the Vowel, for this -ου- was the Long Vowel of Classical -ο- (see p. 184).

(*k*) *Crasis* (or Fusing together).

For 'Crasis' with the Article, cp. ἡ ἠώς (cp. aurōra) → ἕως, ἡ ἡμέρᾱ (cp. ἦμαρ) → ἡμέρᾱ, see p. 95.

In a wider sense, 'Crasis' would include καὶ εἶτα → κᾆτα, καὶ ἄν → κἄν, and certain other common Combinations. As a rule the careful Classical writers avoided letting a word ending in a Vowel come before a word beginning with a Vowel, the rule being τὰ φωνηέντα μὴ συμπίπτειν.

(*l*) *Deaspiration*.

In Greek we find

(i) 'Aeolic', and sometimes Ionic, objecting to initial ʽ: cp. 'Aeol.' ἠρώων (ἡρώων), Ion. οὖλον (ὅλον); see pp. 32, 36;

(ii) Greek in general objected to combinations like θριχός (cp. θρίξ), which lost their first Aspirate (τριχός): this is called Grassmann's Law (p. 123), and an instance of it is seen in Buddha from *bhudh*- (cp. Greek πυθ-έσθαι);

(iii) in Latin there was an occasional tendency to drop the h, especially in the Conversational and 'Vulgar' Language (cp. French heure from hora): for Classical instances cp. anser from hanser (χήν), and arēna. Sometimes the 'Vulgar' Language also added the h-, like our Cockney-language, as we see in the celebrated poem of Catullus, beginning

> C*h*ommoda dicebat si quando commoda vellet
> dicere, et insidias Arrius *h*insidias.

(*m*) *Dissimilation*.

The objection to having certain similar sounds in close succession has been already seen in θριχός → τριχός: cp. also praestīgiae from -str- (stringō). This is commonest

(α) with the letters *l* and *r*: cp. exemp*l*ā*r*is but mī*l*itā*r*is;

(β) when two *Dentals* came together: between these two

there grew up a sibilant-sound: thus *uid-te* → ἰδ-s-τε (→ ἴστε), *skid-tos* → scid-s-tus → scissus;

(γ) for ἀμφιφορεύς → ἀμφορεύς, see p. 179.

(*n*) *Doublets.*

ens before Vowels would → εἰς (cp. τιθεντσι → τιθενσι → τιθεῖσι), before Consonants it would → ἐς (cp. δεμσποτης → δεσπότης): hence we have both εἰς and ἐς. Similarly in Early Latin we have a*p* templō, but a*b* dīvō. There are some who suppose that οὕτωδ usually → οὕτω (cp. legetōd → λεγέτω legitō), but that οὕτωδ δέ, etc. (see above) → οὕτωδ-ς-δέ → οὕτως δὲ: hence οὕτω and οὕτως; but there are other explanations.

(*o*) *Enclisis.*

Some words seldom if ever stood by themselves: such words are called 'Enclitics' because they leant on other words: they then usually had no Accent of their own. Thus cp. εἴ τις, sí quis, né-ve → neu, audīsne → audīn; cp. also πόσα ττα → ποσ' ἄττα (p. 125). εἰμί and φημί are still Enclitic in the Present Indicative.

Some words often leant on the word which followed: thus cp. ἐκ- in ἐκτείνω: this is called 'Proclisis'.

(*p*) *Epenthesis.*

We have already seen *sperio* (cp. σπέρμα) → σπείρω, teniō (cp. tendō) → τείνω: here it seems that the *i*-sound at first affected the previous Vowel by Assimilation (p. 176), and then was lost in the second Syllable. Cp. also *koruā* → Ionic κουρή, *monuos* → Ionic μοῦνος (p. 32), *pat-nō* (patēre) → pandnō → pandō.

In Greek we find λαθ-ανω (cp. λαθεῖν latēre) → λανθάνω: here, as in μανθάνω, etc., the ν-sound was kept in *both* Syllables.

(*q*) *Loss of Letters, and 'Telescoping' or Syncope.*

For the loss of the Final Syllable by 'Apocope', as in ápo → áp (áb), see pp. 73, 175.

In Greek and Latin we sometimes have one of two similar Syllables disappearing: thus cp. ἀμφιφορεύς → ἀμφορεύς, ? τετράπεζα (p. 133) → τράπεζα, ἡμιμέδιμνον → ἡμέδιμνον, nūtrītrīx → nūtrīx, venēnificium → venēficium, stīpipendium → stīpendium; cp. also εἰδωλολάτρεια and idolatry.

In Latin we find, chiefly owing to the Accent (p. 73), a tendency to 'telescope up' words such as calidus (caldus), válidē (váldē), súbrigō (súrgō), pérrigo (pérgō), pū́rigō (pūrgō), répepulī (réppulī), clā́vidō (cláudō).

In Conversational Latin the tendency was still stronger, as we see in frātrem → *frère*, and (mē)metipsi(ssi)mum → *même!*

(*r*) *Metathesis.*

(*a*) In βασιλέως as compared with Homeric βασιλῆος, ἑστεῶτες → ἑστῶτες as compared with Homeric ἑστήοτες, and πόλεως with πολῆος, we see what looks like an interchange of quantities: in the first two words there was once a *F*, and in the third a *i̯*.

(*β*) In Ionic ἐνθεῦτεν (cp. ἐντεῦθεν), κιθών (cp. χιτών), we seem to have a similar interchange of Aspirates: but it is possible that, in the awkward combinations ἐνθευθεν and χιθων, Ionic dropped one Aspirate and Attic the other.

(*γ*) In σκέπτομαι and speciō we may possibly have an interchange of k and p.

(*s*) *Metrical Convenience.*

The desire to fit certain words into the Verse led to many devices, of which the following are only a few:—

(*a*) ἀθάνατος was scanned as ᾱθάνατος: ἀ- was probably from *n̥*, though some might regard these words as being from *n̥̄* (cp. p. 172);

(*β*) silva (written silua and pronounced *silwa*) could be counted as three syllables: cp. genua, etc.; other letters were *i* and *e*, as in parietis (4 or 3 syllables), alveō θεός (3 or 2): cp. also *glorious* (3) with *bilious* (2);

(*γ*) fugat was fugāt in Early Latin (cp. fugās), and audit

was audīt (cp. audīs): not only did the Poets sometimes use the Archaic forms of these words, but they even used what are called 'false' Archaisms, for the sake of the metre: thus cp. Vergil's pōnīt, where the *i* probably came from ĕ (cp. ἔλεγε legit).

(*t*) *Prothesis.*

Greek ἐ-λαχύς (levis), ἐ-ρυθρόν (rubrum), ὄ-νομα (nōmen), ἀ-μύνω (? mūniō), show a 'Prothetic' letter to facilitate pronunciation, as in Latin estella (Conversational Latin) → étoile; a similar letter may perhaps be seen in ἀ-στήρ (cp. stella), ἴ-σθι (cp. sumus).

(*u*) *Rhotacism.*

The change of *s* to *r* is called Rhotacism: we see it especially in Latin -*s*-, between Vowels and in certain other positions, as in *ǯenesi* → genere (cp. εὐγενές), *wesna* → *verna* (cp. ἑστίᾱ): honor was due to Association with honōrem, etc. (from -*s*- between Vowels). For instances where -*s*- does not → -*r*-, cp. rosa, and see Conway's *Verner's Law in Italy*.

In Laconian and Elean we sometimes find final -s → ρ, e.g. τίρ (τις) τοῖρ (τοῖς).

For the change, see p. 205.

Syncope: see Loss.

PART V.

PRONUNCIATION, ACCENTS, AND SPELLING.

37. Pronunciation of Greek and Latin Sounds.

37. (*a*) *How were the following words and sounds pronounced in Classical times? Give English Equivalents.*

(i) *istis, ara, petes unus non quot iuga vires;*

(ii) *au, ae, eu, oe, ui;*

(iii) ῑφι : ᾱρα : σέ : μή συ, σκῦτος, ὦ, φόνου, ὄζον;

(iv) ει, αι, οι, υι, αυ (about 450 B.C.), ευ, ου (450 B.C. and later).

Latin.

(i) *istīs, āra, petēs ūnus nōn quot iuga vīrēs.*

If we take these two lines

> Ma can't yet make it feel too good,
> No! not yon piece of ear-ring could or would;

we shall have the Latin Vowel-sounds, and some Consonant-sounds also, viz.

ā (ma), *ă* (can't, when unaccented),
ĕ (yet), *ē* (make),
ĭ (it), *ī* (feel),
ū (too, when accented), *ŭ* (good),
ō (no), ŏ (not);
i [incorrectly written as *j*] (yon),
s (piece),
r (ea*r*-*r*ing),
c (could),
v [more correctly written as *u*] (would).

The above Latin Sentence should now be practised by being read *out loud*, again and again, before new instances are tried. It would be something like this in English letters:—

isteece ahrăh pĕ-tayce oonŏos known quot yŏogăh wee-race.

(ii) *au*, *ae*, *eu*, *oe*, *ui* might be illustrated by an English Sentence

Now buy new oil cruits,

which, in Latin letters, would be

nau bae neu oel cruits.

The Diphthongs in Early times were sounded by the pronunciation first of one letter and then of the other: e.g. *au* would be, in an exaggerated form, *ah-oo*, which would get nearer to the sound of English *now*.

But the pronunciation of some sounds differed at different Periods.

Greek.

(iii) *ἶφι*: *ἆρα*: *σε*: here we should have sounds like those in the Latin words *istīs āra pe-*, viz.:

eep-hĭ: *ahrăh*: *sĕ-* (this does not take the Note into account: see p. 193, below);

μή συ, σκῦτος, ὦ, φόνου ὄζον would have its Vowel-sounds approximately represented by the French words

père tu fumes encore;

here we have

η (père, air),
υ (tu—not English),
ῡ (plume—not English),
ο (not),
ω (encore, oar).

The Consonants would be easy, except for *φ* and *ζ*:

φ χ θ may be represented by the English sounds in to*p-h*at, blac*k-h*at, po*t-h*at;

ζ by the English sound in gla*zed*.

(iv) The Diphthongs *ει*, *αι*, *οι*, *υι*, *αυ* (about 450 B.C.), *ευ*, *ου* (450 B.C. and later) might be illustrated by these English Sentences:—

May I oil wheels? Down you go, do,

which in Greek letters would be—

μει (may), *αι*, about 450 B.C. (I), *οιλ* (oil), *υιλς* (wheels): *δαυν* (down), *ευ* (you), *γου* (go), about 450 B.C., but later, *δου* (do).

37 (b). Mistakes in Pronunciation.

(*b*) *Point out the mistakes which are often made in the pronunciation of:*

(i) *ut parvos infans nunc civitas iacet ;*

(ii) ῥῖζαι σοφῶς ἐχύθησαν.

(*b*) (i) We sometimes hear

ut parvos īnfāns nunc cīvitās iacet,

not pronounced like this—

oot parwoss eenfahnce noonk keewitahce yăhket,

but like this—

ut parvus infanz nunk sigh-vitās jassit.

This pronunciation contains more than fifteen mistakes, which should be worked out *very carefully.* The above Sentence, like the Sentences given above, should be thoroughly mastered: it should be *read out loud again and again.*

(ii) We sometimes hear

ῥῖζαι σοφῶς ἐχύθησαν

not pronounced like this—

*rheezdye sop-horse eck-h*ut*-hè-săhn* (*u* being the French *u* in *tu,* and *è* like the French *è* in mère),

but like this—

rye-zye soffoze eck-you-theesan.

This pronunciation contains more than ten mistakes, which also should be worked out *very carefully.*

37 (c). Evidences for Greek and Latin Pronunciation.

(*c*) *Mention some of the Evidences as to the pronunciation of Classical Greek and Latin.*

(i) The *Māter-Language* (p. 10, foll.) gives us some evidence, as being the (great . . . grand-) mother of Greek and Latin: it can be to some extent reconstructed through a comparison of these with its other daughter-Languages, such as Sanskrit, Celtic, etc.;

(ii) these various *Sister-Languages or Cousin-Languages* themselves give some evidence as to the pronunciation of Classical Greek and Latin; and we may add

(iii) the *Descendants* of Greek, and of Latin, especially the Romance Languages: for instance, the sound of *ā* in these Languages (English *ah*) gives evidence against Classical Greek and Latin *ā* being sounded as they are in English l*a*te; moreover, such words as loi, foi, trois, voir, fier are evidence as to *the tendency* of Classical lēgem, fidem, trēs, vidēre, fīdere;

(iv) *Grammarians*, and other Authorities such as Varro, tell us a little: thus it seems that the *ae-* of aequos tended towards the sound of *e-* (of equos) lengthened;

(v) *puns*, such as the famous pun cave nē eās and Cauneās, *and other casual helps*, may be utilised: thus we know that *βη* was not unlike a sheep-noise;

(vi) *Metre* may throw light on some points, e.g. on the weak pronunciation of final *m* in Latin ('elided' before Vowels, or, perhaps, rather 'nasalising' the Vowel just before it), the scansion of *genua* as genwa, and of parietis as paryetis, may also be mentioned;

(vii) *writing* and spelling are also to be noticed, and especially that of Inscriptions, Inscriptions being least liable to alterations and 'modernisings': thus we find *ἀφ' ὧν*, and sometimes *ἀφ' ὧν*, proving that *φ* was *not* our *f*, but rather our *p-h* of to*p-h*at; again, maxumus and maximus, and the new letter introduced by the Emperor Claudius, point to a Latin *u*, *in certain positions* not unlike German *ü*, or the French *u* in une plume;

(viii) *Transliterations* from one language to another must be noticed: thus we find in Early Latin trium*p*us, and Pili*p*us (p. 45), which again show that Greek *φ* was not yet *f*.

37 (d). Advantages of Pronouncing Greek and Latin correctly.

(*d*) *Suggest a few of the advantages of pronouncing Greek and Latin more as they used to be pronounced, instead of pronouncing them like English sounds.*

In favour of the system of pronouncing e.g. the *ā* of *fāta* like the English *a* in *fate*, in may be said

(i) that this is still *customary*: that to change the custom would be a great trouble—to the present generations: this argument is usually brought against *any* proposed reform;

(ii) that English-speaking people find it *easier* to give the English values to letters: but see below (1, 2, and 8);

(iii) that there are *still some problems* to be solved, and that it is better not to change till we change once for all: this argument also is usually brought against any proposed reform, even by those who dare not deny that the reform is in the right direction, and is, on the whole, *nearer to the truth* than the old custom is. We do not refuse to accept Darwin's theory merely because it is not yet perfect: we should accept it *provisionally*, as being more likely than certain older views, but not necessarily final—we should not refuse to go forward because the goal is not yet certain: at any rate we know in which *direction* the goal lies.

(iv) the statement that the 'English' pronunciation 'obscures the quantities of Vowels' seems to me to be off the lines: it is as easy to give the right *quantities* to mensa (Nom.) and mensā (Abl.) by the 'English' pronunciation as by the other—in fact by the former it is easier. The 'false quantities' are not an integral part of the 'English'-method: they are an abuse of it.

1. Against the 'English' pronunciation (e.g. of the *a* of fāta as in English *fate*), it may be mentioned that

(*α*) the English pronunciation of some letters is almost unique, for few other Languages pronounce *ā* as we do in fate;

(*β*) it is often historically inaccurate for Classical Greek and Latin;

(γ) English represents many different sounds by the same letter or sign: thus the *i* of 'I' and 'hit' are very different;

(δ) English uses many different letters or signs to represent the same sound or a similar sound: e.g. cp. the Neutral-vowel sounds in a sentence like this, as it is *sometimes* pronounced:—

Both*er* th*e* vill*ai*n*ou*s auth*or*'s bund*le*s, *ma*ma.

2. The more correct Pronunciation seems to have proved not only possible, but also successful, in America, and to some extent in Scotland, and in Wales; so it might be tried more generally in England.

3. The *Māter-Language* would be easier to reconstruct, if this more correct pronunciation were used, and

4. *the relations between the various Sister-Languages and Cousin-Languages would become clearer;*

5. the Classical Languages might be made *more living*, nearer to what they were when they were spoken: their *rhythm and music*, on which the speakers and writers spent so much time, would be better appreciated;

6. *Accuracy* in general, and useful researches in particular, would be encouraged;

7. at first, it is true, the pronunciation would be harder for English-speaking people, but it would be *easy for people who speak other Languages*, and might help *intercourse* with those people by means of Latin—an excellent medium of Conversation;

8. the learning of other Languages by English-speaking people would become vastly easier: at present how many from a Public School or University can understand or speak such useful Languages as *French and German?* Their Vowel-sounds are made far easier if Greek and Latin be pronounced more correctly;

9. '*False Quantities*' would be less and less frequent in Greek and Latin Verses, if Greek and Latin were read aloud in as near a way as possible to the way in which they were once spoken.

37 (e). Helps to Correct Pronunciation.

(e) How might the more correct Pronunciation of Greek and Latin be helped?

1. *Abstruse points should be avoided* at first.

For instance,

(α) Classical *t* (τ) and *d* (δ) were pronounced with the tongue nearer to the teeth than English *t* and *d;*

(β) Classical *n* (ν) was more 'Dental' than English *n;*

(γ) Latin *-m* was usually a weaker sound than English *-m;*

(δ) the Classical Pronunciation changed from time to time: thus cp. Greek ου p. 184, which changed as in the words 'go to';

(ε) the sounds of Attic σσ and ττ are still doubtful; and other Problems remain to be solved.

The general facts which we *do* know are sufficient for beginners.

2. The start should be made by

(*a*) *a few words,*

(*b*) with *English* equivalents; these few words should be thoroughly mastered

(*c*) by constant *reading aloud*, and

(*d*) by *correction* (by self or by others), till they are

(*e*) absolutely and thoroughly *familiar;* then

(*f*) other words and sentences should be tried.

(*g*) *Long Vowels* should be very carefully marked, especially in Latin (which had not its η and ω): this is most important.

Note.—Reading aloud (for which Prizes might well be offered) should be practised at Schools especially, where it would form a pleasant break in the hour's work: it is a fallacy to regard it as a waste of time, for it is an indispensable help, e.g. towards understanding the rhythm and music, and the meaning, of the original, and towards learning foreign Languages. And this Reading aloud, or Reading aloud to oneself (if the expression may be pardoned), should never be discontinued. Translation of Greek or Latin should **never** be attempted until the Greek or Latin has been read out loud.

3. For *Details*, the reader should carefully study *The Restored Pronunciation of Greek and Latin*, by Arnold and Conway (Cambridge University Press). I owe a great deal of the above to this excellent little pamphlet, with which I heartily agree.

38 (a). Greek and Latin Accents.

38. (*a*) *What was the nature of the Greek* (*as opposed to the Latin*) *'Accents'. Explain the Accent-signs, and*

(*b*) *accentuate the following words, with a few Notes:*
Ζευ, ἰμεν, ἀνα, ειμι, ἀνθρωπος τις, λυσις, θυμος, βαλων and βαλειν, ἀδαματος, ὀνομακλυτος, τροπαιον, ειδεναι, φορουμεν, ἀλλα, πατρος.

(*a*) 'It was a compáct cómpact, was it?'

Say these words, and notice how

1. the *Note* changes: notice how the tune (so to speak) in which we say the statement 'It is', differs from the tune in which we say the Question 'Is it?' The tendency of the tune of our ordinary Sentence is downwards, from the higher note to the lower; in fact, most Sentences (at least in *our* Language apart from Dialect-peculiarities) end unsatisfactorily if they end on a higher note—they sound incomplete. A Question is *meant* to sound incomplete: in fact, an ordinary Question is not a complete Sentence, but is only the beginning of a Sentence which is not ended till the Answer has come: we might say that a Question like 'Where is Jones?' is the beginning of a Sentence ('Jones is ——') which the Answer will complete ('—— in town'). This is called Sentence-Accent, and may have been to *some* extent common to Greek and Latin: see also p. 74.

2. Notice the *Stress* on the first Syllable of cómpact, and on the second Syllable of compáct: cp. also cómpound and compoúnd, cóntract and contráct. In the Accented Syllable we use more force and muscular effort, and often more distinctness. This was the ordinary Latin Accent, which can be best seen

in words like *audín? út sésē córrigat melióribus oboédit, ostentā́tióne dḗpósitā.*

(i) It rarely fell on the last Syllable, except in words like *audín?* (from audīsne), and in Monosyllables like *út* (where the Accent can be regarded as falling on the first Syllable);

(ii) it regularly fell *on the last Syllable but one, if this was Long*, as in *sḗse, oboédit;* but

(iii) it fell on the last Syllable but two, if the last but one was short, as in *córrigat, melióribus.*

These two Accents were most important in the *scansion of the Saturnian* metre (see p. 55).

Thus it seems never to go back beyond *the three Final Syllables:* but there are two exceptions, viz.

(iv) a *Secondary* Accent, which would come *before* this Accent, as in ostentā́tiṓne, where ō had the Main, and ā the Secondary Accent;

(v) in *Early Latin* the Accent, probably *the Main Accent*, fell on *the first Syllable of every Accented word*, and it was this Accent that helped to change *légomenoi* and *légemenai* to *légiminī* (p. 91)

Latin, therefore, had Stress-Accents. Notice, however, that the Accent on fácere did not blur the sounds of the two e's that followed: see p. 183.

Historic Greek, on the other hand, had a Note or Pitch Accent: thus

(*a*) νόμος meant that the first ό was pronounced on a higher, or rather on a rising Note: νομός meant that the second ό was so pronounced;

(*b*) in a Sentence, this second νομός would appear as νομὸ : this ὸ marked a descending Note, and ὸ may (for practical purposes) be considered as if it had no Accent-sign at all: in fact, we might write the word νὸμὸς or νομος;

(*c*) the *Circumflex* reveals its origin when we split up ᾶ or â into άὰ: there was first a rising Note and then a descending Note.

Was the sign of a Short Vowel (ă), in its origin, this Circumflex *reversed* and turned upside down?

The Classical Greek Accent was therefore not a sign of Stress but a sign of Note, though in Greek, as in Sanskrit, there was *a tendency for it to become, by degrees, a sign of Stress.* Modern Greek is scanned by Accent, though it is not the same thing as Stress: in Modern Greek μῆνιν ἄειδε θεὰ Πηληιάδᾱ' Ἀχιλῆος could not be a Hexameter.*

(b) Greek Accentuation.

Note on the Greek Accent.

For further information, see Giles' *Manual*, King and Cookson's *Comparative Grammar*, and various Articles in the *Classical Review*, *American Journal of Philology*, etc.: the subject is most complicated, and only a few views are selected here. Whitney's *Sanskrit Grammar* will also be found useful by those who will take the trouble to study it: Sanskrit gives us very valuable evidence about the Māter-Language Accent. Bloomfield's Article in the A. J. P. (vol. ix.) is worth studying carefully.

Ζεῦ: if we wrote this as Ζέὺ (Sanskrit Dyău), and compared the Nominative Ζεύς with Sanskrit Dyāús, we should clearly see the Accent going back in the Vocative: in the Māter-Language the Accent, in the *Vocative*, regularly fell on the first Syllable of the word: cp. also πατήρ πατέρα, but Vocative πάτερ.

ἴμεν: in the Māter-Language the Finite Verb,

(α) in Main Sentences was Unaccented (see εἰμι below), except when it began the Sentence;

(β) in Subordinate Sentences it was Accented, and the Accent was 'free' (i.e. not confined to the last three Syllables): thus here it would be *imén* or *imés*. Notice the effect of the ′: the Root (*ei-*, *oi-*, *i-*) is in its III-Stage (*i-*), whereas in *eími* or ? *éimi* it is in its I-Stage. See pp. 74-75.

In Greek, *the 'Recessive' Accent* in Finite Verbs, and in some other words (see λύσις below), changed ἰμέν to ἴμεν.

* It is interesting to read the Modern Greek Poems which are scanned not according to the Length of the Vowel but by the Accents.

ἀνα:

(i) as a Preposition, it would be Accented ἀνά, which in a Sentence would become ἀνὰ, i.e. would lose its Accent;

(ii) by 'Anastrophe' (p. 175) it would be Accented as ἄνα;

(iii) as a Finite Verb, meaning 'Up!' 'Rise up!', it would, like other Finite Verbs, have the 'Recessive' Accent, and be ἄνα: for other instances, cp. ἔνι, ἔπι, meaning ἔνεστι and ἔπεστι;

(iv) ἄνα 'o king', from ἄνα(κτ), needs no explanation.

εἰμι.

(i) εἶμι 'I will go' was from *eîmi* or ? *éimi*;

(ii) εἰμι 'I am' is still unaccented and 'Enclitic', when it is unemphatic: this is a trace of the time when most Finite Verbs were unaccented in Main Sentences (p. 194), φημι in the Present being another survival of this: possibly a third was εἰ (from *ei*, Imperative) in Homer's εἰ δὲ ἐπέντυε 'but go (and) equip . . .';

(iii) Emphatic εἰμί probably has not its Māter-Language Accent.

ἄνθρωπός τις (cp. p. 178) shows

(*a*) 'Enclitic' τις throwing back its Accent on to the ὁ;

(*b*) the Accent of ἄνθρωπος going *further back than the three morae*, as they are called; if we work backwards, we find that ο gave one mora, and ω gave two; we might therefore expect ἀνθρῶπος, and there are signs that this may have been the Earlier Accent (cp. Early τροπαῖον, becoming τρόπαιον later on): possibly ἄνθρωπος was due to Association with words Accented like ἄνεμος, where 'the Rule of the three Morae' was adhered to.

λύσις: the Māter-Language Accent was lutís, as we can see from the III-Stage (*lu*) being used (cp. πατέρα πατρός, below). The 'Recessive' Accent seems have spread (e.g. from the Verb) to some Nouns like this, though other Nouns (like θυμός) resisted it.

θῡμός. The Māter-Language Accent is preserved here, though 'Aeolic', like Latin, had the 'Recessive' Accent, i.e.

θῦμος, and (with Stress Accent) fūmus: contrast, however, Attic ἕβδομος, which was from -mós.

βαλών and βαλεῖν. The Māter-Language had the Accent on the last Syllable in βαλών, as we see from Sanskrit: the 'Recessive' Accent did not influence these words, because they were not, in Early times, Finite Verb forms: βαλών was an Adjective and βαλεῖν a Substantive.

ἀδάματος. In the Māter-Language *-tós* was Accented: but in Compound Words like this, and cp. words compounded with ἐπι-, etc., the Accent went back to the Indeclinable Prefix: but the Greek 'Rule of the three Morae' could only let the Accent as far back as the third Syllable from the end.

ὀνομακλυτός: ὀνόμα, and κλυτός (cp. above), would represent the Māter-Language Accents: but in Composition we should have ὀνόμακλυτός, and then, by the 'Rule of the three Morae', ὀνομάκλυτός. The first Accent was sacrificed.

τροπαῖον (Early), later τρόπαιον: see ἄνθρωπος (above).

εἰδέναι. In Sanskrit we find a Case-form *dāvánē* (*ē* representing *-ai*). Apparently as a rule the Dative -ai was Accented, but the 'Locative' εἰδέν (cp. αἰέν) may have influenced the Accent of the Dative-form. The 'Recessive' Accent did not come into play here, as the word was once a Substantive (cp. above).

φοροῦμεν: The Circumflex is explained by the Accents on φορέομεν, the Accent on the έ being the 'Recessive' Accent, and going as far back as the Greek 'Rule of the three Morae' allowed.

ἄλλα as a 'Neuter Plural' needs no explanation; ἀλλά was perhaps once identical with this form, but was *differentiated* from it by the Accent—ἄλλα being set apart for one function, and ἀλλά for another.

πατρός: the Māter-Language form was *pətrós*, the Accent falling on the Case-Ending *-ós;* where the Accent fell on the Suffix, we have e.g. pətérm̥ -> πατέρα. With this compare κυών, but κυνός. See p. 75.

39. Greek and Latin Spelling.

39. *How did the best MSS. spell*

(*a*) *the Greek Words for :—*

'*I knew*', '*thou knewest*', '*he knew*', '*I save*', '*I was going to*', '*I wished*', '*if*' [with the Subjunctive], '*I arrange*', '*with*', '*always*', '*boldness*', '*he dies*', '*thou art said*' : *Give the Greek for* '*I struck*', '*I was struck*', '*I will come*';

(*b*) *the Latin Words for :—*

(i) '*dead*' (*Nom. and Acc.*), '*horse*', (*do.*), '*of the son*', '*towers*' (*Nom. and Acc.*);

(ii) '*yoke*', '*at Rome*', '*pleasant to behold*';

(iii) '*I throw away*'.

(*a*) *Greek Words.*

ᾔδη, ᾔδησθα, ᾔδει, σώζω, ἔμελλον, ἐβουλόμην, ἐάν or ἄν, τάσσει ξύν αἰεί θάρσος (Old Attic, e.g. of Thucydides), τάττει σύν ἀεί θάρρος or θάῤῥος (New Attic, e.g. of Demosthenes), θνήσκει, λέγει or λέγῃ;

ἐπάταξα (not ἔτυψα, nor ἔτυπον), ἐπλήγγην, εἶμι or μέλλω with the Infinitive (not ἐλεύσομαι).

(*b*) *Latin :—*

(i) *Endings—*

2nd Declension—Nom. and Acc. Sing. mortuos, mortuom; equos, equom, or ecus, ecum; Gen. Sing. fīlī not fīliī.

3rd Declension—Nom. Plur. of i-stems, turrēs, Acc. Plur. turrīs.

(ii) *Miscellaneous*—i, never j; u, never v—rule seldom adhered to in Books; no diphthongs, e.g. never æ, œ, but always ae, oe.

(iii) *List of Useful Words* (as spelt in Quintillian's time): abicio, adicio, adulescens (Noun), aestimo, āfui, amoenus, ancora, anulus, auctor, auctōritās, Autumnus, bēlua, beneficium, bracchium and brāchium, būcina, cāecus not coecus, caelebs not coelebs, caelum, caenum, caerimōnia and caeremōnia, caesaries, Camēna, caussa, cēna, cēterum, cēterī, clipeus, comminus, condicio, cōnectō, cōnitor, cōnīveō, cōnubium, coniunx, contio, convīcium, cottidie and cōtidie, dīciō, dīnōscō, ēlegans, emptus, epistula, erus, existimō, exsanguis, exscindo, faenus and fēnus, faenum and fēnum, fēcundus, futtilis, genetīvos, genetrīx, glēba and glaeba, Hādria, harēna probably better than arēna, harundō, hedera, hiems, holus and olus, īlicō, inclitus and inclutus (older), incohō and inchoō, indutiae, intellego, Iūppiter, lacrima and lacruma (older), libet: lubet is the older spelling, littera better than lītera, lītus, malevolos, mercēnnarius, mīlia, mixtus, monumentum and monimentum, multa: mulcta is the old spelling, nactus and nanctus, nāvos neglegō, nē 'verily' better than nae, neglegō, nēquīquam and nēquicquam novīcius, nuntīo, oboediō, obscēnus, onustus, Paelīgni, paene, paenitet, paulum: paullum is the older spelling, percontor, probably better than percunctor, Polliō and Pōliō, pōmerium, prēlum, proelium, prōscaenium, pulcher superseded pulcer, quattuor, quotiēs: quotiens is the older spelling, Raetia, reccīdī, reciperō: recupero is the older spelling rēligiō: relligiō is the older spelling, rēliquiae: relliquiae is the older spelling, repperī, reppulī, rettulī, saeculum, saepes, saepiō, satira and satura (older), scaena, sepulcrum, sescenti, sētius not secius, solacium, sollemnis, sollers, stīlus, sūcus, sulphur and sulpur, suscenseō, suspīciō, taeter, temptō, thēsaurus: thensaurus is the older spelling, tingō and tinguō, trānsmittō, etc., and trāmitto, etc., umerus better than humerus, umor, umidus, better than humor, humidus unguō and ungō, valētūdō not valitūdō, Vergilius, Virginius, vertex; vortex is the older spelling, vīcēsimus, vīlicus, not villicus.

See further, Dr. Reid's Editions of *Cicero*, and Lindsay's *Historical Latin Grammar*, from which most of the above are selected. The Long Vowels are not all marked in this List.

PART VI.

HOW SOUNDS ARE MADE (PHYSIOLOGY).

40. Organs of Speech.

40. *Give some account of the Organs of Speech, showing how sounds are made.*

Sounds are made when air is blown by bellows (the Lungs), through a pipe (called the Trachea): at one part of this pipe the

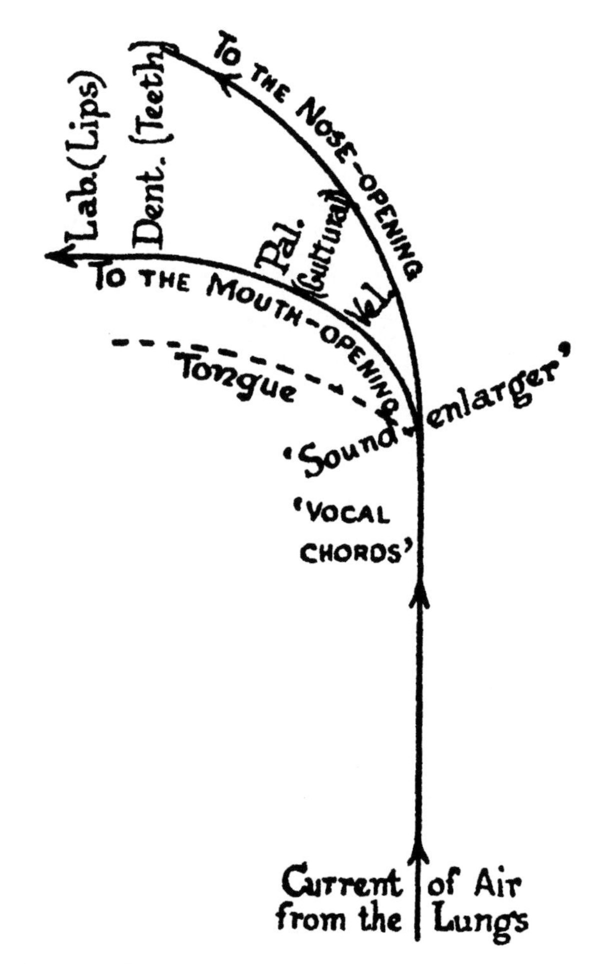

passage can be made narrow or it can be left open: this part is where the 'Vocal Chords' or 'Cords' are, and the tone will depend largely upon the narrowness or openness of these 'Chords'—the narrower opening of course producing a higher Note. Hence the air passes into what has been called the Voice-box, and in this Voice-box it is modified and enlarged. Thence the air comes out, as one sees in the Diagram, either by the Mouth-passage, or by the Nose-passage, or partly by both: for you can breathe either when you hold your nose tight, or when you keep your mouth shut tight, but not when you do both together (except for a little breath that may come through the ears): as a rule you probably breathe through both mouth and nose, though for ordinary purposes the nose-breathing is the better.

In technical Language, the air passes through the Trachea, the Larynx, the Glottis (the slit between the Vocal 'Chords'), and the Pharynx: the air can be breathed-in or inhaled through the mouth and the nose: the latter is better, as the nose both warms and filters the air before letting it pass to the Lungs.

Now by which opening does your breath come out when you speak—through the mouth or through the nose? How can you decide which opening you are going to use? Well, the Nose-opening can be closed by a movable piece of flesh, and I dare-say you have used it when you have drunk something which you did not want to taste, that is to say unless you adopted the plan of holding your nose.

In trying the following sounds you will find it easier to notice what happens, if you *exaggerate*.

(i) Breathe ordinarily, and little or no sound will be heard;

(ii) breathe more forcibly, and you will hear a sound like *her* or *hah;*

(iii) now shut your mouth and try to say '*papa*': probably you will not be able to get much nearer than '*kaka*', for '*papa*' needs the use of the lips: *p* is a *Labial.*

In Ventriloquising one has to begin by sounds like 'Hullo!', and proceed to Guttural Sounds like 'kaka': by degrees one can learn to say something very like 'papa' without moving the lips: for of course it does not do for a ventriloquist to use his lips.

'Papa' has a '*Sharp*' Labial, while *b*aba has a '*Soft* Labial, and *f*ather *v*ery *w*ell have still 'softer' Labials (*f* and *v* being very near to Dentals); now after these sounds (p, b, f, v, w) add the *h*-sound, and we have what are called 'Aspirated Labials', cp. up-hill, ab-hor, Golf-house, etc.

Now say '*Mam*a', and you will find that here also you use the lips: this is called a Labial *Nasal*, but notice that you can say 'Mama' while you are holding your nose: see also (iv), below.

(iv) Now say '*tut-tut*', and notice what happens: you feel your tongue moving, perhaps quite touching your *teeth*, perhaps only nearly touching them: the letter *t* will be a *Dent*al, a sharp Dental.

The distinction between 'Alveolars', 'Dentals', and 'Cerebrals', need not be studied here: see Giles' *Manual*, § 67 and 68.

Here, again, besides the 'Sharp' *t*, we have the 'Soft' *d* in '*d*a*d*a', and 'Aspirated' Dentals in an*t-h*ill and ma*d-h*ouse. In 'Si*ss*y' and 'Li*zz*y' we have hissed or Sibilant Dentals.

In '*Mam*a' we had a Labial Nasal: in '*Nan*a' we have a Dental Nasal. Here, again, you can say 'Nana' while holding your nose quite tight: but this is not the natural way of saying it, and, when you have a bad cold and find it hard to breathe through your nose, the sound of a word like '*moon*' comes out more like '*bood*': this shows that, in pronouncing Nasals, some of the air naturally passes through the nose. The same will apply to the Guttural Nasal of 'king': you *can* say 'king' while you are holding your nose quite tight, but, as a rule, when you say 'king' you send some air through your nose: and when you have a bad cold you will generally say '*kig*' (cp. '*bood*' for 'moon').

(v) Now say '*k*ing' and '*g*et': your tongue is farther back than in 'tut-tut', and of course much farther back than in 'papa': it is nearer to the throat or *Guttur*, and *ng* is the Guttural Nasal: here we have 'Sharp' *k*, 'Soft' *g;* 'in*k*-*h*orn' and pi*g-h*ouse would give 'Aspirated' Gutturals, and 'king' the Nasal Gutturals: these are called *Palatals* (p. 173), and *ng* would be a Palatal.

(vi) If you say 'kong' and 'gone', your tongue will be still farther back: these sounds are called *Velar*, as the tongue is nearer to the Velum, the 'veil' that can close the Nose-passage (see above).

(vii) After these sounds try the words 'trilling' and 'thrilling': these will give the *Liquids*, *r* and *l*.

Is this all for the 'Consonants'? No: for there still remain

(viii) *the sounds which we make in passing from one letter to another:* thus, in saying 'up it goes', we have not only a Labial (*p*), a Dental (*t*), and a Velar Guttural (*g*), but we also have the sounds made in 'gliding' from letter to letter: hence the name '*Glides*'.

Writing does not often represent these 'Glides': on the other hand, English writing especially is fond of preserving certain sounds which are no longer heard, as in the word '*night*'.

In fact, as with human beings, so with letters, each is liable to be influenced by his neighbours, and not by his next-door neighbours alone: this we saw in the case of θριχός (p. 133), where χ changed θ to τ: and see Assimilation (p. 176).

(ix) The *Vowels* also have the tongue in different positions: there is no space to work this out here, but notice the changes when you say *oo*, *oar*, *ah*, *er*, *ay*, *ee*, *eye*.

In order to realise the changes, utter the sounds with great force.

Of the Vowels, according to their Graeco-Latin pronunciation (p. 183, foll.), *a* was Velar, *o* and *u* Velar and Labial, *e* and *i* Palatal and Dental. See further Giles' Table (opp. p. 78 of the *Manual*).

41. Instances of Sound-Changes.

41. *Write Notes on the history of—*

(*a*) *-s- between Vowels in Greek and in Latin ;*

(*b*) *the combination of two Dentals in Greek and in Latin.*

It must be remembered that most Sound-changes were

(*a*) very gradual, and

(*b*) practically unconscious.

The word '*imperceptible*' will give the idea of both (*a*) and (*b*).

(*a*) *-s- between Vowels.* See Conway on Verner's Law (p. 7).

In Sanskrit we find the *-s-*, under certain conditions, getting a sound like the *sh* of 'wishy-washy': thus the word for 'sage' (*ṛṣi*) was pronounced 'Rishi'. Sometimes, however, we find Sanskrit *-s-* → *-r-*, and sometimes we find *s* → *h*, and this reminds one of *ǵenesi* → Latin gene*r*e, Greek γενε῾ι → γένει.

Through what stages did -*s*- between Vowels pass, in order that, in a word like *ǵenesi*, it should become

(i) Latin -*r*- in gene*r*e,

(ii) Greek ῾, and then nothing, in γενε῾ι → γένει ?

At first -*s*- here sometimes became softened to a *z*- or *zh*-sound, *ǵenez*(*h*)*i*.

This *z*(*h*)-sound in Latin (as in English we*r*e, cp. wa*s*) gradually, very gradually, passed into a kind of *rz*(*h*) sound, then the *z*(*h*) became softer and fainter, till it died away and left the -*r*- alone. But another explanation may be possible, viz., that -*s*- → a sound like -*rh*-.

In Greek the *s*- or *z*-sound, between Vowels, as well as at the beginnings of words before Vowels, very gradually passed into a kind of *sh-* or *zh*-sound (not *rzh*): here again the *s-* or *z*-sound became softer and fainter, till it died away and left the *h*-sound alone (cp. septem and ἑπτά); between Vowels this *h*-sound itself died away in Greek (but cp. Laconian μῶά, on p. 32), and often the two Vowels 'contracted': cp. in Latin ni*h*il → niil → nīl.

(*b*) *The combination of two Dentals.*

Sanskrit, as we see in the word Bu*dd*ha, liked certain combinations of Dentals, but Greek and Latin found them harder. English people seldom pronounce these sounds distinctly when they try to talk Sanskrit or one of the Indian Dialects.

In English we find it easier to say 'towar*ds th*em' than to say (distinctly) 'towar*d th*em'; and in Early Greek and Latin we find the *s*-sound actually growing up between two Dentals, so that 'Dental + Dental' → *Dental* + *s* + *Dental.*

In Greek, a combination like ἰδ-ς-τε (from *uid-te*) → ἴστε, the first Dental become merged in the *s*-sound: cp. also πιθτις → πιθ-ς-τις → πίστις.

In Latin we have a different development, for skid-s-tos (from *skid-tos*) → scidssos → sci*ss*us: when the previous Vowel was long, we have only one *-s-*, as in *bheidh-tos* → fīd-s-tus → fīsus.

Greek has something not unlike this in the change of μελιτία to μελιτσα, and thence sometimes to μέλιττα, but sometimes to μελίσσα (cp. our pronunciation of condi*t*ion, which shows a different *s*-sound, however).

In both Greek and Latin we get extension by *Association* (p. 67) with such forms: thus, in Latin, mi*ss*us (cp. mi*tt*ō) and fū*s*us (cp. fun*d*ō) helped to produce pul*s*us rather than pul*t*us (cp. παλτός), and, in Greek, ἴστε (cp. ἰδεῖν) helped to produce ἴσμεν rather than ἴδμεν.

PART VII.

THE ALPHABETS.

Note.—Here, as elsewhere, we shall proceed from the best-known to the less well-known, and we shall take the *English* Alphabet as our starting-point: from this we shall pass to *Latin*, and thence to Greek.

For details about the Alphabets, see Giles' *Manual*, King and Cookson's *Comparative Grammar*, and, best of all, Roberts' *Introduction to Greek Epigraphy*: for a special study, this book is indispensable.

42. Classical Latin Alphabet compared and contrasted with ours.

42. *How did the Classical Latin Alphabet differ from ours?*

The Classical Latin Alphabet was very like our own Alphabet, but

(i) J did not belong to it, for Latin wrote and pronounced the word for 'yoke', for instance, as *i*ugum, with a *y*-sound;

(ii) W did not belong to it, nor yet

(iii) U as distinct from V: in Capitals V, in Cursive-hand *u*, represented the *w*-sound and the *u*-sound of our words '*w*ine' and 'p*u*t' (VĪNVM uīnum, PVTŌ putō).

j and *v* were not introduced into MSS. till Mediæval times, when the pronunciation of the Latin words for '*y*oke' and '*w*ine' had changed.

Now let us *cancel* those letters in which the Latin Alphabet more or less resembled the Attic Greek Alphabet of 400 B.C.; and then we shall see what is noteworthy.

Note.—The resemblance is sometimes in appearance and outward form rather than in sound: but we are discussing mainly the outward form here.

43. Attic Greek Alphabet and its connexion with the later Latin Alphabet.

43. *What was the general connexion between the Attic Greek Alphabet (in the time of Demosthenes), and the Latin Alphabet in the time of the Emperor Claudius?*

The Greeks '*borrowed*' their Alphabet from the Phœnicians, who were not its inventors, however: the Phœnicians were chiefly carriers of the ancient world, rather than originators. Some say that the Earliest Alphabet which Greece had (through the Phœnicians) came from the Egyptians, others that it came from the Babylonians, others that it came from the Hittites (who were probably Mongolians).

The Greeks did not keep this Alphabet unchanged, for it lacked Vowel-signs: they therefore *altered* it.

But all the Greeks did not alter it in the same way: there was

I. an **Eastern** Greek Alphabet, used by most of the Greeks in Greece proper and in Asia Minor, and

II. a **Western** Greek Alphabet (see the plan on p. 17) used especially by the Greeks in *Italy and Sicily*.

From the *Eastern* came the *Attic* Alphabet, with some changes, and from the *Western* came the *Latin* Alphabet, also with some changes.

Attic Greek, [A] [B] Γ [Δ] E Z H Θ [I] K [Λ] [M] [N] Ξ O [Π] [P] [Σ] [T] Υ Φ X Ψ Ω.

Latin (i) [A] [B] C [D] E F G H [I] K (*rare*) [L] [M] [N] O [P] Q [R] [S] [T] V (*u*) X Y Z;

(ii) *Numerals*, CD or M, D, Ψ ⩊ or L, X;

(iii) (*Claudius' Innovations*) Ⱶ (the sound between *i* and *u*, as in max*u*mus or max*i*mus, p. 45: cp. French *une*, German *ü*), Ⅎ (Consonantal *u*, or *w*), ↄ (*ps*, and *bs* which was pronounced like *ps*). These did not continue.

Thus the *Attic* Greek Alphabet was an Eastern Alphabet,

changed in some respects, e.g. by the addition of Ω; the Claudian *Latin* Alphabet was a Western Alphabet, changed in some respects, e.g. by

(*a*) the adoption, later on, of certain Greek letters like Y, and of

(*b*) Claudius' letters (see above).

44. History of certain Letters in the Greek and Latin Alphabets.

44. *Give a short history of the following Letters of the Greek and Latin Alphabets :—*

(*a*) *Greek H, F,*

(*b*) *Latin C, X, Y, Z, the Numeral-signs, Q.*

(*a*) We know the *Attic* Alphabet (see above): how did it differ from the Western?

(i) In 403 B.C., H was adopted to denote the sound of ē (as in *mère*), and Ω to denote the sound of ō (as in *oar*).

Note.—The Long Vowel of ε was now not η but ει, as we see by the Contraction of ἐποίεε into ἐποιει. Cp. ἐχρύσοον and -ουν.

In the Western Alphabet, H represented the 'Aspirate'.

(ii) The Classical Attic Alphabet had no F, though F is found in some Greek Dialects (pp. 32, 38): in the Western Alphabet F was found, but at first not with the value of Latin F, but rather with a W- or WH-sound, somewhat as in our word *which*. See p. 49.

(*b*) (i)—C:

In the Western Alphabet, as in the Eastern, the third letter was Γ (C): in Early Latin this served not only for the *g*-sound but also for the *k*-sound (though k is also found, and survived in K. for Kaesō): later on, *for the g-sound the shape* of the letter *was slightly modified* (G), while the old form still continued to be used with the *k*-sound. As in the initials K. (Kaesō), KK (castra), etc., we have a trace of K, so in the initials C. and Cn. (Gaius and Gnaeus) we have a trace of the *g*-sound of C, a trace of the time when C was more closely connected with its parent, γάμμα or Γ.

G (= *g*) is assigned to about the time of Appius Claudius the Censor (312 B.C.).

(ii)—X:

In the Eastern Alphabet, X was χ (k-h, as in blac*k*-*h*at); in the Western Alphabet X was ξ or x, and came *before* φ: in Early Latin, however, we find the *x*-sound represented by xs, as in saxsum: it is possible that this symbol was also used as a Numeral (10): see below.

(iii)—Y:

To represent the Greek υ-sound, Latin at first used V (*u*), as in Aeg*u*ptus: then Latin invented a modification of Greek Υ, viz. Y, to represent the Greek υ-sound more accurately, and we find Aeg*y*ptus.

(iv)—Z:

The Early Latin Alphabet had Z, and so had Oscan and Umbrian, but S was found sufficient for the sibilant-sound: later on, however, about the time of Cicero, Z was *re-introduced from the Greek Alphabet*, with Y to represent the Greek Z, which till then had been represented by *s* or *ss* (as in Plautus' trapessita, cp. τράπεζα).

(v) *The Numeral-signs.*

Early Latin used ϴ and the last letters of the Western Alphabet as Numeral-signs (cp. p. 210): viz.

ϴ as 100 (perhaps afterwards → C, cp. Centum),

X as 10,

CD as 1000 (afterwards → ꟿ → M, cp. Mille),

D, half of this, 500 (hence the letter D, 500),

Ψ, 50 (afterwards L, perhaps through ⊥).

(vi)—Q:

The Western Alphabet, as distinct from the Eastern, had Ϙ or Koppa, with a *k*-sound: a horse branded with this sign was called *κοππατίας* (Aristoph., *Clouds*, 23). In Early Latin we find Q used, e.g. in peqūnia, but, later on, it was confined to the *qu*-sound, as in quārē.

45. Greek Alphabets (Local).

45. *By what signs would you recognise the Alphabets (especially the Archaic Alphabets) of*

(i) *Cyprus,*
(ii) *Corinth,*
(iii) *Argos,*
(iv) *Boeotia,*
(v) *Laconia?*

(i) *Cyprus:* The *Syllabic* system (by which every syllable ends in a Vowel) is found here: e.g. Στᾱσαγόραν appears as *sa-ta-sa-ko-ra-u*, πτόλιν as *po-to-lī-ne:* see further Cauer's *Delectus;*

Note.—The following peculiarities are of course not found on *all* the Inscriptions of the particular place, but only on one or more. See Roberts, Vol. I.

(ii) *Corinth:* ⊓⊔ (β), C < I (γ), B (ε), ⊟ (h), ≶ (ι), M (σ);

(iii) *Argos:* ⋏ C (γ), E (ε, η), ⊟ (h), M (σ), R (ρ);

(iv) *Boeotia:* ⊟⊟ (θ), ∨ (λ), □ ⊙ (ο), R (ρ), S (σ), Ψ (χ);

(v) *Laconia:* Γ Λ C (γ), X (ξ), R (ρ).

PART VIII.

ETYMOLOGY AND SÉMANTIQUE, OR THE MEANINGS OF WORDS.

Etymology, in one of its senses, is concerned with *the meanings of words, and the ways in which those meanings may change.* Some Principles of change we have seen already: but we have seen them applied to the sounds and forms of words, rather than to their meanings. For instance, we have seen what is meant by a 'Law of Sound-change', and an apparent exception to a Law (p. 66); we have seen what is meant by 'Analogy' or Association (p. 67), and by 'Contamination' or Blending (p. 69), in so far as these Principles affect the sounds and forms of words.

46. Principles of Evolution compared with Principles of Language.

46. *'The history or "Evolution" of the meanings of words is very like the history or Evolution of various things in the world of Nature'. Illustrate and comment on this statement.*

Are the lives of words at all like the lives of men? 'Evolution' tells us a great deal about the 'Heredity' and 'Environment' of men, about the way in which a man is influenced by his companions and his surroundings and in turn influences them; but are there any such Principles to be found in the history of words?

Let us start with an instance.

We have seen that people form groups and that the members of a group are liable to influence one another. Thus, of three men, one may be quiet and the other two may be lively. If these three are often together, the result will probably be either that the one quiet man will become livelier, or that the two lively men will become quieter ; or both these results may go on side by side.

But, it will be said, surely words are not anything like this: surely the words in our minds are not in groups but in pigeon-holes—each in a pigeon-hole of its own.

In answer to this I refer to p. 68, where we have seen that the Greek number for 800 changed its form because it happened to belong to the group of 'numbers for hundreds,' and to come between 700 and 900: ὀκτωκόσιοι became ὀκτακόσιοι by Association (p. 68).

There is, however, this important *difference* between persons and words. As we shall see directly, words, like persons, have their heredity, their environment, their individuality: they may become specialised or fossilised, and in many other respects they may be like persons ; but they have no free choice and no consciousness ; in fact, they are dependent on persons, they cannot use themselves; they must wait to be used.

Science or 'Evolution' tells us about the history of a person.

1. It tells us that he has a certain stock-in-trade given him by his parents, and this is called his '*Heredity*'. With this he starts life.

2. He lives with certain people, and in certain places, and these people and places influence him and he influences them. These surroundings of his are called his '*Environment*'.

3. It is well known that *persons of the same groups may influence one another* very considerably ; and that these groups may change ; thus the baby will be influenced by the home-group, the boy by the school-group, the man by the college-group or the business-group or whatever the group may be. This may be called the influence of *Association*.

4. Owing to these influences, no one man remains what he was to start with. Every one changes and every one changes differently. Every one has something which distinguishes him from every one else, and this is called his *Individuality*.

While still young this person becomes able to do more and more things better and better; but he finds that he does certain things especially well. He is not alone in the world: there are many others besides, with whom he may have to struggle for a good position or for higher things than that, or even for mere existence; and his success will depend largely on how fit he is for his particular life, and on how well he uses his powers.

5. This is called the *Struggle for Existence*, and it results in *the Survival of the Fittest;* for at first, in looking round us, we are apt to say that there are too many people in the world, that there are more than we need for the various purposes of life: where one would be enough, we find several.

6. This person will probably take up some special branch in life—for instance, he will go in for trade or for law or for teaching. This is called *Specialisation.*

7. A person may begin with one branch in life, and then change to another which may be more or less like the first branch. This is called *Change of Function.*

8. If he gets used to this second branch and fitted for it, the process is called *Adaptation.*

His other occupations he may keep on one side for the time being, or he may give them up altogether. For instance, he may give up his games.

9. It is possible that, long after a person has given up some one branch in life, we may still find records of his having taken up that branch, if only we look carefully. Thus, for instance, we may notice a photo of a cricket-team in his rooms, or we may notice that his right arm has certain muscles strongly developed. He does not play cricket now, but the traces of cricket still survive.

We thus see what was once a habit, and very common, preserved only in a few isolated traces. This might be called *Fossilisation*, but the principle will be clearer if we think of some of those specimens of animals of extinct species, which we find preserved in the gum of certain trees. Here we find an animal perfectly preserved, although it is no longer to be found in the living world of nature. This animal is a kind of fossil.

Such isolated traces of things that were once usual are of the greatest importance in History and Science.

10. We said just now that the person becomes specialised and becomes unable to do all things equally well at the same time. For instance, he teaches, but he has no time to play the piano well, or to prepare food; in fact, he cannot do everything all by himself. There is a need of *Co-operation;* he must get others to do certain things for him, and the best people he can get are those who are specialists at the things which he wishes to have done.

Such are some of the principles which we see at work in the evolution or history of persons in the world: and, strange as it may seem, all these principles, as well as many others, are also to be seen at work in the evolution or history of words in the mind. In fact, though it is somewhat incorrect, we may roughly say that 'as people are in the world, so words are in the mind'.

47. Instances to Illustrate Principles of Etymology or Sémantique.

47. *What Principles of Etymology do the following words illustrate: bridegroom, redbreast, see (in 'I see what you mean'), pig (in 'he's a pig'), St. Paul's, pagan, humble?*

(*b*) (i) '*Bridegroom*'.

'Bridegroom' was in Early times a Compound of two words, *bride* and *goom*, which word was derived from a word meaning 'man' and was connected with the Latin word *homo*.

These two words were put side by side, and the exact relation between them, namely the 'man *of* the bride' was not expressed by any sign, but was infused by common sense. These two words became a single word, and started on a new life of their own. They were children of a word 'bride' and a word 'goom', but now as a single word they came to have a new 'environment', and to belong to a new group: they came to mean something like 'husband'.

Thus the word 'bridegroom' now formed part of the group of words for 'man' (? man in an inferior position!), and in this group was the word *groom;* and it was this word 'groom', which was more familiar to most speakers, that altered 'bridegoom' into 'bride*g*room', somewhat as the more familiar words 'sparrow' and 'grass' have often produced '*sparragrass*', instead of the less familiar *asparagus*, in the language of common people. See p. 68.

The principle at work here, then, is the influence of a group of words upon one another.

Supposing the word had remained *bridegoom*, the word *goom* meaning 'man' would have survived here, while it had disappeared elsewhere in language. In other words, it would have been preserved here just as the beetle was preserved in the gum (p. 220), or the fossil in the cliff, when all other animals of the same species had perished. Compound words (see p. 82) are excellent *preservatives* of old forms.

(ii) '*Redbreast*'.

'Redbreast' was also made up of two distinct words: *red* which was both a Substantive and an Adjective, and *breast* which was a Substantive.

Redbreast is now used to denote a special kind of bird which *has a red breast.*

The first principle here is that nothing can be described in full each time we allude to it. We have to invent a short name by picking out some conspicuous part or feature. For instance, 'Bluebeard' was not a full description of the gentleman, but merely described him by mentioning his most prominent characteristic.

This one characteristic becomes the sign by which we clearly denote a particular object. Now a robin has a red breast as its conspicuous feature, and redbreast has come to be a sign and symbol for robins *par excellence:* not for all animals with red breasts but for one particular kind. In other words, instead of describing the whole thing we simply mention a part of it.

The general principle of this is *the desire for shortness*, or Economy.

Another general principle at work is the *Specialisation.* 'Redbreast' might possibly have been used for *any* animal with a red breast, but it has come to be confined to one type of animal only.

With this we may compare 'Longshanks', which came to be the name, not of a particular type of man merely, but of one particular king.

(iii) '*See*', in 'I see what you mean'.

Supposing boys wanted to play cricket and had no wickets, they might choose a tree and agree that this should be used instead of wickets.

The tree was there already, and they would only be putting it to a new use. This is called *Adaptation.*

Now, if this were done often enough, the tree might come to be regarded as a regular substitute for wickets.

So in the case of the word 'see'.

You show some one something which you have made, and he tells you that he sees it with his eyes. You describe to him something which you have done: his eyes cannot see it, but he wants to tell you that he understands it—that the eye of his mind sees the idea or the picture. So he takes the word for seeing with the eye, and uses it for seeing with the mind. He uses it for a new purpose, and adapts it.

Similarly he takes the word for *grasping* things with the hand and uses it for grasping things with the mind.

What we have to notice here is that the sense is now absolutely clear, although the word was once quite a new expression. The old word was used in a new sense and adapted to a new purpose. This process was repeated, and now there is nothing at all strange or new about the word 'see' in the sense of 'understand'.

What was first only occasional has now become usual and habitual. (See Strong, Logeman, and Wheeler's History of Language.)

This is obviously an instance of how people must start with what is easy to understand, if they wish to explain what is not so easy; and the technical word for this in Language is *Metaphor.*

Thus a man is very angry and we say his mind is like a storm or like a fire. The Latins said 'ardet' (īrā, etc.).

Metaphor can be defined in this way. 'A word which is regularly used to express one thing gradually comes to express another thing somewhat like the first: but the first thing is usually easier to understand than the second'.

One would naturally ask, 'What words are easiest to understand?', and the answer would be, words that appeal to the senses, especially to the senses of sight and sound and touch and taste.

It was on somewhat the same principle that the Egyptians, when they wished to denote the idea of 'brightness', drew a little picture of the sun; thus expressing the abstract idea in a concrete form. It is hard to imagine how else such ideas could have been denoted.

(iv) *'Pig', in 'he is a pig'.*

Something like this simple and easy word 'see', is the easy word 'pig'. A pig was known to be greedy, and a pig was a thing which people could see. Hence it became a convenient symbol for *greediness*, which is, of course, a mental quality.

'He is a *pig*', therefore, was a convenient way of stating 'he resembles a pig in being greedy'.

Here again the principle of Economy has been at work: it was shorter and more striking to say 'he is a pig' than to say 'he resembles a pig in one important characteristic'.

(v) *'St Paul's'.*

'St. Paul's' could not have been often used by itself at first; for, by itself, it might have referred, not only to St. Paul's Cathedral, or School, or Station, but also to St. Paul's Epistles.

After a time, however, owing to constant use in such sentences as 'there was a good service at St. Paul's Cathedral', there had ceased to be any need to express 'Cathedral' in certain contexts, and so people have been able to discard it. It is not necessary to discard it; but it is Economical to do so.

In the same way, the word 'Home', when spoken to the coachman, clearly denotes 'Go home', without there being any necessity for expressing the word 'Go'.

The important principle here is that this Economy, or *Ellipse*, as it is called, can make words entirely change their functions, so that 'Home', instead of being a Substantive, is turned into a command, an Imperative.

(vi) '*Pagan*'.

The word *paganus* at first denoted a man of the country or village; and, by contrast with the word Urbanus, which denoted the polished man of the town, it acquired a bad sense of one who was outside the best circle, one who was unorthodox: hence its present sense. Compare also *Villanus* and our English word *villain*, which at first was connected with *villein*, and had no bad meaning. These would be instances of *Degeneration*.

(vii) '*Humble*'.

The word 'humble' illustrates the opposite process, which may be called *Improvement* or *Amelioration*.

At first it meant 'low-lying', being connected with *humus* the ground. Then it came to be used as a term of abuse, but later on, through the influence of Christianity, it was shown that the humble man was so far from being a vile character and despicable, that he was a most excellent character and amiable. The touch of Christianity raised this word, as it has raised so many words, from the low level to the high level. But, on the whole, the process of Degeneration in the meaning of words seems to be the commoner.

PART IX.

SOME IDIOMATIC USES OF GREEK PARTICLES, WITH LATIN EQUIVALENTS.

48. The Function of a Particle.

48. *What is meant by a Particle? Illustrate your answer.*

The word 'Particle' has various meanings: thus sometimes we find Conjunctions like ὅτε and *ut* classed as Particles, as in 49 (below); but the word 'Particle' is here meant to be used rather in the following sense.

An Outline-picture without shading and without colouring may give a rough and vague idea of a piece of scenery; but *shading and colouring* will generally help to make the idea more accurately and more definitely realised: a speech without change of tone and without movement may give a general notion: but modulation of the voice and variety of 'gesture' will generally help to make the notion more interesting and impressive. Somewhat similarly a piece of good Greek without its Particles might give a rough and vague idea, and a general notion, but Particles would usually add a kind of shading and colouring and emphasis—they would serve as a sort of 'gesture' and facial expression: they make the idea less bare and cold, they help it to be more accurately and more definitely realised, they make it more interesting and impressive, they cover the bare skeleton with flesh, and that flesh with clothing: they give *life and warmth.*

The Greeks were especially fond of 'Particles': they loved to give the key-note of a sentence by one of those little words in which some Languages are so poor: thus, if a Greek had been told that the enemy was coming, and had wished to say 'All right, I don't care: *let* them come', probably he would not merely have said 'let them come', but would have used the Particle δ' οὖν: cp. οἱ δ' οὖν βοώντων.

Yet, while we give the Greeks all credit for the subtle shades of meaning denoted by these Particles, let us remember that the French can produce much the same effect by their '*gestures*', and other people by the *tone* of their voice, whereby the idea of anger, scorn, pity, or amusement, can be conveyed: Greeks had the Note of their word to some extent fixed already (see p. 193): there was less chance of conveying ideas by a difference of Note, and Particles were the means they chose, almost of necessity.

49. Some Greek Conjunctions.

49. *What words had the Greek Language, by which it could express*

(*a*) '*but*' (*however*);
(*b*) '*for*' (*because*);
(*c*) '*and*' (*moreover*);
(*d*) '*so*' (*therefore*);
(*e*) '*if*';
(*f*) '*who*' (*Relative*)?

The following List should be enlarged: it may prove useful for Greek Verses, where a metrical variety is of so much importance. See further Paley's *Greek Particles*, or Liddell and Scott's *Greek Lexicon*.

(*a*) '*but*' ('*however*'): . . . δέ, ἀλλά, ὁμῶς, ἀλλ' ὁμῶς, καὶ μὴν, καί τοι, . . . μέντοι, etc.;

(*b*) '*for*' ('*because*'): . . . γάρ, καὶ γάρ (see below), ἐπεί, ἐπεὶ δὴ, ἐπεί τοι ['since, as you know', etc.], ἐπεί [δή] περ, ὡς, ὅτι, etc.;

(*c*) '*and*' ('*moreover*'): καί, . . . δέ, ἔτι δέ, καὶ δὴ καί, etc.;

(*d*) '*so*' ('*therefore*'): . . . οὖν, τοίγαρ, τοιγάρουν, . . . δή, . . . ἄρα [Poetic], ὥστε, etc.;

(*e*) '*if*': εἰ, εἴ γε ['that is to say, if . . .'], εἰ δή ['if it is indeed true that'], καὶ δή [Poetic, καὶ δὴ τέθνηκα 'supposing I *am* dead'], etc.;

(*f*) '*who*' (Relative): ὅς, ὅστις [(*a*) 'whosoever', or (*b*) 'if or since he'], ὅστις γε [(*b*)], ὅσπερ [(*b*), and (*c*) 'the very same man who . . .'], ὅσπερ δή [do.], ὅσπερ γε δή, etc.

50. Some Greek Particles.

50. *What Particles might the Greeks have used to represent the shades of meaning in the following Sentences? Give Latin Equivalents where you can.**

(*a*) '*who on earth . . .?*'
(*b*) '*either . . . or . . .*';
(*c*) '*whether . . . or . . .*';
(*d*) '*some one will object and say . . .; then I answer . . .*';
(*e*) '*the best of all*,' '*far the best*';
(*f*) '*unless of course . . .*' (ironical);
(*g*) '*nay rather, I should say . . .*';
(*h*) '*for instance*';
(*i*) '*be that as it may*';
(*j*) '*forsooth*';
(*k*) '*surely it is . . .?*';
(*l*) '*surely it is not . . .?*';
(*m*) '*here comes A*';
(*n*) '*then and not till then*';
(*o*) '*only on this condition*'.

(*a*) '*who on earth . . .?*': τίς ποτε; καὶ τίς; τίς καί; quisnam?

(*b*) '*either . . . or . . .*': ἤ . . . ἤ . . ., or the first can have ἤτοι . . ., and the second ἢ καὶ . . . 'or else', or ἤτοι . . .

* For many of these idioms I am much indebted to the Rev. A. H. Cooke (of King's Coll., Camb.), and the Rev. Bertram Pollock.

ἢ καὶ . . . can both be used; aut . . . aut . . .; vel . . . vel . . .;

(*c*) '*whether . . . or . . .*': εἴτε . . . εἴτε . . ., or either or both may have εἴτ' οὖν . . ., or the second may have εἴτε καὶ . . .; sive . . ., sive (seu);

(*d*) '*some one will object and say . . .*': ἀλλ' ἐρεῖ τις . . ., or ἀλλὰ γὰρ . . ., or ἀλλὰ νὴ Δία [in Oratory], the two latter introducing the objection in 'Oratio Recta': the Answer ('then I reply') is introduced by ἀλλὰ . . ., and further objection to this by yet another ἀλλὰ . . .; dixerit (or dicet) aliquis (or quispiam), or, at enim [like ἀλλὰ γὰρ . . .];

(*e*) '*the best of all*': ἄριστος, πάντων ἄριστος, ἄριστος δή, ἀγαθὸς εἴ (περ) τις (καὶ) ἄλλος; vel optimus, bonus si quis alius;

(*f*) '*unless of course . . .*' (ironical); εἰ μὴ ἄρα . . ., (sometimes) εἰ μή τις . . .; nisi forte . . .;

(*g*) '*nay rather, I should say . . .*' . . . μὲν οὖν [τοὐμὸν μὲν οὖν 'no! mine']; immō verō;

(*h*) '*for instance*': γοῦν [in the sense of 'at any rate'], γὰρ, αὐτίκα, οἷον [esp. 'Philosophic']; nam or enim (sometimes);

(*i*) '*be that as it may*': . . . γε, . . . δ' οὖν, ἀλλ' ὁμῶς (sometimes); (at)tamen, saltem;

(*j*) '*forsooth*': δή, δῆθεν, δήπου (sometimes); scīlicet;

(*k*) '*surely it is . . .?*': ἆρα . . .; ἆρ' οὐ . . .; οὐ . . .; οὐ γὰρ . . .; πῶς [γὰρ] οὐ . . .; nonne, -ne (sometimes);

(*l*) '*surely it is not . . .?*': ἆρα μὴ . . ., μῶν . . ., πῶς [γὰρ] . . .; quid? (followed by Question); num . . .?;

(*m*) '*here comes A*': καὶ μὴν . . .;

(*n*) '*then and not till then*': τότε δή, εἶτα δή; tum demum;

(*o*) '*only on this condition*': οὕτω δή; ita tandem, sic dēmum.

51. Some Greek and Latin Idioms.

51. *Mention the chief idiomatic meanings of the following:—*

(*a*) δή, καὶ δή, καὶ γάρ, τοι, καί, τις, ὡς, δ' οὖν, γοῦν, ἦ μήν, μή, ἄρα, μὲν οὖν,

(*b*) *īdem, ille quidem, ita . . . ut . . .*,

Vide the *Lexicon*, for details.

(*a*) δὴ: 'then', 'as you see', 'in truth' (εἰ δὴ 'if indeed'), ironical (cp. δῆθεν), emphasising (ἄριστος δή, πολλὰ δή, οὕτω δή, τοῦτο δή, τότε δή, etc.), καὶ δὴ 'supposing', καὶ δὴ καὶ ('moreover'); καὶ γὰρ 'for . . . also', 'for even . . .', 'for in truth . . .', 'in truth';

τοι 'it is true that' (especially in maxims, etc.);

καὶ 'and', 'then', 'even', 'also', 'or' (sometimes), 'or rather' (do.), and emphasising (καὶ πάλιν '*again*', καὶ νῦν '*now*'), καί τοι ('and yet', etc.); καὶ μὴν 'here comes A', καὶ δὴ καί 'moreover', καὶ δὴ [see above], καὶ τοῦτο 'and that too' (idque);

τις: 'some one (will suffer for it)' [implying that '*you* will suffer for it'], 'perhaps' [εἰ μὴ φίλος τις 'unless perhaps a friend . . .'], ὅστις 'whoever' or 'since he', etc.;

ὡς: 'when', 'because' [with Indicative or Participle, e.g. ὡς ταῦθ' οὕτως ἔχοντα 'under the impression that this is so': ὡς δῆθεν ironical: ὡς γέρων 'considering that he is an old man'], ὥσπερ 'just as', etc.;

δ' οὖν: 'be that as it may', 'I don't care' [οἱ δ' οὖν βοώντων 'well! let them shout'], σύ δ' οὖν 'but *you* . . .', [as opposed to ἐγὼ μὲν οὖν 'I . . .'], εἰ δ' οὖν γενήσεται 'but if it *should* happen';

γοῦν: 'at any rate', 'for instance' (sometimes);

ἦ μὴν: 'of a truth' [especially in promises, threats, and oaths];

μή: besides its uses in Negative Commands and Prayers, and in Conditional and some Relative Sentences [e.g. ὃς ἂν μὴ ποιῇ ἀδικεῖ], it is found in οὐ μὴ ποιήσῃς (and ποιήσεις), and in Questions like μή ἐστι 'is it?', etc.;

ἄρα: ' then ', *εἰ μὴ ἄρα* ' unless, of course, . . .', *παρῆλθες ἄρα* ' so you came, did you ? ', *ὡς ἄρα* something like Latin *quod* with the Subjunctive;

μὲν οὖν: ' well then . . .', ' or rather I should say ' (corrective), emphasising *ἐγὼ* (' I for my part '), etc.

(*b*) *īdem*, *ille quidem*, and *ita . . . ut . . .* can all be illustrated by ' he was an excellent man, but an utter fool ':

optimus erat, īdem stultissimus;

optimus ille quidem erat, sed stultissimus;

ita optimus erat ut esset stultissimus;

ita . . . ut . . . can also be used thus:—

ita abiit ut non videret ' he went away without seeing ';

ita abībō ut nōn videam ' I will go away on condition that I do not see ';

ut tu hōc facis, ita ego faciō ' I do it just as you do ';

ut hac re saepe utitur, ita saepe non utitur ' while . . . yet . . .'

PART X.

TEXTUAL CRITICISM, AND HOW TO EMEND.

52 (a). The Meaning of the terms σχόλια, uncials, palimpsest.

52. (*a*) *What is meant by the words σχόλια, uncials, palimpsest?*

For details, see Gow's *Companion to School Classics*, Lindsay's *Introduction to Latin Textual Criticism* (and the works to which he refers), Rutherford's *Thucydides*, Book IV., and Notes to Classical Authors, *ad lib.*: also the various Emendations proposed from time to time in the *Classical Review*, etc.

σχόλια.

Long after Authors had written, much of their Language became hard to understand, and Γραμματικοί or Litterati added Glossaries, Paraphrases or Translations, and Notes: there were not 'Grammarians' in the same sense that Roby and Goodwin are: they had a wider field.

If the word σχόλια is used in its limited sense (see Rutherford, *Thuc.*, IV., p. xxxiii), they are Notes on some word or phrase or passage, saying what seemed to a certain School (especially the Alexandrine School) to be the meaning of this word or phrase or passage. Most Classical Authors had many σχόλια.

The Alexandrian Scholiasts lived about 260 B.C. and later, while Servius and others (of Rome) lived between 300 and 500 A.D.

At first these σχόλια were published separately: some have their Authors' names (e.g. Servius' on Vergil), others are anonymous. Most of the σχόλια that we possess, however, are *compiled* by some 'Scholiast' or 'Scholiasts' from the Notes of previous 'Scholiasts', and are not found separate but in the margin of the Classical text.

Gloss.

A strange word, especially a foreign word, was called a γλῶσσα, and the explanation of it was called a γλώσσημα: later on, the word 'Gloss' came to be used of an easier word to explain a harder word.

The 'Gloss' was written either in the margin, close to the hard word, or else over the hard word.

Sometimes 'Glosses' might either

(i) oust the words which they explained (see τυραννοῦντ' and κοιρανοῦντ', p. 247), or

(ii) creep into the text as well as these words (see κηρεσσιφορητοὺς οὓς Κῆρες φορέουσι, p. 247), or

(iii) blend with these words into a single Construction.

In all three Cases there was liable to be some further alteration for the sake of sense or metre: thus, in (ii), καὶ would often connect the word and its 'Gloss'.

'*Uncials*' in Greek texts mean Capitals, being at first 'inch-high letters': these Capitals tended to become 'rounded off' and abbreviated, when written, so that Σ appeared as C, E as ϵ, M as m; moreover, the letters were often run into one another. Both these processes made writing quicker, and helped the Capitals or Uncials (or Majuscules) to become more like our small letters (or Minuscules), which are called Running or Cursive hand.

The change would therefore be from large angular-looking Capitals [or Uncials or Majuscules] separate from each other, to smaller and rounder letters [Minuscules], written continuously [or Cursively].

Note.—In Early MSS. we do not find Accents, nor yet Divisions between words: thus τὸν δὲ and τόνδε would be written in the same way.

Uncials *in Latin* are not the same as Capitals: some Latin MSS. are entirely in Capitals, others in Uncials, many of which are like the letters of Cursive hand, being

(i) not so tall, and

(ii) not so angular (cp. m and M).

Then came Half-Uncials: then the Minuscules or Cursive hands, of which the most important was the Caroline (see under St. Benedict, below).

Latin Capitals, Uncials, and Cursive hand all show Abbreviations, e.g. $\overline{\text{QNM}}$ (quoniam): see further p. 247.

Palimpsest.

Both Greeks and Romans sometimes wrote on parchment or papyrus, with ink and a quill pen (calamus). A parchment thus written on could be cleaned by a sponge and then again written on: if the cleaning was done directly after the first writing, it was more or less complete, but, if it was only done soon afterwards, traces of the first writing remained; and some of our most useful Texts are 'Palimpsests', i.e. 'first writings' over which something fresh has been written: indeed, we have MSS. on which yet a third layer appears. The 'Instituta' of Gaius had over them some of Jerome's writings.

52 (b). Some Codices.

(*b*) *Explain the following names of Codices: Laurentianus, Mediceus, Palatinus, A, V, P.*

Codex.

A *Codex*, in one sense, was a small wooden tablet (δέλτος) with wax on it; upon this men wrote Notes with a stilus or pointed instrument: *codicillus*, the diminutive form, came to mean a small Note (cp. the codicil of a will).

But in Textual Criticism a Codex meant a kind of book, having its writing on both sides of the pages, but having it

(i) written not printed,

(ii) usually written continuously, not word by word,

(iii) with Notes, either above words or in the margins (p. 238).

Laurentianus. At Florence there was a Library attached to the Church of San Lorenzo: it was composed chiefly of

(α) the Public Library of San Marco, founded in 1444 by *Cosmo de Medici:* besides this it contained

(β) the private Library of the Medicis, and

(γ) some Latin MSS from the Library of Leopold.

Hence the Codices in this Library at Venice were called Laurentiani, Leopoldini Laurentiani, and Medicei (as well as Florentini and Marci).

Palatinus.

(α) The Vatican Library at Rome included many MSS. forcibly removed from the Palatine Library at Heidelberg in the 17th century;

(β) Besides this are the Codices Palatini still at Heidelberg.

For other instances of MSS. of different names, but belonging to the same library now, see Gow, p. 19, foll., from which most of the above is taken.

A (Ambrosianus);
V (Venetus);
P (Parisinus);
but besides these, we have A after various MSS., e.g. Venetus A (of Homer, see below), and Leyden A and B (of Lucretius).

52 (c). Some well-known MSS.

(*c*) *Mention three or four well-known MSS., with dates.*

1. *Laurentianus,* also called Mediceus (see above), contains Sophocles (seven plays), Aeschylus (do.), and Apollonius Rhodius (Argonautica): it belongs to the 11th century. It is not complete, but has plentiful σχόλια (p. 237) and some Introductory Notes.

2. The *Ravenna* MS., also of the 11th century, contains all the eleven plays of Aristophanes, but it is not the highest authority for all of them.

3. The *Ambrosian* MS. of Plautus is one of the oldest Latin MSS., belonging to the 4th or 5th century, A.D.: it does not contain all Plautus, and is a Palimpsest (p. 239).

It is now in the Ambrosian Library at Milan.

4. The *Bembinus* MS. of Terence once belonged to Cardinal Bembo, who died in the 16th century: it was a 5th century MS. and is now in the Vatican.

5. (α) *Vaticanus* was one of the Vergil MSS., which are very numerous: it belongs to the 4th or 5th century, as does

(β) *Palatinus* [now in the Vatican, see p. 240];

(γ) *Mediceus* [or Laurentianus, p. 240] has corrections which were made at the end of the 5th century.

52 (d). Dates of some MSS.

(d) To what dates are most MSS. to be assigned, and for what reasons?

For Details, see Gow (p. 31 foll.).

There are some early manuscripts, such as the three fragments of the Iliad (on papyrus), dating from the 1st century, B.C.

Few manuscripts, however, are as early as the 4th and 5th centuries, A.D. (see Vaticanus, above): more are of the 10th to the 13th, and still more of the 13th to the 15th (see below).

The Date can sometimes be determined by

(i) Historical facts and traditions (p. 240),

(ii) the writing, whither capitals or uncials, with no divisions between the words, and with no punctuation, or minuscules, with punctuation: there are also intermediate stages;

(iii) the spellings, abbreviations and contractions.

There are other evidences also: see, for instance, Thompson's *Palaeography*.

52 (e). The best MSS. of Homer.

(*e*) *What are the best MSS. of Homer?*

There are many MSS. of Homer, as of Vergil, and most of them have σχόλια (p. 237).

1. Aristarchus, the great Alexandrine, prepared two editions, making use of a received text: many of Aristarchus' Notes come to us in σχόλια (see p. 237). The work of Aristarchus largely influenced

2. Venetus A, of the Iliad (10th century); there are also, for the Iliad,

3. a Laurentianus (p. 240) and

4. a Townleianus [so called, like the Harleian MSS., from the person who bequeathed them to the British Museum].

For the Odyssey, of which the MSS. are not as old as those of the Iliad, we have

5. a Venetus (12th century), and

6. a Townleianus (13th century), and

7. an Ambrosianus [so called from the Ambrosian Library at Milan] (14th century).

To these we may add

8. MSS. containing only σχόλια.

52 (f). Some influences of Alexandrine Grammarians and others on learning and on MSS.

(*f*) *Say a few words about the influence, on learning and on MSS., of the following, with approximate dates:*

(i) *The Alexandrine 'Grammarians'*; (ii) *St. Benedict*; (iii) *Alcuin of York*; (iv) *Poggio*; (v) *The Capture of Constantinople*; (vi) *Aldus Manutius.*

(i) *The Alexandrine 'Grammarians'.*

After Alexander had conquered the East, and had founded cities in many places, and had died, his successors, the Διαδόχοι, divided the great Empire of the East among them: a part of this Empire was Egypt, and in Egypt Alexandria (called after Alexander) had its famous Library and was the chief seat of of 'culture'.

In Alexandria flourished Poets, such as Theocritus and Callimachus, and also learned men, and a School of men who interpreted and wrote Notes on various Classical Authors, beginning with *Homer*. Among these men were Zenodotus, Aristophanes, and Aristarchus.

Aristophanes of Byzantium lived about 260 B.C., and was Librarian of the great Library at Alexandria: he was the founder of the School, and interpreted Homer, writing σχόλια (p. 237), and Notes on the authenticity, the punctuation, and the Accents and 'breathings'. He also edited other Authors, e.g. Pindar and Plato.

Zenodotus wrote about such subjects as Dialects, Poetic Constructions, meanings of words, the Article, and the Dual and Plural.

Aristarchus of Samothrace lived considerably later, being, in fact, a pupil of the School of which Aristophanes was the founder: he revised the text of Homer, arranged it in books, removed interpolations, paid attention to words, metre, and Accents, and wrote Notes on mythology. He also edited other Authors, e.g. Pindar, Aeschylus, Sophocles, and Aristophanes.

(ii) *St. Benedict*, who was the founder of the Benedictine order of Monks, and died before 550, saw that in monasteries, as elsewhere, 'Satan finds some mischief still for idle hands to do'; so he founded, near Naples, a model monastery, in which MSS. were to be copied: this was to be part of the regular routine. It was all the more creditable, as he was not himself a learned man.

It was in the copying-rooms or Scriptoria of this monastery and of many others which followed in Western Europe, that the Classics were reproduced and multiplied, and that Cursive hand (p. 238) was developed. A *Scriptorium* is still to be seen at Gloucester.

(iii) *Alcuin* had a School at York: the work done by this School was very narrow and 'theological', for

(*a*) 'music' meant 'Church-chanting',

(*b*) 'astronomy' meant 'the calculation of Easter',

(*c*) poetry was discouraged; but still there was some benefit from the teaching of Grammar, Logic, Rhetoric, Arithmetic, etc.; so that when the illiterate Charlemagne, who lived about 800 A.D., wished to introduce 'culture' at Tours, he asked Alcuin to found a School for him: other Schools followed, e.g. at Lyons and Rheims.

Soon after 800, the Schools and Universities grew quickly.

(iv) *Poggio* Bracciolini, who died shortly after 1450, was one of those learned Italians who, by some means, or rather by *any* means—for they bought, begged, borrowed, or stole—got possession of all the Classical MSS. they could in the Benedictine Monasteries or elsewhere, and, at the Pope's bidding, brought them back to Italy.

This keenness on the Classics was mainly due to the Italian Literature founded by Dante, Petrarch, and Boccaccio (about 1300 to 1350).

(v) *The Capture of Constantinople by the Turks*, in 1453, drove many learned Greeks, and with them many valuable MSS., to Italy: thus the Revival of Learning or the Renaissance began, and then from Italy spread, through the Pope's infiuence, over Northern Europe.

(vi) *Aldus Manutius* and his family lived in Venice between 1450, when printing was invented, and 1600: they, with other publishing 'firms' (e.g. in Florence), provided Greek books, with Latin translations and Notes, and also Greek Grammars, thus putting the Greek Classics within the reach of Scholars everywhere.

53. Causes of the commonest mistakes in MSS.

53. *How have the commonest mistakes in MSS. arisen? Invent or quote instances.*

Copyists were and are human: often ignorant, sometimes lazy or sleepy, with little encouragement to think of what they were writing down, and occasionally wishing to write down sense where they could see no sense, and altering accordingly—do we wonder that they have made so many mistakes? Do we not rather wonder that they have made so few?

Some simple instances will serve as an introduction: for details, see the books referred to on p. 237 (above).

Most of these instances are from copies of some Papers of mine by a clerk, who had had a fairly good general education, and wrote well, but did not know anything about the Classics.

1. Alterations made by the clerk: See on 3 below, 'St. Henery', and possibly on 2, TUPANNIE;

2. [In an Essay on Greek Tyrants]:

(*a*) [Heading of the Essay] TUPANNIE;

(*b*) [quotation from the Essay] 'the Greek Tyrants also introduced new State-*warships*';

3. [this occurred in orders for Books] 'please send *In a Garden* . . . and the *St. Henery* Edition of Sir Walter Scott';

4. [Technical term] 'capitis *dēminūtō*';

5. [in some Grammar Notes] 'dīgnus notārī "worthy to be *brandied*"';

6. [in some Philology Notes, see p. 62]

(*a*) 'according to Grimm's Law, *g* became *cork*';

(*b*) *vide bimus*;

7. '*the the* city';

8. (*a*) [Aesch. Ag. 549]

τρίτον δὲ τὸν νῦν τυραννοῦντ᾽ ἐποψομαι,

(*b*) [Iliad, viii., 528]

κηρεσσιφορήτους οὓς Κῆρες φορέουσι :

9. [in some Roman History Notes]

'the order of the letters *SPOR* is in itself a sign of the Senate's position';

10. [do.]: 'the Consuls were liable to be *tired* after holding office for a year';

11. Combinations of mistakes: see below, p. 247.

1. It is possible that both No. 2 (*a*) and No. 3 will include No. 1 (Alterations made by the clerk).

In 2 (*a*) the clerk ought to have written TVPANNIC: but he wrote V and C wrong, producing TUPANNIE. Probably he thought this was an English title, and altered to U and E so as to connect the word with 'twopenny!'

In 2 (*b*) there was again the mistake of a letter, 'w*o*rships' being written as 'w*a*rships'.

In 3, we have *mistakes due to dictation*: for 'Enoch Arden' does not look like 'In a Garden', nor 'St. Henery' like 'Centenary': here, again, it is possible that the clerk put in the H of 'Henery' to 'make sense': it probably was not in the dictated word.

It must be remembered here that 'Dictation' will include words which the clerk first read, and then '*said aloud to himself*', and then wrote down according to the sound.

4. Here the clerk left out a letter: he should have written dēminūt*i*ō.

5. In 'worthy to be brand*i*ed' on the other hand, he has *put in a letter*.

6. (*a*) 'According to Grimm's Law, *g* became *c* or *k*' was the original: here there has been a *Wrong Division*, as also in (*b*), vidēbimus, where perhaps the clerk was thinking of the more familiar vide 'see'.

8. (*a*) Here τυραννοῦντ', which will not scan, was a *Gloss* (p. 238) on the less common word κοιρανοῦντ', and it appears in *the place of* this word ; whereas

in (*b*) the explanation of κηρεσσιφορήτους, viz. οὓς Κῆρες φορέουσι, appears in addition to the original word.

9. Here ' SPQR ', the *Abbreviation* for Senatus populusque Romanus, has been mistaken for ' SPOR ' [see 2, above] ;

10. ' *tired* ', instead of ' *tried* ' shows the letters *i* and *r* in the *wrong order*. I recently had the word ' weird ' put as ' wired ', in a printer's Proof.

11. Gow gives some excellent instances of *Combined Errors :* e.g.

(i) [Sen. de Prov.] : laeti fluentem *e lorica sua* sanguinem : here fluentemeloricasua → fluentem*m* [repeated letter, 7] el*i* [inserted, 5, perhaps owing to a glimpse of the following *i*] oricasu [*a* omitted, 4] : besides this, we have of course a changed division of words, 6, and a correction by a copyist, 1 ; possibly the stages were fluentem-*m*elori-casua → fluentem-mel*i*ori-casu ;

(ii) [Sen. Epp., xiv. 14] : videbimus an *sapienti opera r. p. danda sit :* here sapientioperarpdandasit → sapientior [letters omitted, 4] a*per* [changed order, 10, and letter inserted, 5, and changed division, 6] d*e* [corrected, 1] nda sit. Possibly the stages were sapienti-opera-r-p- [rei publicae] danda-sit → sapienti*ora*-rpdanda-sit → sapientiora-*per*d*e*nda-si(n)t ;

(iii) [Pl. Pers. 546] : quia specie quidem : here quiaspecie-quidem → quiaspe*x* [corrected, 1] iequidem [changed division, 6], the stages being quia-specie-quidem → qui-aspeci-equidem → qui aspe*x*i equidem.

We may now consider some of these in more detail.

1. *Alterations.*

Most alterations were made because the copyist wished to give better sense, or (what he believed to be) a better form or better grammar : thus, in 11 above, it would be natural to correct sit to sint, because of sapientiora. Thucydides' text has suffered terribly, because copyists and editors have 'corrected' and modernised his forms; Homer has perhaps suffered still more. In the case of Thucydides, the comparison of an Inscription with the text in which he quotes it shows a very large number of small modernisings.

If a copyist had omitted a line, he would often put it in at the bottom of the page: this would itself be an alteration, and might lead to a serious mistake on the part of the next copyist.

Some few alterations have been due to a less honest motive, as when the text of one Gospel has been altered so that it may agree with the text of another Gospel, or in the well-known instance where the Athenians were said to have altered Homer (Iliad, 2, 553-555) so as to give themselves glory.

2. *Mistakes where something has been wrongly seen* ('warships').

Greek and Latin Capitals and Cursive-hand may give at least four different forms for a single letter, e.g. Δ D δ d: and these four classes must usually be considered separately. For instance,

(i) *Greek Capitals* A, Δ, Λ; ΑΛ, M, IN, ΔI, etc., might have been confused: but

(ii) *not Greek Cursive-hand* α, δ, λ; αλ, μ, ιν, δι, etc.;

(iii) *Latin Capitals* C, G; but

(iv) *not Latin Cursive-hand* c, g.

It will be good practice to take each of the Alphabets, bearing in mind such forms as the Uncials C Є (Σ E), and to take each Letter *per se*, and consider other Letters with which it might have been confused. Or take instances from Notes on Classical Authors, and classify these.

For instance, under

(i) [*Greek Capitals*], notice the confusion of AN and ΔH, which might explain away certain 'hard' uses of ἄν; notice, however, that ἄν and δή would not be confused so easily as ἄν and αὖ.

The distinction is not always of importance, for, as we know by personal experience, it is often enough that one word should look 'rather like' another: thus see Marcus Aurelius (Rendall's Appendix to his *Translation*), where we find ὁλοσχερῶς for δυσχερῶς (ix. 3), and perhaps φύσει for φησί (v. 6). Gow quotes φόνου and φόβου, nimium and minimum, etc.

Proper names would be especially liable to corruptions: see Gow, p. 56.

3. Mistakes where something has been *wrongly heard* ('St. Henery Edition').

We cannot tell how frequent these may have been, but the constant confusion of η, ει, ι, of αι, ε, etc., point to this origin: thus in M. Aurelius we find ἀποληφθέντων for ἀπολειφθέντων.

4. *Omissions* (dēminūtō).

Madvig's pretty Emendation in Seneca (de Tranq. An., 5, 5) is quoted by Gow: in 'aiebat malle se esse mortuom quam vivere' he inserts nequam after quam: here the word had been omitted because the eye passed from the quam of ne-quam to the quam which looked like the end of nequam: this similarity of ending is called Homoeoteleuton. So in M. Aurelius (iv. 24) we have μόνον omitted after ἄμεινον.

The omission of single Letters is very common, and of course is liable to lead to further errors: thus fac scias could → faccias → facias, 'st cito could → scito, quia si could → quasi, ὑποδύρεσθαι (M. Aurelius, ii. 2) could → ὑποδύεσθαι.

The same will apply to whole lines, especially when the eye passes from the end of one line to the similar ending of the next line, and so omits this second line altogether.

5. *Insertions* ('brand*i*ed').

The converse of these instances is equally easy, e.g. quasi could → quia si. Thus M. Aurelius (i. 17) where καὶ τὸ τοῦ may have been supplanted by καὶ τούτου.

6. *Wrong Division* (cork).

These mistakes are especially liable to lead to others: thus see p. 247 above.

The neatest emendation is Madvig's, to Seneca (Epp. 81, 4), where philosophia unde dicta sit apparet, ipso enim nomine fatetur: *quidam et* sapientiam ita quidam finierunt ut dicerent . . . is corrected to . . . fatetur quid amet ('confesses what it is that it loves', *τί φιλεῖ*). See further, Gow, p. 54, where submoveret ipsa is quoted, for sub vomere et ipsa (Verg. Georg. 2, 356): here the letter *e* is also omitted.

7. *Repetitions* ('the the city').

Gow also quotes celebrabitur for celabitur (Hor. Sat. ii. 4, 11).

8. *Glosses, etc., entering the text.*

See Gow (p. 56), and Rutherford, *Thuc.* iv. (passim).

9. *Abbreviations and contractions* (SPOR).

In M. Aurelius (i. 57), ἄλλοις was read as $\overline{\text{ανοις}}$, an Abbreviation for ἀνθρώποις. Gow mentions that Acts xiii. 23 shows (in two MSS.) $\overline{\text{CPIAN}}$ (σωτηρίαν) for $\overline{\text{CPA}}\overline{\text{IN}}$ (σωτῆρα Ἰησοῦν), where we also see Wrong Order (10).

For a useful list of Latin Abbreviations, see Lindsay, p. 92, foll.: a few may be mentioned here.

ē (em, est, or et),

n̄ (nōn, or nam),

ap̶ (apud),

p̶ (prae; slight signs will make it stand for other words); for 'suprascripts', cp. $\overset{o}{\text{m}}$ (modo), $\overset{c}{\text{n}}$ (nec).

10. *Wrong Order* (t*ire*d).

Et and *te*, *ut* and *tu*, *tamen* and *tamne*, flumina and fulmina, omnia and omina, and hundreds of other instances might be mentioned.

11. *Combinations:* see p. 247.

12. *Unavoidable Faults* will be found where some part of the MSS. was destroyed or obscured: the copyist who was copying from it could not be expected to do more than copy what he found before him. Sometimes, however, if the gap

was small, he would try to fill it up: another copyist might fill it up in quite a different way.

Verses by which the above Classes of Errors may be remembered:

Mistakes may be in letter, line, or word,
if things are altered, wrongly seen or heard,
left out, inserted, or divided wrong,
or else repeated; or if words belong
to Gloss or Comment, entering the text
through carelessness; Abbreviations next,
Contractions, and Wrong Order; oft we find
two or more classes of mistakes combined.

54. When Emendations are most probable, and How to Emend.

54. *When is an Emendation most plausible, and how should one proceed to emend a corrupt passage?*

An Emendation of a passage in an Author is most plausible when

(*a*) it restores good sense (in the given Context), and—in Poetry—

(*b*) restores metre,

(*c*) in accordance with the style and vocabulary of the Author; and also

(*d*) keeps near to the given text,

(*e*) accounts for the corruption having arisen, and

(*f*) does not go against what we know about MSS. in general, and these MSS. of this Author in particular.

Now, supposing we had to emend an English sentence like 5 (*a*): 'according to Grimm's Law, g became cork', what should we do?

First of all we should try to get sense, and—if possible—we should look at the context. Then we should try to find the wrong word or words: here obviously the word *cork* stamps itself, for we know that Grimm's Law deals with the letter g.

Then we should draw a thin line through *cork*, and try to find a word or words which would make sense and be as near as possible to *cork*, i.e. to the word in the text: we should try alternatives, as if it were a Missing-word Competition.

We should choose the Answer which best explained how

the mistake or mistakes might have arisen: thus, *c* or *k* would not only make sense, but it would be very near to the text, and would easily give rise to the mistake, i.e. by Wrong Division.

The following method, then, might be found useful:—

1. First read the passage through and *get the general sense* as far as you can. It is needless to say that the meaning becomes far clearer if you know the context.

2. Then try to *find the wrong word or words.*

3. Copy out the passage or the corrupt part, first of all in capital letters, and then in ordinary writing, but don't divide up the passage into words; write *consecutively.*

4. Draw a thin line through what you think to be the wrong word or words, and treat this '*gap*' as a kind of 'missing word' in a missing-word competition. At first don't trouble about the form but only about the *sense* which is required.

5. Put down alternative words which seem to you to give the required sense.

6. Then try to reconcile the sense and the corrupt forms: that is to say, *insert tentatively new words which will give the right sense and be as near as possible to the wrong form.*

7. This restored word, or these restored words, must of course, as a rule, contain about as many letters as the missing word or words, and must fit in with the metre, if it is poetry, and anyhow must be in harmony with the syntax and the style and vocabulary of the author.

8. Then try to find the various *causes* of those errors which would be illustrated by this instance. Especially common would be the changed divisions of words, with alterations or omissions or additions, and frequently with glosses creeping into the text. You must also allow for later alterations. State how your emended passage became the corrupt passage.

9. Illustrate the various errors and changes as far as possible.

10. It is needless to say that a knowledge of *MSS.* in general, and of the MSS. of the particular Author, and their

Dates, their commonest errors, their spelling, and their abbreviations, is of the greatest importance: to this may be added a knowledge of how to *compare* various MSS.

11. Both σχόλια (p. 237) and Glosses, of which there are large collections, are also not only helpful but indispensable: thus cp. Rutherford's *Thucydides*, especially.

These *Verses* may help to fix this method in the mind:—

First get the *sense*, then find the flaw,
the word or words you'd fain restore:
these in a bracket now should stand
in capitals and cursive-hand.
Then try to change them for the best.
The faulty words by sense are guessed,
by metre, style of Author, next
by nearness to the given text.
Show reasons for the alterations,
then add appropriate illustrations,
[N.B.] Learn all you can of MSS.:
then danger of mistakes is less.

Practice in Textual Criticism and Emendation.

1. *Notice* the mistakes which *you yourself* and others make in copying out *anything:* and classify these mistakes. You will be most likely to understand these, and to be interested in them, and to remember them.

2. Take a collection, or make a collection, of *Emendations:* first try to find the right solution *by yourself*, and compare your result with the 'Fair Copy'; then *work out the different stages backwards and forwards*, from the correct to the corrupt and from the corrupt to the correct. See p. 248.

3. Rather than do thousands of different instances, *do a few very thoroughly* and again and again, for instance those on p. 247 foll., until you know all their ins and outs.

4. Take the *Letters of the Alphabet* one by one, first Greek Capitals, then Greek minuscules, and so on, and work out for yourself the Letters which might *look like* any given Letters· e.g. see p. 248 above, for Α Λ Δ, etc.

5. It might be worth while to do the same with certain *sounds*, especially such sounds as Greek ει.

PART XI.

A FEW SCHOLARS AND PHILOLOGISTS, AND THEIR SERVICES.

> " *Look unto the rock*
> *whence ye are hewn.*"

55 (a). Some leading Philologists and their services.

55. *Mention a few of the services done by the following to*
(*a*) *Philology ;*
(*b*) *Scholarship. Give the date of the death of each under* (*b*).

(*a*) (i) *Philologists of the New School;* (ii) *Greek and Latin Philologists;* (iii) *Sir W. Jones;* (iv) *Leibnitz;* (v) *Hermann;* (vi) *Schlegel;* (vii) *Bopp;* (viii) *Grimm;* (ix) *Pott;* (x) *Schliecher;* (xi) *Georg. Curtius.*

(*a*) (i) *Philologists of the New School*, of whom Brugmann may be taken as a type, have the following characteristics :—

1. they try to show the relations of the various members of the Indo-European or Māter-Language, and to reconstruct it: see p. 159, foll.;

2. they do this by examining the *Data*, which are

α. the Historical Data in Single Languages, i.e. the Comparison of Earlier and Later forms: cp. p. 44;

β. the Dialects and Spoken Languages, as well as the Literary Languages (see p. 27);

3. they employ Scientific Methods and Principles, e.g.

α. the Comparative Method (not confining themselves to any one or two Languages): see p. 20;

β. the proceeding from the known (e.g. how Latin became the Romance Languages, p. 28) to the unknown: see p. 62;

γ. Phonetic Laws or Laws of Sound-change (p. 66), as opposed to such theories as that *s* 'sometimes' became *r* in Latin;

δ. Association or Analogy (p. 67). For further details, see notes on the Semi-vowels (p. 171), Gutturals (p. 173), etc.

(ii) *Greek and Latin Philologists.*

The Greeks

1. regarded all other Languages as 'barbarous'; the field for study was at present too narrow;

2. they treated Language 'philosophically', with more regard to its origin (see Plato's *Cratylus*), and to *the constructions* and meanings of words (see Zenodotus, p. 243), than to the Analysis of words. But

3. the Alexandrine School did good work with regard to Homer and the Greek Dialects, etc.

Latin Philologists also had too narrow a field, not taking other Languages into account, and not considering even their own Inscriptions as valuable evidence (see p. 56).

(iii) *Sir W. Jones.*

Before the study of Sanskrit by Englishmen, near the beginning of this century, the field of research was narrow: in fact, in the previous centuries Hebrew had been regarded as the parent of all Languages: this was due to the Theological bias.

The study of Sanskrit not only showed more clearly the relation of Greek and Latin to Indian, but also introduced a new kind of Grammar, viz. the *minute examination of forms*: every tiny thing was of importance in the sacred writings of the Brahmins, the Vedas.

Sir W. Jones and T. H. Colebrook noticed how Sanskrit resembled Greek and Latin

α. in its Vocabulary, or words: see the list on p. 85 foll.;

β. in the arrangements and uses of words in Sentences (Syntax); and

γ. in the parts of words (Analysis).

They decided that Sanskrit, Greek, and Latin, had some common source, perhaps no longer extant: they founded the Asiatic Society.

At first Sanskrit was supposed to be the Mother-Language of Greek and Latin: then Zend (old Persian) was discovered, and a new theory had to be found: see Schlegel and Bopp (below).

(iv) *Leibnitz* said that we must work from the known to the unknown: we must not merely apply theories, but must collect facts and get theories from them. This is the Inductive Method, which is so prominent a feature of the New School's work.

(v) *Hermann* examined the Ancient Grammarians and the Greek Dialects, and applied 'Philosophical' Principles to Language: he erred in supposing that people set about changing a Language as consciously as they set about building a house. His method was not either Historical or Comparative (p. 259).

(vi) *Schlegel* suggested an origin for *Inflection:* he said that some Languages were organic, expressing meaning by changes in the Root itself, while others—degenerated from these—were inorganic, expressing meaning by adding to the Root other elements (words or particles) from outside the Root. Apart from the difficulty of seeing what he means, we must notice his fallacy of supposing that modern Languages are 'degenerate', because they are more 'Analytic' (see below). Bacon also fell into this fallacy.

(vii) *Bopp* said that Endings were additions to a Root from the outside (e.g. to the Root γραφ- would be added -ήσεται): he said that in *Chinese* we see Roots alone, not coalescing with one another; that in *Semitic Languages* we see Roots, sometimes modified, and sometimes coalescing with one another to form Compound Words; that in the Indo-European Language we also see this Coalescing or Composition: thus he said that the *-s* of λόγο-ς was once a separate word meaning 'he', the -ος of μένος a separate word meaning 'be(ing)', and that λυθήσομαι (cp. p. 127) was made up of several words, e.g. -θη- of τίθημι.

He also looked on Modern Languages as 'decayed'.

He introduced something like the idea of Laws, but he called them Laws of Gravity, and he did not make them sufficiently strict: see p. 66.

Bopp also made contributions to Comparative Syntax, such as the Local Theory of the Cases.

(viii) *Grimm* was

1. the first 'Historical' Grammarian (though he specially studied the Teutonic Languages), and

2. the first to insist on the importance of the Spoken as opposed to the written Language;

3. he also first introduced the real 'idea' of Law, though not in its strictest form: see Verner's Law (p. 63).

(ix) *Pott* studied Phonetics and the derivations of words: he also tried to find the relations between the different Indo-European Languages; thirdly, he insisted more strictly on 'Laws'.

(x) *Schleicher,* like Bopp, had a tendency to treat Languages as if they were plants: he carried the analogy too far.

He said that the earliest Languages were Radical or Isolating, consisting of separate Roots; that then came the Agglutinative stage, when these Roots could be combined, but were not yet combined permanently: they were at present only glued together; that thirdly came the Inflexional Stage—here the Roots (especially those which had once been Pronouns) had often become permanently fixed on to Verbal Roots, so as to form a single word with them (cp. λόγος, p. 107); that then came Degeneration and Decay—the 'Analytic' stage, when we say '*I* give *to* you' rather than the Inflexional dōnō vōbis.

The views are open to severe criticism: he did not produce any instance of a Radical Language becoming Agglutinative, or of an Agglutinative Language becoming Inflexional: neither did he prove that our method of speaking is Degenerate.

His great service was to collect and arrange the work of others, and to insist more strongly on 'Laws'. He also tried to reconstruct the Indo-European Language: but he gave it *a* (not *e* and *o* as well), and gave it no Aspirates (gh, bh, dh, etc.) in its Earliest period, and no Semi-vowels (p. 171), and no Velar Gutturals (p. 173).

(xi) *Georg. Curtius* suggested the Principles of Etymology, and Analysed the Greek Verb, and said that the *a*-sound split up into *a*, *e*, and *o* in 'European'. But he had not yet realised the strictness of 'Laws' (p. 66), and made changes too 'conscious' (cp. pp. 205, 261).

55 (b). Some leading Scholars and their services.

(*b*) (i) *Bentley*; (ii) *Boeckh*; (iii) *Erasmus*; (iv) *Aulus Gellius*; (v) *Munro*; (vi) *Porson*; (vii) *Scaliger*; (viii) *Wolf*.

For a good list of Scholars, see Gow, p. 66; and for details, see Appendix.

(i) *Bentley* (-1742) [Cambridge].

Bentley was the father of the Eighteenth Century School of Scholars;

a. he was great at collecting and emending MSS (e.g. those of Horace and Terence);

β. he showed his extraordinary learning when he exposed the spuriousness of the so-called 'Letters of Phalaris': he ruthlessly demolished the arguments by which Boyle had tried to prove these Letters genuine;

γ. as Master of Trinity he tried to sweep away various abuses.

(ii) *Boeckh* (-1867) [Berlin].

a. He defined Philology as all knowledge about Antiquities, e.g. History and Religion;

β. he edited Pindar, with special attention to Metres;

γ. his *Public Economy of Athens*, and

δ. his *Corpus of Greek Inscriptions*, have helped to make him famous.

(iii) *Erasmus* (-1535) [London, Cambridge, Basle].

α. Erasmus wrote a Latin which was not purely Ciceronian, but was a living Language, natural and full of vigour;

β. his *Colloquia*, *Encomium Moriae*, and *Adagia*, had an enormous circulation: a great work of his was

γ. his Latin Version of the New Testament.

See, further, Jebb's 'Erasmus'.

(iv) *Aulus Gellius* (180 A.D.).

Wrote *Noctes Atticae* (so-called because they were written at Athens during the evenings and nights); they were 'a medley of literary, grammatical, and antiquarian gossip' (Wilkins).

(v) *Munro* (-1885) [Cambridge].

α. He translated and edited *Lucretius* and *Catullus*, and he was to some extent the founder of the modern system of Notes to the Classics; these Notes are so commonplace to-day that it is hard to realise a time when they were a new departure.

β. He wrote beautiful compositions (e.g. Lucretian Hexameters).

(vi) *Porson* (-1808) [Cambridge].

Porson is famous for

α. his textual criticisms and emendations,

β. his Grammatical commentaries,

γ. his attention to Metres.

δ. He edited Euripides. Like Bentley and Scaliger, he was a scathing critic.

(vii) *Scaliger*.

α. (-1558) [Agen]. The Elder censured Erasmus' *Ciceronianus*—very unfairly, for he misunderstood Erasmus' point of view. He wrote the first scientific Latin Grammar.

β. (-1609) [Leipzig]. The Younger edited Catullus, Tibullus, and Propertius, besides doing good work on Chronology.

(viii) *Wolf* (-1824) [Halle and Berlin].

His 'Prolegomena' to Homer maintains that in Homer's time writing was unknown: that therefore the whole of Homer could not have been composed all at once: that there were once numbers of separate Lays, recited first by Rhapsōdists, and then by Homeridae: that these separate Lays were not collected till 500 years' later, i.e. by Pisistratus. He supports this by saying that the Poems themselves are not organically connected, the *Iliad* with the *Odyssey*, and the different parts of the *Iliad* with one another.

APPENDIX.

LIST OF USEFUL BOOKS (MOSTLY IN ENGLISH).

List of useful books.

The following List is short, and is practically confined to books in English or Latin, except in the case e.g. of Greek Etymology (Prellwitz) where little knowledge of German is required. For further Lists, see Victor Henry's *Comparative Grammar*, and other Text-books, and Mayor's admirable *Guide to the Choice of Classical Books* (with Supplement).

On English.

Earle—several works;

Sweet—Do.

* Skeat, *Etymological Dictionary of the English Language.*

On Greek.

Monro, *Homeric Grammar ;*

Prellwitz, *Etymologisches Wörterbuch der griechischen Sprache ;*

Wharton, *Etyma Graeca ;*

Winer, *Grammar of New Testament Greek.*

On Greek Dialects and Alphabets.

Ahrens, *de Graecae Linguae Dialectis ;*

Cauer, *Delectus Inscriptionum Graecarum ;*

* Roberts, *Introduction to Greek Epigraphy ;*

Smyth, *Greek Dialects : Ionic ;* and see further p. 31 foll.

On the Indo-Europeans.

* Ihering and Drucker, *Evolution of the Aryan ;*

Schrader and Jevons, *Prehistoric Antiquities of the Aryan Peoples ;*

*Schrumpf, *A first Aryan Reader ;*

I. Taylor, *Origin of the Aryans.*

On Latin.

Bréal and Bailly, *Dictionnaire Etymologique Latin;*
Conway, *Verner's Law in Italy;*
* Lindsay, *Short Historical Latin Grammar;*
Wharton, *Etyma Latina.*

On Latin Inscriptions and Italic Dialects.

* Allen, *Early Latin;*
Conway, *Italic Dialects, and Exempla;*
Egbert, *Introduction to the Study of Latin Inscriptions;*
* Lindsay, *Latin Inscriptions;*
Wordsworth, *Fragments and Specimens of Early Latin.*

On Greek Particles.

Paley, *Greek Particles;*
and Notes to Classical Authors by various Editors, e.g. see Riddell's Edition of *Plato.*

On Physiology.

Behnke, *Mechanism of the Human Voice.*

On the Principles of Philology.

Paul, *Principles of the History of Language;*
Max Müller, *Science of Language, etc.;*
Sayce, *Principles of Comparative Philology;*
* Strong, Logeman, and Wheeler, *The History of Language;*
Trench, *The Study of Words;*
* Wheeler, *Analogy, and the Scope of its Application in Language.*

On the Pronunciation of Greek and Latin.

Purton, *Pronunciation of Ancient Greek;*
and see p. 183 foll.

On Sanskrit.

* Max Müller, *Sanskrit Grammar;*
Peile, *Notes on the Tale of Nala;*
* Whitney, *Sanskrit Grammar;*

On Leading Scholars and Philologists.

The Encyclopædia Britannica;
Obituary Notes in Papers;
Pamphlets and short books, e.g. by Jebb (on Erasmus).

On Sound-changes generally.

Brugmann, *Grundriss ;*
Conway, *Verner's Law in Italy ;*
Darbishire, *Relliquiae Philologicae ;*
* Giles, *Manual of Comparative Philology ;*
Halsey, *Etymology of Latin and Greek ;*
V. Henry, *Comparative Grammar of Greek and Latin ;*
L. Horton-Smith [various Pamphlets published by Macmillan & Bowes] ;
King and Cookson, * *Comparative Grammar*, and *Sounds and Inflections ;*
I. Müller, *Handbüch*, vol. ii. ;
and innumerable Pamphlets, and Articles in various Papers, such as the *Classical Review* and the *American Journal of Philology.*

On Correct Spelling.

Lindsay, *Short Historical Latin Grammar ;*
Reid's Editions of *Cicero ;*
Rutherford, *New Phrynichus, etc.*

On Textual Criticism.

Bentley, *Phalaris ;*
Cobet, *Variae Lectiones, etc. ;*
Madvig, *Adversaria Critica ;*
Thompson, *Manual of Greek and Latin Palaeography ;*
Westcott and Hort, *New Testament ;*
and see p. 237.

* The asterisk marks the most useful works for those who are not Specialists.

INDICES.

I. GENERAL INDEX.

C.

D.

E.

II. GREEK INDEX.

The Dialect forms will be found on the following pages: *Doric* (23), *Ionic* (32), Old and New *Attic* (33), *N.T.* (33), '*Aeolic*' (36-37), *Homeric* (38-39); Exercises (40-41).

The **Dialect** forms will be found on the following pages: *Doric* (23), *Ionic* (32), Old and New *Attic* (33), *N.T.* (33), '*Aeolic*' (36-37), *Homeric* (38-39); Exercises (40-41).

The Dialect forms will be found on the following pages: *Doric* (23), *Ionic* (32), Old and New *Attic* (33), *N.T.* (33), '*Aeolic*' (36-37), *Homeric* (38-39); Exercises (40-41).

The **Dialect** forms will be found on the following pages: *Doric* (32), *Ionic* (32), Old and New *Attic* (33), *N:T.* (33), '*Aeolic*' (36-37), *Homeric* (38-39); Exercises (40-41).

The Dialect forms will be found on the following pages: *Doric* (23), *Ionic* (32), Old and New *Attic* (33), *N.T.* (33), '*Aeolic*' (36-37), *Homeric* (38-39); Exercises (40-41).

III. LATIN INDEX.

The **Early Latin** forms will be found on p. 44 foll., the *Italic* forms on p. 55, and Latin Spelling on pp. 197-198.

The **Early Latin** forms will be found on p. 44 foll., the *Italic* forms on p. 55, and Latin Spelling on pp. 197-198.

The **Early Latin** forms will be found on p. 44 foll., the *Italic* forms on p. 55, and Latin Spelling on pp. 197-198.

The **Early Latin** forms will be found on p. 44 foll., the *Italic* forms on p. 55, and Latin Spelling on pp. 197-198.

IV. INDEX OF ENGLISH, FRENCH, ETC.

V. PHILOLOGISTS, ETC.

See also, pp. 269-271.

Printed in the United States
41309LVS00003B

9 780766 178502